MW00911789

Jordan and the Holy Land

Revised and Updated

**by
KAY SHOWKER**

FODOR'S TRAVEL PUBLICATIONS, INC.
New York & London

Fodor's Jordan and the Holy Land

Editor: Andrew E. Beresky
Maps and City Plans: Pictograph
Photographs: Kay Showker
Drawings: Sandra Lang
Cover Photograph: Bruno Barbey/Magnum

Cover Design: Vignelli Associates

CONTENTS

iii

CONTENTS

FOREWORD

Jordan may possibly be the most underrated tourist destination in the world. Although its name is as familiar to us as the Bible, Americans have almost no mental picture of the country. And though Jordan's King Hussein is a frequent and familiar visitor to the U.S., we have only a vague idea about the land and the people he governs.

Jordan is not only the heartland of the Middle East and the Arab world; it is the very spot where man first developed the communal life that launched Western civilization. Here, at this crossroad, three of the greatest religions of mankind—Judaism, Christianity, and Islam—flowered. Here, too, the great empires—Egyptian, Hittite, Babylonian, Assyrian, Greek, Roman, Persian, Nabataean, Byzantine, Arab, Crusader—conquered and destroyed, ruled, built, and created. Some of what they built can be seen today. The people and their culture are the mosaic they created.

As do all the countries of the Middle East, Jordan abounds with important historical and Biblical sites, any of which could be the subject of a book. But this is a guidebook, not a textbook. It is meant to be a concise and practical guide for the modern traveler.

We have tried to highlight the most important places and direct the newcomer through the maze of hills, tells, digs, temples, churches, castles, mosques, etc., that cover the country. If your interest is stimulated to learn more, then this guide will have served a useful purpose.

The transliteration of Arabic words into English is a continuing problem; consistency is almost impossible. The following variations will serve as examples: Moslem or Muslim; Koran or Qu'ran; Muhammad, Muhammed, Mohammed, Mohamed, Mohammad, Mehemet or Mehmet.

We have tried to be practical. Place names, shops, hotels, etc., are written as they appear locally so that a visitor will recognize them. Historical names are given in their commonly accepted forms. Terms that might be used by a

v

traveler are rendered simply and as closely as possible to their English equivalents, without the use of symbols or diacritics. Without some knowledge of Arabic or linguistics, the use of elaborate systems is usually more confusing than helpful.

A book such as this is never a one-person effort. It requires the help of many—more than there is space to name; but I would particularly like to thank Jordan's former minister of tourism, Ghaleb Barakat, and Director of the Office of H.R.H. Crown Prince al Hassan bin Talal, Michael Hamarneh, whose interest and help made my task easier; Ali Ghandour, chairman and president of Royal Jordanian Airlines, whose continuing interest and enthusiasm helped me get the job done; and at the Jordan Information Center in Washington, D.C., Akram Barakat, director, and Helen Khal, who was there every step of the way. The contribution of Dr. Graham Leonard of UNRWA, Yousif Dajani, and freelance writer/photographer Joanne Zembal in helping to update the material has been invaluable.

Although every care has been taken to ensure the accuracy of the information contained in this guide, the publishers cannot accept responsibility for any errors that might appear.

All prices quoted in this guide are based on those available to us at the time of writing. In a world of rapid change, however, the possibility of inaccurate or out-of-date information can never be totally eliminated. We trust, therefore, that you will take prices quoted as indicators only, and will double-check to be sure of the latest figures.

Similarly, be sure to check all opening times of museums and galleries. We have found that such times are liable to change without notice, and you could easily make a trip only to find a locked door.

When a hotel closes or a restaurant produces a disappointing meal, let us know, and we will investigate the establishment and the complaint. We are always ready to revise our entries for the following year's edition should the facts warrant it.

Send your letters to the editors of Fodor's Travel Publications, 201 E. 50th Street, New York, NY 10022. Continental or British Commonwealth readers may prefer to write to Fodor's Travel Publications, 9–10 Market Place, London W1N 7AG, England.

FACTS AT YOUR FINGERTIPS

HOW TO GET THERE. By air: Royal Jordanian Airlines has direct flights to Amman from New York, Houston, Chicago, and Los Angeles on Boeing 747s. It was the first Arab airline to connect the United States with the Middle East on a regular basis and by direct, nonstop flights.

Several European airlines have direct flights from Europe to Jordan. Flying time is 5 hours from major European cities and 10½ hours from New York.

Royal Jordanian also links Jordan with other Middle Eastern capitals, with daily flights to Cairo, Baghdad, and the countries of the Gulf—Bahrain, Kuwait, Qatar, Saudi Arabia, and the United Arab Emirates. Most of these flights take from 1 to 2 hours. The carrier offers service to six countries in the Far East and is planning to start service to South America.

Air Fares

Among the more confusing aspects of travel these days is the matter of air fares, and perhaps none are more confusing than those that apply to the countries of the Middle East. The following fares were valid at the time this book went to press, but, judging from past experience, prices will probably have changed by the time the ink is dry on the page.

All prices are round-trip between New York and Amman:

Individual Fares

	IATA Fares	Royal Jordanian Fares Only
First Class	$3,950 year-round	$2140
Business Class	$2,354 year-round	$1,570
Unrestricted Economy	$1,908	
Restricted Economy	$1,858	$1,290

Royal Jordanian 6–60-day Apex (advance purchase): Tickets must be purchased in advance. One stopover. $821 basic, $941 peak (June 1–July 31).
Royal Jordanian 10–120-day Excursion: $910 basic, $1,035 peak (June 1–Aug. 31).

By car: An interesting overland route from Europe through the ancient lands of Turkey and Syria enters Jordan at Ramtha, about 70 miles north of Amman. Driving time from Damascus is about 4 hours (allow 1 to 2 hours for border crossings).

Regular shared-taxi service is available between Damascus and Amman and costs JD 4. Petra Taxi Company, with offices in Damascus and Amman, has cars leaving about every hour from Damascus for Amman. You should telephone the day before to reserve a seat.

For the return to Damascus by taxi, the companies in Amman that offer regular service are Hadad Taxi, Feras Taxi, and Hilal Taxi. For long journeys by shared taxi you may want to buy 2 seats for yourself, since the price is so cheap. This way the car is less crowded and the ride will be more comfortable.

By bus: The newest "overland" route is a bus-and-ferry service between Amman/Aqaba and Nuweibah/Cairo. Operated from Jordan by JETT (Phone: 664146; 894-872 for JETT services outside of Jordan.) and Jordan National Shipping Co. (Aqaba Phone: 315342), and from Egypt by Delta Line, buses leave Amman and Cairo twice daily. The JETT bus with hostess departs from Amman at 3 A.M. to connect with the ferry which departs from Aqaba at 11:00 A.M. for Nuweibah in Sinai. From there the ferry continues to Cairo. The complete journey takes 20 hours. Cost is JD 16. Snacks are sold on the bus; lunch can be purchased on the ferry. A second ferry departs from Aqaba at 4 P.M. The ferry-only price is JD 12.250 or LE 33.75. Car with driver is JD 21.500 or LE 61.25 for a small car; JD 35.250 or LE 102.50 for larger ones. Between Amman and Damascus there are coaches twice daily, leaving from each city at 7 A.M., and 3 P.M. The service is handled by Karnak in Damascus and by JETT in Amman. The price is JD 3. Coach service is also available to Baghdad at 10 P.M. for JD 10 one-way. Low-cost transportation either by bus or shared taxi is available to many places throughout Jordan. These are detailed later in this chapter.

By train: Jordan's only rail line is the narrow-gauge, single-track Hejaz Railway, built in the early 1900s for pilgrim traffic between Damascus and Medina. Much of it was destroyed in World War I during the Arab Revolt against the Turks led by Sherif Hussein, the great-grandfather of the present king, and Lawrence of Arabia. Sectors have been reconstructed, and a new branch has been added that extends to the port of Aqaba. Basically, it carries only freight, although we are told passengers willing to forgo all comforts have been taken aboard.

By sea: Several cruise lines include Aqaba on itineraries from the Mediterranean through the Suez to the Red Sea and up the Gulf of Aqaba. These include Epirotiki, Royal Viking Line, and Sun Line. Passengers visit Petra on a day tour.

Another car-and-passenger ferry service is available between Aqaba and Suez on regularly scheduled ships, which carry mostly cargo. The line is run by the Telestar Maritime Agency (tel. 660213) with offices near Firas Circle on Jebel Hussein in Amman. Mail address: P.O. Box 9360. Cable: TELSTAR. Telex: 1604 Telstar.

WHEN TO GO. Spring and autumn are the best times to visit Jordan; the weather is wonderful for travel throughout the country. However, we would not dissuade anyone from going at other times of the year.

The country's climate is as diverse as its scenery. Daytime summer temperatures are hot, but nights are cool. Winter often brings snow on the mountaintops. Spring carpets the countryside with beautiful wild flowers and the valleys with pink oleander. Rain falls from November to April, but the rest of the year there is sunshine every day. Fall and spring are long and pleasant, though occasionally a strong desert wind blows in spring. July and August are hot in much of the country. From December through February Amman and the surrounding area can be cold, but Aqaba, on the Gulf, is a warm and sunny winter resort.

Average Temperatures in Major Tourist Centers

	Winter			Spring			Summer			Fall		
	Jan.	Feb.	Mar.	Apr.	May	June	July	Aug.	Sept.	Oct.	Nov.	Dec.
Amman F.	46	48	53	60	69	74	77	78	74	69	59	50
Aqaba F.	60	62	68	75	83	89	90	91	86	80	71	62

WHAT TO TAKE. Pack with a plan so that you will not be burdened with useless items. Limit baggage to what you can carry—and leave enough room for the gifts and souvenirs you are sure to buy in Jordan.

Although Jordan is thought of as having a hot climate, you will be surprised to discover how much the temperature varies within a given day or from one month to the next. Jordan has 4 well-defined seasons. Hence, your wardrobe should be planned according to the time of year and the extent of your itinerary.

In early summer (May, June) and fall (September, October), cotton and dacron dresses and slacks for ladies and slacks and suits for men are comfortable, provided they are made of the type of fabric that breathes. In the dead of summer (July and August) only pure cotton dresses, blouses and skirts, shirts and trousers are recommended, especially for those who suffer from the heat.

Winter (December through March) can be cold with some rain, especially in the highlands. Women will need light wool or knitted suits and dresses with long sleeves or jackets. Gentlemen should have medium-weight suits and warm sweaters. Even April can be cool, especially in the evening. Women should be sure to include a versatile dress with jacket or a polyester knit with long sleeves. Include a lightweight coat or cape, a warm housecoat, nightgown, and warm slippers, as floors are usually laid in tiles. A stole or warm wrap for evenings is useful year-round. It is amazing how even in the middle of summer, when the sun goes down after a hot day, there is sometimes a chill in the air. You will feel it all the more because the day was so warm. Moreover, older houses, hotels, and guesthouses are not centrally heated, and it is frequently cooler inside than outdoors. Hats, except as protection against the sun, are seldom worn. A mantilla is appropriate for mosques and churches.

Jordanians are accustomed to foreigners and to the bizarre ways some tourists dress. Nonetheless, it is still a conservative country as far as women are concerned. Slacks are readily accepted; shorts and bare sunback dresses are not. Unless you want to attract attention to yourself, modesty in dress and decorum in manner is wise.

For men, there is not a great deal of emphasis on formality, but dress is conservative. Hotel laundry service is usually fast and reasonable, so you do not need to burden yourself with a great deal of clothing.

Useful items to include in your suitcase are small binoculars, a small flashlight, a washcloth, disposable premoistened facecloths, insect repellent, collapsible hangers, face soap (keep it in plastic bags), packaged soap powders, moisture cream, and a collapsible drinking cup. Always have a generous supply of facial tissues on hand—you will be amazed at their many uses, and only deluxe hotels supply them in your room. If you do not want to be bothered with packing all these items, they are readily available in Amman.

Sunglasses are a must, and a shade hat for sightseeing in the open, in the desert, and for the beach is advised, especially in summer. Be sure to bring comfortable, flat walking shoes, summer or winter. Sneakers are wonderful for walking and climbing around monuments and sites of antiquity, especially at Jerash and Petra. A raincoat will be necessary in January, February, and March. A bathing suit for sunbathing or for swimming should be included year-round—and don't forget to pack the suntan lotion.

PACKAGE TOURS. In almost every case, tours from the U.S. to Jordan include other Middle Eastern countries. The great majority are Holy Land tours, which use Jordan as a gateway. Generally, this type of tour spends 2 days in Jordan, with rushed visits to Petra and Jerash.

As part of a Middle East and Holy Land tour, the following general interest, nonpilgrimage tours are samples of what is available. Hotels, most meals, and sightseeing are usually included; airfare is *additional* unless otherwise stated.

Adventure Center (Encounter Overland, London), 5540 College Ave., Oakland, CA 94618: 56 days; Treks & Safaris, Cradles of Civilization.

Consolidated Tours Organization, 777 Cleveland Ave., #208, Atlanta, GA 30315, tel. 404–767–2727: 10-day tours of the Holy Land and Jordan (Amman, Jerusalem, Galilee, Bethlehem, and Petra); also 11-day packages to the Holy Land, Jordan, and Cairo. Via Royal Jordanian Airlines. Call agency for details.

Foreign Independent Tours, 2125 Center Ave., Fort Lee, NJ 07024: 3- to 7-night packages Jordan/Petra, Holy Land; can be combined.

Hemphill-Harris Travel, 10100 Santa Monica Blvd., Los Angeles, CA 90067 offers two Middle East combinations, each 24 days that includes 2 days in Amman and 1 in Petra; prices from $3,660.

Jackson Tours, Box 6600, Tyler, TX 75711, tel. 214–597–1187: 10- and 12-day Holy Land tours begin in Amman. Visit Jerusalem with day trips to Galilee, Bethlehem, and sites in between. One program adds Cairo, another adds Rome and Vienna.

Nawas International, 20 East 46th St., New York, NY 10017: 17 days in Egypt, Jordan, and the Holy Land.

Olson-Travelworld, 5855 Green Valley Circle, Culver City, CA 90230: 21 days, Best of the Middle East combines Egypt, Jordan, the Holy Land, and Turkey.

Polo Travel, 271 Madison Ave., New York, NY 10016, has a 15-day tour combining Egypt, Jordan, and the Holy Land. Priced from $1,889 (low season) and $1,398 for children under 12 traveling with 2 adults. It includes airfare, breakfast, and lunch or dinner daily. Hotels are first class, rather than deluxe.

Regaltours, 29–09 Bridge Plaza North, Long Island City, NY 11101; 718–786–8033: A 10-day, all-Jordan program to major sites of the country; from $1,199, including airfare from New York on Royal Jordanian Airlines, 6 nights deluxe hotel and breakfast in Amman, and 2 nights at Petra. Extensive sightseeing with guides and other amenities.

Sunny Land Tours, 166 Main Street, Hackensack, NJ 07601: 15 days in Egypt, Jordan and the Holy Land, from $1,495; and series of 7-day programs of Jordan and other Middle East countries, which can be combined for individual travelers.

Swan Hellenic/Esplanade Tours, 581 Boylston St., Boston, MA 02116, tel. 617–266–7465: 17-days visiting the art treasures of the Ancient Near East: includes Aqaba, Petra, Amman, the Holy Land, and Egypt. Also 15-day tours, Jordan and Jerusalem. Call for details.

Travcoa, 4000 MacArthur Blvd. #650E, Newport Beach, CA 92660: 25-day Classic Holy Land tour, Amman, Jerash, Petra, Istanbul, Athens, from $4,295; and 30-day Grand Middle East tour, Amman, Jerash, and Petra, $5,095. Both can be combined with Egypt and other Eastern Mediterranean countries.

Other tour operators with programs to Jordan are *Compass Dive Tours, International,* 2022 Powers Ferry Rd., #230, Atlanta, GA 30339; *Compass Tours,* 330 Seventh Ave., 19th Floor, New York, NY 10001; *Jolis Voyage,* 5200 B. Rolling Road, Burke, VA 22015; *Royal Tours,* Box 302, Amman, Jordan; *Travelink Tours International,* 3166 Des Plains Ave., Des Plaines, IL 60018; *Vista Travel,* 135 West 36th St., New York, NY 10018; and *World Pilgrimages,* 2300 Henderson Hill Rd., #325; Atlanta, GA 30345.

Christian pilgrimage tours are offered by a number of firms who specialize in these programs. They are almost always led by a clergyman. Among the firms are *Calvary Tours,* 270 Madison Ave., NYC 10016; *Catholic Travel Center,* 444 W. Ocean Blvd. #1210, Long Beach, CA 90802; *Catholic Travel Office,* 4701 Willard Ave. #226, Chevy Chase, MD 20815; *DTA Tour & Travel,* 1610 Eastgate Dr. #S, LBJ/NW Hwy, Garland, TX 75041; *Wilcox World Turns,* 1705 Northwestern Bank Bldg., Asheville, NC 28801; *Wholesale Tours International,* 387 Park Ave. South, NYC 10016; *World Mission Tours,* 641 De Soto Dr., Miami Springs, FL 33166. In **Canada,** *Christian Fellowship Tours,* P.O. Box 266, Niagara on the Lake, Ontario L0S 1J0; *Distant Horizons Tours,* 206 Bloor St. West #4, Toronto, Ontario M5S 1T8.

TIPS FOR BRITISH VISITORS The Jordan Tourist Board, 211 Regent St., London W1R 7DD, tel. 01–437–9465 will give you information on vacations to Jordan and the Holy Land.

Passports. You will need a valid passport and a Tourist Visa (cost £21) which you can get through the Jordanian Embassy, 6 Upper Philimore Gardens, London W8 7HB, tel. 01–937–3685.

Customs. (See Customs Regulations below for entering Jordan.)

Returning to the U.K. you may bring home (1) 200 cigarettes or 100 cigarillos or 50 cigars or 250 grams of tobacco; (2) two liters of table wine and, in addition, (a) one liter of alcohol over 22% by volume (most spirits), (b) two liters of alcohol under 22% by volume (fortified or sparkling wines), or (c) two more liters of table wine; (3) 50 grams of perfume and ¼ liter of toilet water; and (4) other goods up to a value of £32.

Insurance. We recommend that you insure yourself to cover health and motoring mishaps with Europ Assistance, 252 High St., Croydon, Surrey CRO 1NF, tel. 01–680–1234.

Tour Operators. *Bales Tours,* Bales House, Barrington Rd., Dorking, Surrey RH4 3EJ; 12 days in Jordan plus Jerusalem, £759; 8-day escorted tour of Jordan £588.

Kuoni Worldwide, Kuoni House, Dorking, Surrey RH5 4AZ; 7 days, Amman/Aqaba, £424; or Amman only, £388.

Prospect Art Tours Ltd., 10 Barley Mow Passage, London W4 4PH; 9 day art tour of Jordan from £695.

Sovereign Worldwide, British Airways holidays, Trafalgar House, 2 Chalk Hill Rd., London W6 8DN; 9-day Jordan and Jerusalem tour from £547; Cairo, Jordan, and Jerusalem from £672.

Thomson Worldwide Ltd., Greater London House, Hampstead Rd., London NW1 7SD; 14-night Red Sea Triangle tour £846; 14-night Egypt, Jordan and the Holy Land from £932.

Voyage Jules Verne, 10 Glentworth St., London NW1 5PG; 17-day fully escorted Land of the Bible tour from £1,245.

Electricity. 220V AC 50Hz. Take an adaptor along for your portable electrical appliances.

PLANNING YOUR SIGHTSEEING. What to see in Jordan largely depends on the amount of time one has to spend. The country is compact and travel is easy. Many highlights can be seen in three days, but it takes at least a week to cover all the main attractions. Most places can be visited in a half day from Amman; the others require a full day.

With a few exceptions, all historic or otherwise interesting sites can be reached by paved road in an ordinary automobile or bus.

On a long trip it is wise to start with a full gas tank and to carry a supply of drinking water. The Ministry of Tourism and Antiquities distributes free maps and literature.

For a 3- to 4-day visit we suggest the following itinerary, which can be expanded to a week by adding other attractions or by dividing the first day into 2 half days:

A city tour of Amman covering the Citadel, the Antiquities Museum, the Roman Theater, and folk museums will consume a morning. In the afternoon, a visit can be made to Jerash and, depending upon one's time and interest, it can be combined with a drive through the Debbin (Dibbeen) Park to Ajlun.

A second day will take in Madaba, Mt. Nebo, and a drive through the Wadi Mujib to Kerak. To reduce travel time, one can return from Kerak by the desert road for an overnight in Amman. Other possibilities are to remain in Kerak or continue to Petra for overnight, though the latter makes for a long day. If this itinerary is chosen, it is essential to get an early start and to move along at a brisk pace.

Alternatively, one can drive to Petra via the desert road and return to Amman on the second or third day via Kerak and Madaba. We should also point out that since Madaba is so close to Amman, it can easily be visited on a short trip from the city and does not have to be part of a longer itinerary.

A third day can be spent in Petra. Many tours offered by U.S. operators unfortunately spend only a few hours in Petra. The minimum time needed to see the ancient city is 2 full days; anything less is cheating yourself of seeing properly one of the greatest sites in the world. Even 3 or 4 days is not too long for enthusiasts. Petra is spread over a large area, and simply cannot be covered in a hurry.

If you have the time, it is convenient to continue south from Petra to Aqaba, particularly if you would like to have a day or two on the beach.

From Aqaba a short trip can be made into Wadi Rum, and for those with adequate time, a camping trip—with or without a camel caravan—can be arranged.

Another excursion from Amman takes you to the Desert Castles east of the capital to Azraq. The complete circuit can now be made in a half day in a car over a newly paved road that eliminates the once hazardous drive over desert track.

These are the most important attractions in Jordan, but, as you will see in the following pages, there are many lesser-known places to visit. To include them would require a stay of 2 weeks.

Additional information and assistance in planning your tour is available from the Ministry of Tourism and Antiquities. Publications of the Ministry and such books as Lankester Harding's *Antiquities of Jordan* and Eugene Hoade's *East of the Jordan* (available at most bookshops) will also be useful. For those with academic or archeological interests, the annual reports of the Department of Antiquities are valuable.

HEALTH REGULATIONS. Anyone coming from epidemic or endemic areas is required to have an inoculation certificate against cholera. Cholera vaccinations are required for travelers, except children under 1 year of age, coming from infected areas.

PASSPORTS AND VISAS. To visit Jordan, travelers need a valid passport or a recognized travel document and a visa issued by Jordanian Consulates abroad. Tourists may also obtain visas upon arrival at Jordanian frontier posts and airports.

A multiple-entry tourist visa, valid for 2 years, may be issued upon request. Your visa application should be accompanied by one passport-size photograph and a stamped, self-addressed envelope. For U.S., Canadian, and Australian citizens there is no visa charge; for British citizens, the cost is $42 or £25 for a single visit; $102 or £60 for two years. Visa fees vary for citizens of other countries. Payment should be made to the Jordan Embassy by money order or certified check only.

For business visas follow the same procedure as above, with the addition of a letter from the company or employer stating the purpose of the visit.

A Group or Collective Visa is available for tour groups providing the group stays in Jordan 2 or more days.

Travel Between Jordan and Israel

Travel between Jordan and Israel is permitted by a 2-way crossing from Jordan or a 1-way crossing from Israel. (If you enter Jordan via Israel, be sure that no Israeli visa is affixed to your passport.) You must leave Jordan directly or via neighboring Arab countries; as of this writing you will not be allowed to return to Israel.

It is important to remember that Jordan government offices are closed on Fridays, Israeli government offices are closed on Saturdays, and the American and British Consulates in Jerusalem are closed on Sundays.

Tourists going to Israel from Jordan can obtain a permit to cross over to the West Bank from the Ministry of Interior in Amman or through a travel agent. The permit is a separate document that allows you to cross over and return. Remember, it is important that you do not allow Israeli authorities to stamp your passport in any way.

So long as you are in a group, the crossing between Jordan and the Israeli-occupied West Bank is likely to be easy and uncomplicated. Your travel agent will have already made the necessary arrangements and will have the proper documentation in hand for the group.

If you are traveling on your own and not making your travel arrangements through a stateside agent, then on your arrival in Amman you should go in person with your passport to the Ministry. You should do this immediately upon arrival, as the paperwork takes a minimum of 2 days. You should plan to take a taxi (JD10) or taxi-service (JD 2) from Amman to the Jordanian security post, where you board a bus for the river crossing. Taxi service from Abdali station is available. The drive from Amman to the security post takes about 50 minutes.

American and other foreign tourists of Arab origin, no matter where they were born, must secure permission from the Ministry of Interior. This may take longer to process, although it can usually be speeded up if you have a good agent working on it. Usually processing at the border by Israeli authorities takes longer and often includes an extensive search of personal effects.

The crossing itself is time-consuming and may be unpleasant and uncomfortable. The bridge closes at 1 P.M. daily and is completely closed on Saturdays, the Jewish sabbath. It's necessary to begin your journey early (via taxi) to reach the Jordanian security point, where you must board a bus, the only vehicle authorized to make the crossing. You cannot cross over in a taxi or your own car. The last bus leaves the security point (on both sides) at 11 A.M.

On arrival at the Jordanian security post you present the papers issued by the Ministry of Interior and, after clearance, wait for the next shuttle bus to take you across the bridge. Passports are checked at the bridge itself (located approximately 2 miles from the security post) and a military escort boards the bus to accompany it to the middle of the bridge, where his West Bank counterpart takes over and gives a briefing to passengers on Israeli entry formalities.

The ride will be a memorable experience. The bus is completely full, neither air-conditioned nor cushioned, and rather old. Passengers are frequently loud and lively with lots of children, and plenty of food will be passed around—and offered to you. Local passengers try to be helpful to tourists, and they will certainly be friendly.

JETT has bus service that makes the crossing directly from Amman to the Israeli military station, eliminating the need to change buses or to change from a taxi to a bus provided you have obtained the necessary permit from the Ministry of Interior. Cost is JD 2.500. The bus departs from Abdali Station at 7:30 A.M. and returns from the bridge at 1:30 P.M.

Upon arrival on the West Bank, there are 2 separate security points, one for tourists and another for the local Arabs. Security officials may sometimes be unpleasant, though tourists are generally treated courteously. Your luggage (and your person) will be thoroughly searched. Some items, such as shoes and anything suspicious, are x-rayed and might even be confiscated—all a grim reminder that there is still a war on in the Middle East.

Once you have passed through Israeli security, there are taxis to take you into Jerusalem or anywhere else you may wish to visit. The crossing procedures can take 3 to 4 hours.

CUSTOMS REGULATIONS. Normally, all articles classified as traveling requirements are exempt from customs duty. In addition to your personal clothing, you are allowed the following items duty free: 200 cigarettes or 200 grams of tobacco, sporting equipment, cameras, films, typewriter, and 1 liter of wine or spirits.

Printing or sound reproduction equipment and phonographs and records (including portable and used) are subject to duty. A radio is exempted from duty when imported for less than 6 months.

Generally, as a tourist you may bring in gifts in small quantities and of low commercial value duty free. The exemption, however, is subject to the discretion of the customs officer. When you arrive by plane in Amman, the red/green (Nothing to Declare) European system is used.

Security Formalities: Before disembarking from a plane or on arrival at the frontier, you are asked to fill in a standard international form to be presented to immigration authorities. Basically, the form asks for passport information and the length and purpose of your visit.

Baggage is subject to inspection and tourists are often requested to open luggage. If any questions should arise, Tourist Police are near at hand to assist visitors.

At the borders the Jordanian officials are generally very courteous. There is a rest house at Ramtha where one crosses into Jordan from Syria. Drinks and refreshments are sold there and toilet facilities are available.

Customs review is the most severe on tourists entering Jordan from Israel or returning to Jordan from there. Particularly, customs officials will confiscate books and tapes that appear to them to have a political intent, even if in fact they do not.

HOW TO GET AROUND. By Middle Eastern standards, taxi drivers in Jordan are fairly tame. You might wonder, though, how their flowing headdress, known as a *kafiya,* does not get caught in the car mechanism. Then, too, as in all the Middle East, you may sometimes wish the automobile horn had never been invented.

Buses operate in Amman and between cities and villages throughout Jordan. An average bus ride in Amman costs 70 fils.

You need not be timid about trying the bus system. English is the second language in Jordan and widely spoken. Jordanians are extremely kind and hospitable to strangers and eager to help. If you are unsure, ask the bus driver or a passenger. You might also carry a piece of paper with your destination written in Arabic as an aid for such times when language does become a barrier.

Even though buses are easy and cheap, you will probably prefer to use taxis, which are reasonably priced, or the *taxi-service* system, which is efficient and inexpensive. *Service* (pronounced *servees*) are 5-passenger cars, each passenger paying for one seat as on a bus. The *service* runs along set routes in town and to outlying areas. The cost is 70–100 fils per seat.

Inside Amman, most *taxi-services* leave from the main downtown square on King Faisal St. or adjacent side streets. If you plan an extended visit in Jordan, you will find it worthwhile to learn the bus and *taxi-service* system.

Taxis are all privately owned and operate within Amman and between cities, towns, and villages. They can be recognized by their green license plates. Those with a white square on the front door and a white light on the roof are *taxi-services*. The white square indicates, in Arabic, the route and destination. Cars with a yellow square on the front doors and a yellow light on the roof are regular taxis, and cost about JD 1 from one Jebel (or hill) to another. The name of the taxi firm is usually written in English as well as Arabic on the door of the taxi. City taxis run on meters.

Intra-city *taxi-services* operate with set rates from fixed points in Amman, depending on the destination. All northbound *services* leave from Abdali Station, King Hussein St., and Shab Sough St. (downtown behind the Gold Market). The southbound ones leave from Wahdat (near Amman New Camp).

Private taxi companies also offer seats-in-a-taxi to points inside Jordan as well as to the neighboring countries of Syria and Lebanon.

Sample *service* prices: Southbound: Madaba, JD 1; Kerak, JD 2; Wadi Musa (Petra), JD 3. Northbound: Jerash, JD 1.

Northbound taxi companies, which also go to Damascus, are Hadad, Feras, and Hilal. Southbound ones are Aqaba, Kabriti, and El Janoub (which also have buses).

JETT buses to Aqaba depart Amman at 7 and 9 A.M., 2:30, 3:30, and 4 P.M. and return from Aqaba at 7, 8 and 9 A.M., 1:30 and 4 P.M. Cost is JD 3.

Car Rental: These are some of the car rental companies in Amman; a complete list is available from the Tourism Authority.

	Phone	Telex
Arabian, Jordan Inter-Continental	641–350	21363
Avis-Jarrar, Queen Alia Airport	(08) 651–071	23678
Avis-Jarrar, Holiday Inn		663–100
Budget, Jerusalem International Hotel	604–231	24197
Europcar, Amman Plaza	674–267	21410
Europcar, Marriott	601–350	21410
Firas, Shmeisani	676–856	24295
Satellite, Al Abdali	601–767	21513

Rates for a small Japanese car are approximately JD 20 for a Chevrolet, JD 28, with insurance and unlimited mileage. On another basis, a small Japanese car is JD 13 for 150 kms, with each extra km being 36 fils. A large European car, such as a Volvo, is JD 32 with insurance, unlimited mileage, and air-conditioning. Compare prices; Local automobile rental agencies may be cheaper than international ones, such as Avis and Budget.

A car can be hired through hotels and travel agents. Or, you may hire a car and driver for the day from any taxi company. A taxi with driver for the day in Amman should be about JD 25 from 8 A.M. to 6 P.M. or JD 4 per hour. Outside Amman the price depends on distance. The following sample prices (given in Jordanian Dinars) were provided by Barq Taxi at the Jordan Inter-Continental Hotel and are probably among the most expensive in town. For example, several taxi companies charge only JD 20 for the Damascus trip. You should be able to arrive at more favorable rates with some bargaining—and never hesitate to bargain on taxi prices *in advance.*

From Amman to

Jerash	& return	half day	15
Jerash, Ajlun	& return	three-quarters day	24
Madaba, Mt. Nebo	& return	three-quarters day	15
Madaba, Kerak	& return	three-quarters day	30
Petra	& return	via King's Highway	45
		via Desert Rd.	35
Aqaba	& return	full day	50
Dead Sea	& return	half day	15
Desert Palaces	& return	half day	35
King Hussein Bridge	one way		10
Damascus	one way		25
Airport	round trip		6

By train: There are no passenger trains in Jordan, although we have been told the freight train will take passengers willing to forgo all comforts. Plans to rebuild the Hejaz Railway to Medina are being studied by a committee from the Ministries of Transportation of Jordan, Syria, and Saudi Arabia.

The railway, built over an 8-year period by nearly 6,000 Turkish soldiers, started running in 1908. From Damascus to Medina the trip took 3 days, a vast and miraculous improvement in those days to Moslem pilgrims, who previously had to spend 40 to 50 days traveling in the fastest camel caravan.

The railway remained in full use for only 6 years, until 1914. With the outbreak of World War I and the Arab revolt against the Ottomans, it became an important military target and was repeatedly attacked. By 1917 most of the line was out of use, although the Ma'an (Jordan)–Damascus stretch continued to operate and is still running.

Reconstruction of the old line could cost $1 billion. Efforts to revive the line have been made several times in the past 40 years—in 1935, 1938, and 1955. It was not until 1964, however, that actual work began. It resulted only in laying a stretch of new track from Ma'an to the Saudi border, still some distance from Medina.

The present plan is more ambitious. The intention is to build an entirely modern railway, replacing the old narrow-gauge track with the standard gauge now in use throughout Europe.

By air: The only regularly scheduled internal air service in Jordan is Royal Jordanian's flight to Aqaba which operates daily. Round-trip fare for up to 10 days is JD 18. One-way fare is JD 13.

Arab Wings, Royal Jordanian's executive jet service, is available for local and long-distance flights.

Transportation from the Airport. Amman's Queen Alia International Airport is a modern multi-million-dollar facility with a wide range of services and features. It is located 25 miles southeast of the capital. The 4-lane highway that leads to the airport is part of the national highway system leading south to Aqaba, east to Madaba, and north to Amman.

An airport taxi service is available in the South Terminal. Taxis start their meters at JD 1.500, with a charge of 100 fils for each kilometer — making the average charge to a midtown hotel approximately JD 5–6. The ride to a midtown hotel takes about 35 to 45 minutes, depending on the time of day and the traffic. There is also a city bus service to and from Abdali Station in town. Cost is 500 fils.

An airport tax of JD 7, which must be paid in Jordanian Dinars, is charged on departure from Jordanian airports. Remember to leave yourself enough Jordanian currency to pay this tax on departure. If you should run out, however, don't be concerned. You can exchange money at the airport.

Transportation to Nearby Countries. Jordan Express Tourist Transport (664146) has daily bus service to Damascus. It leaves from Abdali Road at 7 A.M. and 2 P.M. One way costs JD 3. There is a departure tax of JD 3 per person.

Private Automobiles. You may bring your automobile duty free into Jordan for a maximum period of 1 year upon the presentation of a triptych issued by a recognized automobile club. If you sell the automobile in Jordan, the duty must be paid. You need a license for the vehicle. A valid U.S., British, or international driver's license may be used for up to three months. Foreigners planning to live in Jordan must obtain a local driver's license.

Third-party automobile insurance is compulsory. Annual rates are JD 25 for American cars and JD 20 for non-American cars (subject to increase according to increase of limits of liabilities).

Comprehensive coverage is strongly recommended and can be purchased locally. Price is based on car type, value, horsepower, and model. For specifics, contact an insurance agency in Amman.

Road Conditions. Jordan has over 10,000 miles of excellent roads, many of which were added only in the past decade. The main highways run the length of the country, north-south, and its breadth, east-west. From these major arteries into and out of Amman other roads branch to give access to all the populated towns of the country.

With a few exceptions, most of the historic or otherwise interesting sights in Jordan can be reached over a paved road in an ordinary automobile or bus, on a half- or full-day tour.

Two highways lead from Amman to Aqaba, the King's Highway and the Desert Highway. A third road along the Dead Sea connects with a new road through Wadi Araba to Aqaba.

Jordan's main highway connecting the East and West banks runs from Amman to Jerusalem across the Jordan River at the King Hussein Bridge. It is open daily except Saturday from 7 A.M. to 1 P.M. *Service* from Amman is JD 2 to the security point at the bridge; taxi fare is JD 4. Another road via Salt crosses the river further north at the Prince Muhammad Bridge and continues to Nablus. It is open the same hours, but is not used by tourists.

There are no security regulations banning motoring in any part of Jordan, but there are several check points on major roads where you may be asked to show identification.

Caution should be used in driving in those parts of the desert where there are no roads. It is absolutely foolhardy to strike off on one's own to remote areas of the desert; you could get lost. Now that the road across the desert to Azraq is surfaced, the trip, which once took all day, is an

easy morning's excursion. The ease of such a journey could give the uninitiated a false sense of security. The desert is hostile terrain for the automobile, especially after rain and in the dead heat of summer. Hard desert
tracks can suddenly turn into mud or soft sand into which car tires sink—
and it takes several very strong people to pull them out. This is not meant
to frighten anyone—travel in the desert is fabulous—but only to warn you
to be careful and plan properly.

The Desert Police Patrol, who can be easily recognized by their splendid
uniforms of khaki with red trim and red-and-white checked *kafiya,* are
cooperative in arranging an escort for travel to remote areas of the desert
where tourists are likely to lose their way. For your own protection, you
are asked to check in at police posts stationed in the desert. You should
comply with these requests.

Gasoline and Service Stations. In town, gas and service stations are
ample, but on the open road they are scarce. Be sure you have plenty of
gas before starting, and for trips into the desert carry along an extra supply. Gasoline costs JD 3.600 for 20 liter regular, JD 4.200 for super.

Servicing is adequate on most Japanese, American, and European cars.
Low- and medium-priced cars give the best road service, as repairs are
less likely to be needed and spare parts are more readily available.

City Maps and Walking. Maps of Amman can be purchased from
bookstores and hotel giftshops, and the Tourist Office has a complimenta-
ry but slightly out-of-date map as well. Since Amman has very few name
signs for streets in Arabic and even fewer in English, you should try to
learn a few landmarks in town to enable you to find your way around
quickly. Except for the very heart of downtown, Amman is not a city for
walking as it is built on seven steep hills. Each section or district is designated by the "Jebel" or hill where it is located. In the district where many
of the hotels are situated—Jebel Amman—locations are designated by a
series of roundabouts—*i.e.,* First Circle, Second Circle, up to the Eighth
Circle. The American Embassy and the Jordan Inter-Continental Hotel,
landmarks for American travelers, are located near the Third Circle on
Jebel Amman.

TOURIST FACILITIES. The main organization in Jordan to facilitate
tourism is the Tourism Authority of the Ministry of Tourism and Antiquities. Main Office: Jebel Amman, P.O. Box 224, Amman, tel. 642311/7.
The Tourism Authority has a new office in the Arrivals Building at the
Queen Alya International Airport, located near the exit doors in the baggage retrieval area. Department of Antiquities: P.O. Box 88, Amman, tel.
644336.

Tourist Guides: Guides in Jordan are required to pass an examination
prepared by the Tourism Ministry before being licensed to practice. You
may ask to see a guide's license before engaging him. Guides who speak
English are available through reliable travel agencies at JD 10–15 per day.
During heavy tourist seasons it is wise to ask your agent to book a guide
in advance of your arrival.

Tourist Police: Jordan has well-trained, extremely pleasant, and cooperative Tourist Police. They are stationed at major tourist sites and the air-

port to assist visitors when the need arises. Although they are trained to act as guides, this is not their primary function.

In addition, the government Rest Houses at major tourist sites act as information centers.

Travel Agencies: Any travel agency in Amman will be able to arrange automobile transportation and a guide to the major sightseeing attractions. Prices are regulated, but you should agree on the fee before departing. If several persons are traveling together, hiring a car for the day is the best way to tour the country.

For someone traveling alone, however, this is expensive. Several companies advertise individual fares for daily tours by bus or car depending on the time of year. Jordan Express Tourist Transport Company (JETT) has a bus leaving Amman for Petra daily at 6:30 A.M. and departing Petra at 4 P.M. for the return. Cost is JD 15 from Abdali Station per person for round trip, lunch, horse, and guide. For bus only (no services) to Petra, the fare is JD 6 round trip. Also, there often are other persons traveling alone who are eager to share taxi costs. As soon as you arrive in Amman, go to one of the travel agencies in town and inquire.

Major Travel Agencies in Amman

Name	Address	Telephone
Atlas Travel & Tourist	King Hussein St.	624262
Attaher Tourist & Travel	King Hussein St.	622128
Ayoub Caravan Tours	King Hussein St.	638836
Bestours	Prince Mohammed St.	637171
Bisharat Tours Corporation	Jordan Intercontinental Hotel	641350
Blue Bell Tours	Grand Palace Hotel	661913
Concord Travel & Tourism	King Hussein St.	623536
Crown Tours	King Hussein St.	636919
General Tours	King Hussein St.	624307
Grand Travel & Tourism	King Hussein St.	624363
Guiding Star Agency	Prince Mohammed St.	642526
Halaby Tourist Company	King Hussein St.	639540
International Traders	Shmeisani	661014
Jerusalem Express Travel	King Hussein St.	622151
Jordan Express Company	Police College St.	664146
Jordan Resources Company	King Hussein St.	636772
Jordan Travel Bureau	King Hussein St.	625585
Khoury Travel Tourist	King Hussein St.	623430
Lawrence Tours	Grand Palace Hotel	664916
Nawas Tourist Agency	King Hussein St.	622184
Near East Tourist Center	Jordan Inter-Continental Hotel	641906
Orient Tours	King Hussein St.	625471
Pan Pacific Travel & Tourism	King Hussein St.	621688
Petra Tours	King Hussein St.	637380
Philadelphia Travel Agency	King Hussein St.	630800
Royal Tours	Jordan Inter-Continental Hotel	644267

Name	Address	Telephone
Seikaly's Travel & Tourism	Prince Mohammed St.	622147–8
Telstar Travel & Tourism	Jebel Amman	640213
Terra Santa Tourist Co.	King Hussein St.	625203
Wazzan Travel & Tourism	King Hussein St.	623180
Ya'ish Travel & Tourism	King Hussein St.	630610
Zaatarah Tourist Company	King Hussein St.	636011
JETT Tourist Buses	Abdali Street	664146

HEALTH PRECAUTIONS. Water in Amman is usually safe to drink in deluxe and first-class hotels that have their own filtering systems. If you have any doubts, ask for bottled water, which is available in hotels and restaurants. An excellent bottled water, Kawthar, is bottled from the springs at Azrak by a joint venture with Evian of France. It costs JD 1.600 per dozen of 1.5 liter bottles in groceries; in hotels and restaurants it can cost 2 or 3 times that much, although many hotels provide it free to guests in their rooms. On trips to the desert and to small villages take along water or bottled soft drinks. You will find it handy to include a collapsible drinking cup in your hand luggage for such occasions.

Hotels serve both European and Jordanian dishes. Jordan has a wide variety of good fruits and vegetables. Eat what is in season. Peel the fruit and vegetables until your system has had time to adjust. More important, eat lightly. Tourists become ill from overeating—and overexerting themselves sightseeing—more frequently than from the food itself.

Should you feel any stomach illness coming on, Lomotil is the most immediately effective medicine if taken promptly. It is readily available from local pharmacies without prescription.

MONEY. The monetary unit in Jordan is the Jordanian Dinar (JD), which is divided into 1000 fils. One dinar is equal to about $2 or £6. In reverse, $1 equals about 500 fils; £1 is 925 fils. The JD was reevaluated in 1988; therefore, prices quoted in this book are subject to fluctuation. Ten fils are also called a piaster (pt.). Thus $1 equals 37 pt.

Jordanian money appears in the following denominations:

Banknotes: JD 50, 20, 10, 5, 1, ½ (500 fils).

Silver: 250 fils (25 piasters), 100 fils (10 pt.), 50 fils (5 pt.), 25 fils (2.5 pt.), and 20 fils (2 pt.).

Copper: 10 fils and 5 fils.

There are no restrictions on the amount of Jordanian currency, foreign banknotes, travelers' checks, or gold visitors may bring into or take out of the country. Special authorization is required for the import and export of stocks and bonds.

Foreign currency, drafts, and travelers' checks, should be exchanged at banks and at authorized money changers. Exchange facilities are provided in the arrival lounge at the airport in Amman and at the border guard at Ramtha. In Amman, most banks and money changers are located downtown on the main street and near or in hotels. Hotels and merchants will accept travelers' checks.

Major credit cards are used in Jordan, but their acceptance is limited to hotels and restaurants and a few merchants and travel agencies. Do not expect to use them to cover your costs. Also, personal checks are difficult to cash. To avoid problems, carry travelers' checks. In out-of-the-way places, carry Jordanian currency in small denominations, as change may not always be available. The American Express representative is "International Traders," Shmeisani, across from the Ambassador Hotel, tel. 661–014. There is also an office in Aqaba, but emergency check cashing is only available in Amman. Open 8 A.M.–1 P.M. and 3–6 P.M.; closed Fridays.

TIPPING. Most hotels and restaurants add a 10 percent service charge (12 percent in deluxe places), but the people who actually do the work expect tips. As a guide, try this formula: on departure from a hotel, your total tips should not exceed 10 percent of your bill before the service charge is added.

Taxi drivers do not expect tips, but be sure to agree on the fare in advance if the taxi does not have a meter.

HOLIDAYS. National: May 1, Labor Day; May 25, Independence Day; Aug. 11, His Majesty King Hussein's Accession to the Throne; Nov. 14, His Majesty King Hussein's Birthday.

Moslem holidays: The Moslem (Hegira) calendar is a lunar one, the first year corresponding to the year of the Prophet Muhammad's flight from Mecca to Medina (622 A.D.). Since the Moslem year is 13 days shorter than the Gregorian year, its holidays vary from year to year, and it is difficult to know precisely on which day in the Gregorian calendar a Moslem feast will fall.

Eid el Fitr, a 3-day feast, celebrates the end of Ramadan, the holy month of fasting. *Eid el Adha* (or *el Kabir*) celebrates the end of the *Haj,* or pilgrimage to Mecca, commemorating Abraham's offering of his son. The feast lasts 3 days and is the most important one in the Moslem faith. *Muharram I* is the Moslem New Year, the first day of the Islamic calendar. *Moulid el Nabi,* which falls on the twelfth day of Rabi I, is the birthday of the Prophet. *Rajab 27* is the Feast of *al Miraj,* commemorating the Prophet Muhammad's nocturnal visit to heaven. *Sha'ban 9, Arab Renaissance Day,* commemorates the Arab Revolt against Ottoman rule.

On major feasts Jordanians tend to make a long holiday of it. Government offices and many businesses close down for several days. Businessmen in particular should try to avoid a visit during long holidays and especially during Ramadan.

Friday is the sabbath in Jordan, according to the tradition in most Moslem countries. Government offices and most but not all business offices and shops are closed.

Christian holidays: At Easter, celebrations of the Western and Eastern churches in Jordan fall according to the Eastern church date, which can be as much as a month after the Western one. These are the most impressive and moving services of the year. For Eastern Christians Easter is a bigger and more important feast than Christmas.

Christmas is observed by the Roman Catholic, Protestant, and Orthodox Churches on December 25. In Bethlehem and Jerusalem special services begin on Christmas Eve, December 24, and continue through the following day. It should be noted also that the Coptic and Abyssinian Churches celebrate Christmas in mid-January.

The Moslem Calendar 1989

Gregorian	Moslem
January	Jumada II
February	Ragab
March	Shaban
April	Ramadan
May	Shawal
June	Thul-Kida
July	Thul-Higga
August	Moharram
September	Safar
October	Rabi I
November	Rabi II
December	Jumada I

The Moslem months have alternately 29 or 30 days, and the year has 354 days, so that they do not coincide precisely with the Gregorian calendar from year to year. For example, Ramadan will fall on Apr. 11 in 1989, and on Apr. 1 in 1990.

LANGUAGE. Arabic is the official language of Jordan; however, English is widely spoken at every level throughout the country, and educated Jordanians are almost always bilingual.

TIME. For Amman, Greenwich Mean Time plus 3 hours in summer; 2 hours in winter. For Jerusalem, GMT plus 2 hours in summer; 1 hour in winter. Eastern Standard Time plus 7 hours; Daylight Saving Time plus 6 hours.

BUSINESS HOURS. Government offices are open daily, except Friday, from 8 A.M. to 2 P.M. Banks are open to the public from 9:30 A.M. to 1:30 P.M. During Ramadan, the hours are 9 A.M. to 1:30 P.M. Business offices follow the same hours, but some close on Sunday. Shops and other businesses are open from 9 A.M. to 1 or 1:30 P.M. and from 3 to 6:30 or 7 P.M.

TELEPHONE. Amman and the main towns in Jordan are connected by automatic dial system. Telephones occasionally go out of service, and one may encounter delay in getting through to the party one is calling. Recently, the entire system was expanded and new numbers installed in much of the city. If the number you have dialed does not answer, check with information. It is probably an old number. A city phone book is available. There are coin-operated telephones (50 fils) in many downtown locales such as small grocery stores and newsstands.

Jordan is connected by direct dial to most of Europe, the U.S. and Arab countries. Dial 00, then the country code and local number. Phone calls *cannot* be made from Jordan to Israel.

For telephone information, dial 12. English-speaking operators are available to assist you. For domestic calls and Middle East calls dial 10, and for overseas calls dial 17.

Anyone planning to live in Jordan should be aware that telephones are difficult to obtain in some quarters of the city where demand outpaces supply.

MAIL, FAX, AND TELEGRAMS. In Amman the Central Post Office is located on Prince Muhammad St. in the center of town, and there are branches conveniently located throughout the city. You may buy stamps between 8 A.M. and 8 P.M. at the main Post Office. The branch at the Jordan Inter-Continental Hotel is open 8 A.M.–7 P.M.; closed Fridays.

Airmail postage to the U.S., Canada, Australia, and South America is 240 fils for letters, 120 fils for postcards; to Europe, Africa, and Asia 160 fils for letters and 250 fils for postcards. International airmail to or from the U.S. takes above 5 to 7 days. Airmail letters to all Arab countries and Pakistan are 80 fils, 60 fils for postcards.

You may send telegrams and cables and purchase stamps from leading hotels or post offices in Amman. The cost of cable to the U.S. is 108 fils per word; to Britain, 92 fils; Italy, 116 fils; West Germany, 138 fils. There is no night-letter rate.

You may send a package from Jordan after filling out a customs declaration and clearing it with the local customs office. Packages should be left open for custom officials to check their contents. For ordinary tourist gifts, ask the gift shop to mail your purchases for you. Airmail parcels to the U.S. cost JD 24.100; and to Britain, JD 16.800 for two kilos. By sea per two kilos: JD 6.445 to U.S.; JD 4.450 to U.K. Facsimile service is available at all major Amman post offices and most large hotels. And, there is a good express mail service at Abdali, called "Al Bareed Al Mumtax." It guarantees worldwide delivery within a short period of time.

PHOTOGRAPHY. Jordan is a pleasure for photographers. The weird shapes and color-rich rocks of Petra and Wadi Rum, the drama of the Jordan Valley, the sunset at Jerash, and the panorama from Kerak are only a few of the delightful subjects.

Bring all your film with you and plan to have it developed when you return home. Film—color and black and white—is available, but American film is more expensive than in the U.S. For example, Kodacolor Gold 100 (36 exposures) is JD 2.200 and Ektachrome 100 (36 exposures) is JD 4. Also, you cannot always be sure that the type of film you need will be available, especially film for some of the newest instant and self-developing cameras. European film is also on sale.

If you want to photograph local color, you should remember that what sometimes appears picturesque to strangers might be merely poverty to the local inhabitants. Avoid embarrassing Jordanians, especially women, or yourself; ask permission first. They are often delighted to oblige—and you might want to offer them a little token for their cooperation. Military installations, including bridges, may not be photographed.

Slides of important sites are on sale at leading hotels and gift shops and at sites of antiquity and museums. The quality of the color varies from one vendor to another.

Serious amateur photographers should carry a light meter; unless you are familiar with desert conditions, you will be likely to overexpose film. The sun is deceptively bright, especially at sites of antiquity, and there is an enormous amount of reflected light, particularly during midday. When in doubt, use one stop below the normal setting.

For black and white film, a yellow filter produces good results. Tri-X, 400 ASA, or other fast film is terrific for inside shots, but is often too fast for normal outside shots in the bright sun.

As for color, wonderful results can be had with low ASA film like Koda-chrome 25 or 64 because lighting conditions are ideal. Except that your photographs will have shadows, the best times of the day for picture-taking are early morning and late afternoon, when colors are deeper and antique stone is mellow.

Should you need passport-size photographs in a hurry, they can be made at any of the photo shops on or near King Feisal Street. Most offer second-day service. It is possible to get one-hour developing service for color prints. Try Al-Fanar in the Housing Bank Centre, Shmeisani.

ELECTRIC CURRENT. 220 A.C. volts, 50 cycles. Wall plugs are the round, 2-prong European type (adapters for American products are available locally). Transformers are required for American products, but not for British ones.

CONVERTING METRIC TO U.S. MEASUREMENTS

Multiply:	by:	to find:
Length		
millimeters (mm)	.039	inches (in)
meters (m)	3.28	feet (ft)
meters	1.09	yards (yd)
kilometers (km)	.62	miles (mi)
Area		
hectare (ha)	2.47	acres
Capacity		
liters (L)	1.06	quarts (qt)
liters	.26	gallons (gal)
liters	2.11	pints (pt)
Weight		
gram (g)	.04	ounce (oz)
kilogram (kg)	2.20	pounds (lb)
metric ton (MT)	.98	tons (t)
Power		
kilowatt (kw)	1.34	horsepower (hp)
Temperature		
degrees Celsius	9/5 (then add 32)	degrees Fahrenheit

CONVERTING U.S. TO METRIC MEASUREMENTS

Multipy:	by:	to find:
Length		
inches (in)	25.40	millimeters (mm)
feet (ft)	.30	meters (m)
yards (yd)	.91	meters
miles (mi)	1.61	kilometers (km)
Area		
acres	.40	hectares (ha)
Capacity		
pints (pt)	.47	liters (L)
quarts (qt)	.95	liters
gallons (gal)	3.79	liters
Weight		
ounces (oz)	28.35	grams (g)
pounds (lb)	.45	kilograms (kg)
tons (t)	1.11	metric tons (MT)
Power		
horsepower (hp)	.75	kilowatts
Temperature		
degrees Fahrenheit	5/9 (after subtracting 32)	degrees Celsius

USEFUL ADDRESSES. *Embassies and Consulates:* Jordan Mission to the United Nations, 866 United Nations Plaza, New York, NY 10017, (212) 759–1950; Embassy of the Hashemite Kingdom of Jordan, 3504 International Dr., N.W., Washington, DC 20008, (202) 966–2909; 100 Bronson Ave., Ottawa, Ontario K1R 6G8, Canada, (613) 238–8090; 6 Upper Phillimore Gardens, London W8 7HB, England, 937–3685.

Jordan Information Center, 1701 K. St., N.W., Washington, DC 20006, (202) 659–3322. *Alia Offices:* New York City: 535 Fifth Ave., tel. (212) 949–0060; or (800) 223–0470, or Washington, D.C.: 1925 K. St., N.W., Suite 501, (202) 857–0401. Atlanta: 229 Peachtree St., N.E., Suite 2415, (404) 659–2542. Houston: 3336 Richmond Ave., Suite 216, (713) 524–3700. Chicago: 104 S. Michigan Ave., Suite 215, (312) 236–1702. Los Angeles: 6033 W. Century Blvd. #760, (213) 215–9627. Detroit: 6 Parklane Blvd. #122, Dearborn, (313) 271–6663. Toronto: 150 York St. #908, (416) 862–7527. Montreal: 1801 McGill College Ave., Suite 1160, (514) 288–1647. London: Sales Office, 177 Regent St., London, W1, 734–2557/8/9/50.

Emergency Telephone Numbers. First Aid, 661111; Fire 198; Police 192; Ambulance (Government) 195, Civil Defense Rescue 661111; Fire Headquarters 622090; Jordan Electric Power Co. 636381/2; Munici-

pal Water Service 625943; Police Headquarters 685111; Roving Patrol
Rescue Police (English spoken) 24-hour emergency 621111/637777.

Other Useful Numbers. Airport Information, 08–53200; U.S. Embassy
644371 (open for business of U.S. citizens Sunday–Thursday 8 A.M.–4 P.M.);
British Embassy 832100; Australian Embassy 673246; Canadian Embassy
666124; British Council 636147; French Cultural Center 637009; Goethe
Institute 641993.

BY WAY OF BACKGROUND

An Introduction to Jordan

Jordan in Arabic is *Al Urdan.* It is known officially as the Hashemite Kingdom of Jordan.

Located in the heart of the Middle East and the Arab world, it covers an area of approximately 37,300 square miles (about 35,100 square miles are on the East Bank, 2,165 square miles on the West Bank). The area is about the size of Indiana.

Jordan is bordered on the north by Syria, on the east by Iraq and Saudi Arabia, and on the south by Saudi Arabia and the Gulf of Aqaba, its only sea outlet, which gives access to the Red Sea. On the west its boundary is the uneasy frontier with Israel established by the United Nations Armistice Agreement of 1949. In the subsequent war of 1967, the West Bank of the Jordan came under Israeli occupation.

Jordan's borders with Saudi Arabia were established in a series of agreements made by Great Britian in 1925. In an exchange of territory in 1965, Jordan's coastline on the Gulf of Aqaba was extended by about 12 miles. This border, which passes through almost rainless and unpopulated desert, established a zone where Jordan and Saudi Arabia would share revenues on an equal basis should oil be discovered in the area.

Physical Features

The country's major river is the famous Jordan, which starts from the melting snows of Mount Hermon in Syria and collects the waters of the Yarmuk and lesser streams on its journey south. After winding snakelike for 200 miles through the Jordan Valley, it reaches the Jericho oasis and empties into the Dead Sea, at 1,306 feet below sea level, the lowest point on the earth's surface.

The Jordan Valley (El Ghor), together with the Dead Sea and Wadi Araba, forms one continuous depression through the country from north to south and is part of the Great Rift Valley of Africa and the Middle East. The depression is warm year-round, and with new irrigation it has enabled Jordan to develop a new agricultural base to its economy.

Rising out of the Jordan Valley to an average altitude of 3,000 and up to 5,400 feet are the hills of Biblical history. West of the Jordan, the hills of Judaea stretch from Samaria in the north to Beersheba in the south.

East of the river the mountains are divided into four districts by three steep gorges (wadis) with perennial streams. The four districts correspond roughly to the Kingdoms of the Old Testament: *Ajlun* (the Biblical land of Gilead) lies between the Yarmuk and Wadi Zerqa; *Balqa* (part of Moab and the lands of the Ammonites) is the area between Zerqa and Mujib; *Kerak* (the land of Moab) extends from Wadi Mujib to Wadi al Hasa, and *Ma'an* (the land of the Edomites and later of the Nabataeans) stretches from Wadi Hasa to the Gulf of Aqaba. Beyond the eastern highlands the ever-encroaching desert extends into Iraq on the east and Saudi Arabia on the south.

The Yarmuk River, the main tributary of the Jordan River, forms the border between Israel on the northwest, Syria on the northeast, and Jordan on the south. The Zerqa River, the Jordan's second main tributary, rises and empties entirely inside the East Bank. It has been developed in recent years to provide irrigation for the lower eastern Jordan Valley.

Jordan's population is concentrated in the northern highlands of the country, where the major towns are located near the Jordan River system, and where rainfall is sufficient to support cultivation.

With 80 percent of its land as desert, needless to say arable land is the country's most valued resource. The East Ghor Canal, completed in 1966, has brought much of the Jordan Valley under irrigation. Additional projects in the Jordan Valley are aimed at further land reclamation, greater exploitation of water resources, and infrastructure development including construction of roads, bridges, dams, and electrical plants to improve the quality of life for the farmers of the region and enable them to achieve maximum productivity from their efforts.

Jordan consists of a high plateau divided into ridges by valleys and gorges. Repeated earthquakes through the ages are evident throughout. In the north, toward the Syrian border, there are fields of broken lava and basaltic rock. The greater part of the country east of the Rift depression is desert, arid and sparsely populated. Most of the land is part of the great Syrian or north Arabian desert, consisting of salt flats and broad expanses of sand and dunes, particularly in the south.

The rolling hills and the low mountains support a meager and stunted vegetation most of the year, except in spring when these brown hillsides are carpeted with green grass and flowers. Toward the depression in the western part of the East Bank, there is a rise that evolves into the Jordanian highlands, a steppe of high limestone plateaus and an area of *wadis* that are dry except in the short winter rainy season.

Wheat, barley, and other cereals as well as corn, tobacco, peanuts, fruit, and vegetables are the chief crops in this area. The market furnished by the neighboring oil-producing countries has stimulated the cultivation of cash crops, including tomatoes, citrus fruit, and potatoes. Government-sponsored agricultural extension work to prevent soil erosion and flash-flooding has also stimulated agricultural production. The development of dams and outlets for tributary streams from the plateau is significantly increasing the region's agricultural potential.

The People

The population, which numbers about 2.8 million, is preponderantly Arab in origin and Sunni Moslem in religion. The main schism in Islam occurred early in its history over the question of the rightful succession to the Prophet Muhammad. The orthodox group is called *Sunni* and the dissenting one *Shiite.*

About 7 percent of Jordanians are Christians. The country also has many distinctive ethnic groups such as Circassians, who are Sunni Moslems from the Caucasus.

The majority of the population lives in or near the capitals of Jordan's five main administrative districts: Amman, 1,180,000 (including the country's capital); Irbid, about 582,000; Balqa, 134,000; Kerak, 111,300; and Ma'an, 53,000. Population growth exceeds 3 percent annually, and half the population is under 15 years of age.

About one-third of the population are residents of what was formerly Transjordan; another 40 percent are Palestinian refugees from the wars of 1948 and 1967. About 11 percent of the population are nomadic or seminomadic tribes, *i.e.,* Bedouin.

The original Jordanians are members of several hundred tribes that have lived in the area for centuries. Some came from Hejaz, the home of the Prophet Muhammad, and were soldiers and followers of the Arab armies who carried the banner of Islam out of Arabia in the 7th and 8th centuries. Others wandered into the land across the River Jordan from Palestine or from the south from Egypt or Yemen. Still others were pushed into the area by wars from the north or the south, or tracked across the Syrian desert from the Mesopotamia Valley in the east. Some have come from Hauran and Damascus in Syria and from Lebanon.

Those who trace their origins to antiquity do so through legends and poetry, the Arab's greatest body of literature. With the great movement of tribes, land ownership changed hands many times.

The Bedouin

To be a Bedouin or to come from Bedouin stock is a matter of pride for many Jordanians. The Bedouin virtues and values are an important part of the Jordanian character—the traditional freedom of the desert, a sense of honor, pride in noble blood, bravery, generosity, hospitality, protection of the weak, and emphasis on the importance of the family. Although some of the Bedouin of Jordan are still nomads, most are in the transitional stage toward becoming settled villagers.

There are an estimated 40,000 Bedouin in Jordan. Their camps are found mainly east of the Desert Highway in an area approximately 248 miles long and 155 miles wide. Settlements of semi-nomads are located near the Qaal Jafr and Azraq oases. The former is the site of a government-sponsored agricultural project. A similar settlement has been established near Al Hasa, the center of the phosphate industry, and several villages along the desert highway between Amman and Aqaba.

The following are among the main Bedouin tribes:

—Beni Attiya, who wandered gradually into Transjordan from the Hejaz.

—al Majalli, who came to the Kerak district about 1759 to take refuge after a quarrel within the tribe.

—al Huweitat, who inhabit southern Jordan and claim descent from the Prophet through his daughter Fatima. They are thought to be descendants of the Nabataeans.

—al Isa, who claim to be an offshoot of a large tribe near the Euphrates.

—Beni Khalid, who claim relationship with a tribe of southern Iraq and who moved into Jordan about 100 years ago.

—al Sirhan, an ancient tribe said to originate in the Hauran (Syria), where they had established a semi-autonomous state, which was overthrown by tribes pushing northward from the Hejaz. The easternmost desert of Jordan on the border of Iraq is known as Wadi Sirhan.

A description of the Bedouin way of life will be found in the chapter on the Jordanian way of life.

The Circassians

The non-Arab Sunni Moslem minority known as Circassians (or *Sharakisah* in Arabic) settled in Jordan in the late 19th century. They trace their origins to two Indo-European Moslem tribes, the warrior Iassi and the Kossogs of the Caucasus, and are said to be akin to the Mameluks, who ruled Egypt from the 13th century to the Ottoman period.

In the wake of the Russian conquest of the Caucasus from the 10th to the 19th century, there was a southward migration of Caucasian tribes. In the late 19th century, under Turkish Sultan Abdel Hamid as the traditional protector of all Moslems, a large number of Circassian refugees were settled on land in Turkey, Syria, and Jordan. The first Circassian community reached Amman in 1878; others settled in Jerash, Naur, and Wadi Seer.

In Jordan the Circassian tribes are known as the *Adigah*. They number about 25,000, and consist of several groups: the Kabardian tribes in Amman and Jerash; the Bzadugh and the Abzakh in Naur and Wadi-Seer. Another group, the Chechens, or Shishans, are politically and socially identified with the Circassians in Jordan but speak an entirely different language. Chechen settlements are found in Suweilih, Ruseifa, Zerqa, Sukhne, and Azraq. The community numbers about 5,000.

The two seats allotted to the Circassians in the Jordanian Parliament are always occupied by a member of each community. With no common tribal language between them, the two communities use Arabic to communicate.

The Circassians are credited with helping to recreate Amman, which was all but abandoned when they arrived in the late 19th century. They helped also to establish the first government and police force in Jordan, introduced a system of agriculture, and helped to act as a settling influence on the surrounding area.

The Circassians today are predominantly agricultural and urban landlords, high government officials, and top ranking army and air force officers. Said al Mufti, the best known of the community, was prime minister and a prominent member of the senate. A Chechen has been the Imam of the Zerqa mosque; another, the mayor of Zerqa.

Although the traditional tribal hierarchy is fading, it is still an important factor in marriage. On the other hand, as the Circassians change from an agrarian to an urbanized and culturally Arabized community, their intermarriage with Arab Jordanians, too, has increased.

The community's social and cultural life centers in the Circassian Charitable Association located in Amman. The Circassians have produced many of Jordan's best athletes.

Other Minorities

In addition to the Circassians there is also a small community of Turcomans and another of Bahais, who came from Iran in 1910 to settle on land purchased in 1879 by Abdul Baha Abbas, head of the Bahai faith.

Two small tribes, the Layathna of Wadi Musa and the al-Bdul in the hills around Petra, are Moslem. Because they have retained some Jewish customs, some scholars suggest they may be the descendents of the early Hebrew tribes.

Jordan's Christian population is divided into tribal groupings also. Many are descendants of the early Christian converts in the area and of the Greeks, Romans, and Crusaders who ruled it. Some trace their origins to Egypt, Syria, Lebanon and, of course, to Nazareth, Bethlehem, Jerusalem, and the West Bank towns, which have been predominantly Christian for centuries. The Christian denominations include Greek Orthodox, Catholic, and Protestant. There is a small community of Armenians.

Also not to be overlooked is the country's fast-growing communities of Americans, Europeans, and other foreigners. The largest single group of Americans are those married to Jordanians—an estimated 300. After the war in Lebanon many American and British companies moved their regional headquarters to Amman because of its central location and easy access, comfort, and relatively low cost of living, as well as the prevalence of spoken English and of trained or trainable personnel.

The Palestinians of Jordan—Refugees and Citizens

As noted earlier, about 40 percent of Jordan's population are Palestinians who came during and after the wars of 1948 and 1967. Some live in the ten refugee camps on the East Bank administered by UNRWA, the United Nations Relief and Works Agency for Palestine Refugees in the Near East. Four camps were set up in 1949 and six emergency camps were created after the 1967 war.

It is difficult to come by an exact count of the Palestinians in Jordan. The number of refugees who fled from the West Bank to the East Bank in the months following the war of 1967 is as controversial as the number of refugees following the war in 1948.

Uprooted from their homes and villages in 1948, and from their wretched camps of tents and mud and tin shacks in 1967, the refugees have twice exploded onto Jordan's economy and forced rapid urbanization, particularly in the Amman area.

From the outset, no distinctions were made in official Jordanian statistics between the settled population and the newcomers. Jordan gave all the refugees immediate citizenship. It has also offered the Palestinians greater opportunities for participating in political and economic life than has any other Arab state. They have been granted the same political rights as other citizens; they may purchase or rent homes or farms outside the camps and many engage in business and all forms of employment. Palestinians today hold dominant positions in industry, commerce, finance, civil services, educational and health services, and other sectors of the economy.

The direct cost of providing basic services for the refugees is borne by UNRWA, various international aid programs, governments, and welfare agencies. Although its budget did not label specific allocations, each time Jordan has increased its expenditure for the Ministries of Education, Health and Social Affairs, Labor, Information, and Development and Reconstruction to extend these services and benefits to the refugees.

At this writing, the future of the West Bank is anything but clear. Jordan adheres to U.N. Resolution 242 as the basis of any peace negotiations.

Government

Jordan is a constitutional monarchy with a bicameral legislature. It is headed by King Hussein, who succeeded to the throne in 1952. The King's younger brother Prince Hassan was named Crown Prince in 1965. The official religion of Jordan is Islam.

Legislative power is vested in the National Assembly and the King. The National Assembly consists of two houses, the Senate and the House of Representatives. The latter has 60 members elected by direct secret ballot of all citizens over 18 years of age. Thirty of the members come from the East Bank and 30 from the West Bank. Members are elected for a four-year term of office.

The Senate consists of 30 members who are appointed by the King upon recommendation of the Cabinet. Senators must not be related to the King, must be over 40 years of age, and are chosen from present and former prime ministers, other ministers and past ambassadors, and from the members of the civil and *shari'a* courts (Islamic law courts). They may be retired army generals or former members of the House of Representatives. Senators are appointed for four years and may be reappointed.

The King approves laws and promulgates them. He is empowered to declare war, conclude peace and sign treaties, which must be approved by the National Assembly. He orders the holding of elections, convenes and adjourns the House, and appoints the prime minister and the speaker of the Senate.

The prime minister selects his cabinet; he and the cabinet are responsible to the Parliament.

The Council of Ministers, consisting of the prime minister, president of the council and his ministers, conducts all affairs of state both internal and external.

The Constitution provides that the cabinet be responsible to Parliament. The King is empowered to dissolve Parliament and delay calling elections for a period of 12 months.

The Constitution provides that there be no discrimination on account of race, religion, or language among Jordanian citizens and that there be equal opportunities in work and education. It provides for individual freedom, a free press, the establishment of schools (provided they follow a recognized curriculum and educational policy), and free and compulsory elementary education.

Administratively, the East Bank is divided into five major districts, known as *Muhafezate* (governorates) or *liwa:* Amman, Balqa, Irbid, Kerak, and Ma'an. The West Bank is divided into the three governorates of al-Quds (Jerusalem), Nablus, and al Khalil (Hebron). Each governorate is centered around a major town that is the political and economic hub of the surrounding area.

Great Britain recognized Transjordan as a sovereign independent state by a treaty signed in London on March 22, 1946. Emir Abdallah, King Hussein's grandfather, assumed the title of King on May 25, 1946. In June 1946, upon ratification of the Anglo-Jordanian treaty, the name of the territory was changed to the Hashemite Kingdom of Transjordan. Following the armistice in 1949 Central Palestine, as the West Bank was known, joined Transjordan in 1950.

Economy

Jordan's gross national product has grown from about JD 199 million in 1971 to 1.6 billion in 1984. Few countries in the world can match such a record, and when one considers the country's meager resources, it can be seen as nothing short of a miracle.

Although only about 10 percent of Jordan's land can be cultivated, agriculture is one of the most important sectors of the economy, accounting for 10 percent of the gross domestic product but employing over half of the population. In the development of agriculture, Jordan has put its greatest emphasis on expanding the irrigation facilities in the Jordan Valley. The Jordan Valley Development project, begun in 1958, has brought 30,000 acres under cultivation and will have a total of 90,000 acres available when all stages are completed.

At the time of the 1967 war an estimated 80 percent of the fruit-growing area, 45 percent of the vegetable area, and 25 percent of the cereal area were on the West Bank. Jordan's development of the East Bank of the Jordan Valley over the past decade has, however, altered the relative significance of these percentages.

Agriculture is carried on in three regions.

The Jordan Valley, known as Al Ghor, is part of the Dead Sea Basin. It will have 100,000 acres available for cultivation when current projects are completed. The entire area is below sea level and watered by irrigation. It lies between the Yarmuk River in the north, the Jordan River on the west, the Dead Sea in the south, and the Eastern Highlands. Because of its climate, two crops are produced annually, and it has the potential for three. The region's early production capability, compared with other areas and neighboring countries, also gives it a commercial advantage. The Ghor produces a wide variety of fruits and vegetables, a large part of which are exported to the oil-producing countries of the Arabian Peninsula.

The Ghor region is divided into two main parts, the North Ghor, with about 81,250 acres of cultivable land, and the South Ghor, with 15,000 acres. The Dead Sea lies between. The main source of water in the North Ghor is the Yarmuk River and tributaries of the Jordan River. The annual discharge of water is approximately 660 million cubic meters. Water in the South Ghor comes from the Mujib and Hasa Valleys and a number of lesser streams and springs. The annual discharge is around 90 million cubic meters.

The Highland region, which is dependent on rainfall, grows mainly wheat, barley, beans, and tobacco. Terracing and planting of some fruit trees has been started. For the most part land holdings are fragmented and small. Soil erosion and erratic rainfall are the major problems, but afforestation programs have been started to help combat the problem, and exploitation of springs and groundwater are helping to regulate water supplies.

The Highland region lies between the Yarmuk River and the Syrian border on the north, the Ghor and Wadi Araba in the west, Wadi Musa in the south, and the Badia region in the east and south. Average rainfall is 200 to 600 mm. in the north and middle parts; 200 to 300 mm. in the southern part of the region. The average annual rainfall in the Highlands represents 44 percent of the total annual rainfall in Jordan. Other sources of water are scattered springs and small amounts of groundwater throughout the highlands. Around 15,000 acres are irrigated by springs, while about 3,250 acres are irrigated from groundwater.

The Badia, or desert region, is by far the largest in terms of area and is used mainly for grazing of sheep, goats, and camel in the valleys and rain-fed areas. This region lies south and east of the Highland region and occupies 87 percent of Jordan east of the Jordan River. Research has shown that underground water is available to irrigate 7,500 acres in the north, but only 4,250 acres are presently utilized. In the south, groundwater could irrigate an estimated 22,000 acres of which less than a thousand are presently utilized.

Tourism, which was Jordan's most important source of foreign exchange prior to the war of 1967, suffered a crushing blow with the loss of Jerusalem and other sites on the West Bank. In the past few years, however, it has made a comeback and has surpassed its pre-1967 level. Income from tourism after the Israeli occupation of the West Bank in 1967 dropped to JD 4.6 million in 1968 as compared with JD 11.3 million in 1966, which had been the peak year. But by 1974 it had reached JD 17.3 million, an increase of 53 percent, and by 1976 receipts from tourism were JD 68.86 million and the number of visitors was 1,063,294—compared to 617,000 in 1966. By 1982, the number had exceeded two million. These figures include transit visitors.

New projects have included the completion of a new airport at Aqaba in 1971, the Queen Alya International Airport in Amman in 1983, a completely new highway system throughout the country, and many new hotels. Hotel capacity increased from 1,553 rooms in 1976 to about 6,000 rooms in 1988.

Industry, concentrated in Amman, Irbid, and Zerqa, is recent and accounts for approximately 12 percent of the Gross Domestic Product. Its growth is limited to some extent by the country's lack of certain raw materials and a small home market. However, its real growth is as a manufacturing and distribution center for the Middle East. Industry is playing an increasingly important role in the economy and growing annually as a source of revenue. Jordan's new five-year plan aims at an annual growth rate of 22 percent in the industrial sector.

Phosphate rock, located at Wadi al Hasa, 90 miles south of Amman, is Jordan's most important mineral resource, with reserves estimated at about 3 billion tons. It is mined at Al Hasa and Ruseifa; most is exported. Another of the country's major minerals is potash, which is extracted from an area along the east bank of the Dead Sea.

Oil has not been discovered in any commercially feasible quantity in Jordan, although geologists believe that there is oil here and the government continues to encourage oil companies to explore for it. If oil is discovered in commercial quantities, the government will take a 65 percent share and the company 35 percent.

A large proportion of local demand for refined oil products is met by the Jordanian Refinery Company at Zerqa, with an output of about 828,000 tons per year. The refinery is supplied from Tapline, which runs through the country from Saudi Arabia to Lebanon.

Jordan may be the poor kid on the block when it comes to oil, but it is rich in minerals—more than two dozen of them, in addition to phosphate and potash, can be exploited commercially. The major one is copper—about 55 million tons—in the Wadi Araba, the site of mines exploited before King Solomon. The manganese ore in the Dead Sea area is said to have a high copper content, and there are copper deposits near Aqaba. Among other known minerals are cobalt, iron ore, and uranium.

The target of the first five-year plan was to increase Jordan's income from mineral sales from JD 45 million in 1975 to JD 144 million in 1980, or an average annual increase of 26 percent. This sector received 30 percent of the planned investment for the country under the plan and accounted for over 28 percent of the GDP by 1980.

Manufactured and processed goods include cement, batteries, cigarettes, matches, and some processed food, and there has been significant expansion into new industries such as clothing, pharmaceuticals, marble, soaps, olive oil, toys, and beer. Work is under way to establish large factories for the production of paper, ceramics, processed food, detergents, woolen cloth, and steel tubes, as well as a vehicle assembly plant, among others.

A footwear manufacturing company was the first wholly private Jordanian-American joint industrial venture. International Leather Products Co., Inc., is owned equally by Wolverine World Wide, Inc., and the Jordan Tanning Company. Its 25,000-square-foot facility is capable of producing 250,000 pairs of shoes a year for the Middle East market. The Jordan Tanning Company, located in Amman, owns and operates one of the most modern cowhide tanneries in the Arab countries. Wolverine World Wide, headquartered in Rockford, Michigan, manufactures and markets Hush Puppies and a variety of other footwear. The joint-venture company is licensed to produce and market footwear under the Hush Puppies and Wolverine labels.

In the 1976–80 development plan, JD 100 million was earmarked for a phosphate fertilizer complex in Aqaba; JD 140 million for potash extraction at the Dead Sea by the Arab Potash Company and expansion of the cement factory at Fuheis; establishment of another cement factory costing JD 21.3 million; and a textile factory at Zerqa costing JD 3 million. Combined government and private investment in the mining and manufacturing sector under the five-year period of the plan reached over a billion dollars.

By 1984, phosphate production had reached 6.2 million tons; fertilizer production at the recently completed Aqaba plant and potash at the Arab Potash Company were both over half-million tons, while the latter plans for production to exceed one million tons by 1987.

The Amman Stock Exchange, the first in Jordan and one of the few in the Arab World, opened for business in January 1978. All transactions in shares of listed Jordanian companies must be conducted through licensed brokers on the floor of the Exchange. Private trades between shareholders outside the company are exempted.

During the 1950s and 1960s, the government placed great emphasis on the development of a modern transportation system. There are good all-weather roads from Amman to Aqaba, Azraq,

Jerusalem, Damascus, and Mafraq on the Iraqi frontier. Other roads that have been developed run from Yarmuk to the Dead Sea, Safi-Aqaba, Ma'an-Rum, and Azraq to the Saudi border.

The railway consists of a 52-mile line between Amman and the Syrian border, a 93-mile line between Amman and Hasa, a 157-mile line between Hasa and Aqaba through Hittiya, and a 24-mile line between Ma'an and Ras Naqab.

Amman is growing so fast that telephone lines are insufficient, but the system continues to be expanded. Direct dial is now available to many countries in Europe, the Arab States, and the U.S.

Jordan has long been dependent on foreign aid. Its budget deficits are largely financed with loans and grants from the oil-rich Arab Gulf states and the West. U.S. aid has jumped sharply from JD 10 million in 1982 to over JD 100 million for the years 1985–1987. Additional budgetary assistance is provided by other Arab countries, chiefly Saudi Arabia and the Gulf states. U.N. agencies, the Kuwait Fund, and a number of Western countries— notably Great Britain and West Germany—also provide assistance.

The 1981–1985 plan called for investment of JD 2.8 billion and an annual growth rate in GDP of 10.4 percent. However, due to the regional problems and the slowdown in the world economy, Jordan was unable to maintain the rapid growth she had enjoyed, and in 1981 the annual rate fell to 7.5 percent, and by 1984 it was down to 3.8 percent. The next Five-Year Plan (1986–1990) has had to scale back growth and development plans considerably.

It should be noted that, meager as Jordan's resources may be, one of its most surprising aspects to a visitor is its vitality. The accomplishments of this young nation are amazing and have come as a result of the ingenuity, resourcefulness, and sheer determination of its people and the leadership of King Hussein. Jordanians deserve our profound admiration.

JORDAN—TEN MILLENNIA

A Brief History

The Hashemite Kingdom of Jordan is, politically, only 40 years old. Yet, as a land where people have lived, Jordan is as old as civilization itself. Indeed, here in the Jordan Valley the earliest evidence of man's communal life is found.

Archeologists tell us that Jordan was occupied by settled communities, such as Beida and Jericho, as early as 7000 B.C. Virtually all migrations and conquering armies of ancient times had to cross this land bridge which connected Asia and Africa. Over the centuries many of their numbers settled in the Jordan Valley and the surrounding highlands.

Jordan first appears prominently in the Bible with the arrival of Abraham in the Land of Canaan. The event probably corresponds with the great migration of a northwestern Semitic tribe, the Amorites, who appeared in Jordan about 2000 B.C.

During the 17th century B.C., North Palestine, as it was later called, was conquered by the Biblical Horites, later to be pushed out by the Edomites (Gen. 36:20). The southern portion was taken over by the Hyksos (the Shepherd Kings), who introduced horse-drawn chariots and subsequently revolutionized the art of war. Culturally and politically, Palestine was part of the Hyksos Empire of Egypt until the Hyksos were expelled from Egypt in 1550 B.C.

Less than a century later, during the reign of Egyptian Queen Hatshepsut, Palestine and southern Syria again came under the control of Egypt. A revolt against the Egyptians was put down by Hatshepsut's successor, Thothmes III, and for another century Palestine remained under Egyptian rule. Most of what is known about the period comes from a cache of a hundred or more letters found at Tell al-Amarna in Upper Egypt. These letters, which had been sent from Palestine to Egypt in the 15th and 14th centuries B.C., revealed that Egypt's main interest in Palestine was to use it to defend Phoenicia and southern Syria against the Hittites advancing from the north. In the 13th century, the Hittites were finally checked by Ramses II at Kadesh on the Orontes in Syria.

At about the same time the Phoenician coast was invaded by the "Sea People" from the Aegean, called the Philistines. Within 150 years after the settling of the coast, the Philistines (from whom Palestine gets its name) had conquered all Palestine. Simultaneously, three other groups settled east of the Jordan: Edomites in the south, Moabites east of the Dead Sea, and Ammonites east of Gilead on the edge of the Syrian Desert.

According to the Bible, the Edomites were the descendants of Esau (Gen. 36:9) and the Moabites and Ammonites were descended from Lot (Gen. 19:37, 38). The Ammonites are described as having taken their land from the Zamzummim, a giant race, and established their capital at Rabbath Ammon, present-day Amman (Deut. 2:20).

Another prominent Biblical tribe, the Amorites, were located at Heshbon (Hisban), their capital, and their territory extended from the Dead Sea to the Lake of Galilee. Their king was Sihon, who defeated the King of Moab (Num. 21:26).

Another Amorite Kingdom, Bashan, had its capital at Edrei (Dera'a). Its King was Og, and its territory was situated north of the Ammonites, from Jabbok (Wadi Zerqa) to the Yarmuk (Deut. 3).

The period introduced the next important episode involving Jordan in Biblical history. In the late 14th or early 13th century B.C. the Israelites left Egypt, and after their long wandering in the wilderness moved north into the land of the Edomites. The Edomites refused them permission to pass through their land and forced them to detour northeast through the desert to reach the Arnon River, the north boundary of Moab (Num. 21:21). The weakness of the local rulers made it easy for the newcomers to occupy the hill country of Transjordan.

Historians and archeologists vary widely on the dates of the Philistine invasion, the settlement of the Edomites, Moabites, and Ammonites, and the Exodus. Some authorities date the Exodus as early as the 15th century B.C. Many, however, call Ramses II the Pharaoh of the Oppression and his successor, Meremptah, the Pharaoh of the Exodus. This, then, would place the Exodus in the mid-13th century B.C.

After defeating the Amorites and King Og of Bashan, Moses moved south to conquer Moab. He then allotted the newly won lands of Transjordan to the children of Reuben, Gad, and half the tribe of Manasseh.

After the death of Moses, Joshua with the 12 tribes crossed the Jordan (whose waters divided as did those of the Red Sea) and conquered Jericho. (Kathleen Kenyon in *Digging Up Jericho* dates the fall of Jericho to Joshua in the last quarter of the 14th century.)

By the success of his campaigns in the south and north, Joshua became master of the whole territory and divided the land among the tribes.

In the two centuries following Joshua's death, the Israelites were constantly at war with the Philistines. The slaying of Saul, who had been made king of all Israel in 1020 B.C., signaled Israel's defeat. The final blow came when the Philistines captured the Ark of the Covenant, symbol of unity in the Israelite tribes.

Under the leadership of David (c. 1000–961 B.C.), Israel's strength returned. After consolidating his position in Palestine, David crossed east over Jordan and conquered the three states of Edom, Moab, and Ammon (2 Sam. 10). Later he seized part of Syria and established his control over the nomadic tribes as far east as the Euphrates River.

David was followed by Solomon (c. 961–922), whose reign was the high mark in Israel's political history and economic expansion. With the aid of the Phoenicians, Solomon developed trade between the Mediterranean, Red Sea, and African coasts. By using the camel caravan he extended his trade in the Arabian Peninsula as far south as Sheba (Yemen). The copper mines of Edom were exploited and refineries constructed at Ezion-Geber (Tell al-Khalifa, near Aqaba).

Solomon's lavishness had been maintained by heavy taxes and conscription. Resentment over the burden led to revolt in the northern part of Israel after his death. (Eugene Hoade, in *Guide to the Holy Land,* places Solomon's death in 930 B.C.) Meanwhile Judah, the southern part, formed an alliance with Syria against north Israel. War broke out between the two groups, and in the struggle that followed, north Israel lost Ammon, Moab, and Edom. For the next two centuries, the northern part was known as Israel, the southern part as Judah.

During the 9th century B.C., at the time of the great prophets Elijah and Elisha, a new capital was built at Samaria. Omri's son, Ahab, married the infamous Jezebel, a Phoenician princess. Under her influence worship of the pagan gods returned to Israel. As a result, Ahab was alternately hero and villain in the stories of the prophets.

Ahab was defeated about 850 B.C. by Mesha, King of Moab. The story is recorded on the famous "Moabite Stone" or Mesha Stele found at Dhiban. The Omrite dynasty ended amid torrents of blood and was followed by the dynasty of Jehu, which lasted until the mid-8th century.

Within a few years after Arpad in Syria had fallen to the Assyrian king Tiglath-Pileser III (745–727 B.C.), all Palestine and Jordan were in Assyrian hands, who "carried them away even the Reubenites, the Gadites, and the half tribe of Manasseh" (1 Chron. 5:26). Lastly, Samaria fell to the Assyrians under Sargon II (721–705 B.C.), and Israel became extinct politically. Assyrian records of this period make reference to the Nabataeans, who occupied the territory south and east of Edom. These are the earliest historical mentions of the Nabataeans found to date.

In the following century, Judah, the sole heir to the glories of David and Solomon, revived under the moral guidance of Isaiah and the kingship of Josiah, only to fall later to the armies of Nebuchadnezzar (2 Kings 24:1–4). Jerusalem was destroyed in 587 B.C. and the Jews were taken captive to Babylon. The Prophet Jeremiah, having foreseen these events, repeatedly warned his people.

After Cyrus came to power in Persia in 539 B.C. and extended his empire to Syria and Palestine, he allowed the Jews to return to Palestine and to rebuild the temple in Jerusalem.

During Alexander the Great's campaigns in the East, Palestine was merely a corridor to Egypt. His armies confined their attacks to the coastal cities that might have been used as bases for the Persian fleet.

After Alexander's death, his empire was divided among his generals. Palestine and parts of Syria and Phoenicia fell to Ptolemy, who established a dynasty in Egypt that lasted 300 years. The northern boundary of Palestine was set at Tripoli (Lebanon) on the Nahr el-Kabir. Syria went to Seleucus, who disputed Ptolemy's claim to Palestine and Phoenicia. The dispute resulted in war five times within a century, and was only settled when Palestine passed into the hands of the Seleucids in 198 B.C.

Early in the following century the Seleucids under Antiochus invaded Egypt, and later attacked Jerusalem. They seized the city's wealth, forbade many religious practices of the Jews, and set up an alter to Zeus in the Temple of Jerusalem. This last act was resisted by a section of the population under the leadership of Judas Maccabaeus. Later, because of the corruption of the high priests and the weakness of the Seleucids, Judas' followers were able to establish a dynasty. They were granted the office of high priest and in time were recognized as secular rulers as well.

Upon the death of Antiochus Sidetes, the last great Seleucid king, John Hyrcanus I (135–104 B.C.) extended the boundaries of Judea and Samaria. His successors further enlarged the territory and expanded their rule over Transjordan and the coastal cities. Upon his death, however, his brothers, Aristobulus and Hyrcanus II, quarreled over the succession and appealed to Rome for assistance.

The Romans under Pompey took Damascus in 64 B.C. and Jerusalem in 63 B.C., ending the Seleucid Kingdom. Hyrcanus II was appointed high priest without the title of king. Pompey taxed the Jews and curtailed their domain. After Pompey's death, Antipater (governor of Idumaea, supporter of Hyrcanus II, and father of Herod the Great) was granted Roman citizenship in return for his services to Julius Caesar and awarded the title of Procurator of Judea. His sons were made governors of Jerusalem and Galilee.

In 40 B.C., Parthian troops unexpectedly occupied Palestine. They favored Antigonus as the legitimate heir in Judea, and installed him as king and high priest. Herod escaped to Rome.

In Rome, Herod was recognized as King of Judea by the Senate with the approval of Octavian and Mark Antony. He returned to Palestine in 39 B.C., and with the aid of Roman troops expelled the Parthians. Under Herod's long reign (37 B.C.–A.D. 4) Palestine enjoyed a period of peace and prosperity. Only in his last years did he become the vicious figure tradition has made so familiar.

On Herod's death, rule of the country was divided. A period of unrest followed, and finally erupted in A.D. 66. The following year the Roman army of Vespasian and his son, Titus, captured Galilee. Four years later Jerusalem fell and the Temple was destroyed. Palestine became the Province of Judea, administered by the Commander of the tenth Roman Legion.

At first, the Romans attempted to reconcile the Jews by a policy of leniency. When this failed, Hadrian (in Syria) issued an edict to the Jews that led to another outbreak in 132. Hadrian put down the revolt, turned Jerusalem into a Roman colony, built pagan temples on Mount Moriah and Mount Golgotha, and renamed the city Aelia Capitolina.

About the time of the Persian occupation in the 6th century B.C., the Nabataean Arabs became prominent in south Jordan. They established their capital at Petra, and for 600 years held the land formerly occupied by the Edomites. The location of their territory astride the southern and eastern trade routes from south Arabia and Egypt to Syria enabled them to demand high tariffs for protecting the caravans. Taking advantage of the frequent wars between the Seleucids and the Ptolemies, the Nabataeans extended their land north into Moab, west into the Negev, east to the Euphrates, and south along the Red Sea.

At the time of the Nabataean expansion in the south, a confederation of ten cities situated on both sides of the Jordan came into being in the north. The Decapolis, as it was called, was patterned after Greek cities in language, culture, and religion.

The original cities were probably Seythopolis (Beisan), Pella (Khirbet Fahil), Dion (Husn), Gadara (Um Qais), Hippos (Fiq), Gerasa (Jerash), Philadelphia (Amman), Kamatha (Qanawat), Raphana (Al Rafah), and Damascus. All except one were east of the Jordan. Apparently the cities were never a fixed group of ten; cities joined and withdrew. Among them were Arbila (Irbid), Capitolias (Beit Ras), Edrei (Deraa), and Bosra (in Syria). Pella, Dion, and Gerasa are thought to have been founded by Greek soldiers. The others were older towns.

On the arrival of Pompey, the Romans formed the towns of the Decapolis into a military alliance for self-protection against the Jews, the Nabataeans, and the desert tribes. Later the Emperor Trajan joined Perea, the district between Arnon and the Decapolis, with the latter to create the Province of Arabia (A.D. 90).

The capital of the new province, Arabia Petraea, was first at Petra and then at Bosra in Syria. The third legion (Cyrenaica) was posted in the north, and the fourth (Martia) in the south of the country. Two great camps built to accommodate the latter, at Lajjun near Kerak and Adhruh near Petra, can still be seen. The great road from Bosra to Aqaba was begun by Trajan and finished under Hadrian.

Christianity gained a foothold in Palestine and Jordan between the 2nd and 3rd centuries and spread rapidly after the conversion of Constantine in the 4th century. Under the Byzantines the area enjoyed a period of peace and prosperity for 200 years. During the reign of Justinian (527–565) a large number of churches were built and pilgrimage was fostered. East of the Jordan approximately 20 places were episcopal sees in the Byzantine period, and many of them still have titular bishops.

The country's tranquility ended abruptly in A.D. 614, when the Persians, aided by Jews who wanted to avenge their misfortunes, swept through the country, devastating it as they went.

Coming of Islam

Not long after the Persian conquest a new faith was born deep in the heart of Arabia under the leadership of the Prophet Muhammad. Fired with the zeal of Islam, the new converts marched out of the desert, and within less than a century after Muhammad's death in 632 had conquered the lands from the Atlantic on the west to the Indus River on the east. The empire they established was more extensive than Rome's at its zenith. More important, the religion of Islam and the culture of the Arabs left an indelible mark on the history of the lands they conquered, especially in North Africa and the Middle East.

The weakened state of the Byzantine Empire had enabled the Arab armies to move swiftly. The first battle between the Moslems and Byzantines took place in 629 at Mautah (near Kerak), where the Moslems were defeated and three of their leaders—Zaid ibn Harith, Jaafer ibn Abu Talib, and Abdallah ibn Ruaha—were killed. They are buried in Mazar, where a mosque enshrines their tombs. The battle might be called the Arabs' Dunkirk, for it forced them to return to Medina to regroup and plan. They were at this time under the leadership of Khalid ibn Walid, who was to become one of history's greatest military geniuses.

The following year Muhammad himself led an expedition against the oasis of Tabuk. He made agreements with neighboring settlements granting the people security and the right to retain their property and religion on condition that they paid an annual tribute. These settlements were Ailah ('Aqaba), whose population was Christian; Maqna, south of Ailah, with a Jewish population; Adhruh and al-Jarba, north of it, also Christian. These were the only places outside of Arabia where Islam reached during the lifetime of the Prophet; all are in present-day Jordan.

In A.D. 633 the Arabs launched an invasion of Jordan and Syria, beginning their 100 years of conquest. The first engagement took place in the Wadi 'Araba, where Yazid defeated Sergius, the patriarch of Palestine. The country was soon overrun, and only some towns, such as Jerusalem and Caesarea, west of the Jordan, held out. The Emperor Heraclitus with an army of 50,000 marched south to meet the Moslem troops at the juncture of the Yarmuk and Ruqqad, near the present al Yaqusah, on August 20, 636. The Moslems won and the rest of the country surrendered, and by 640 all Palestine and Syria were under Moslem control. Mu'awiayah, the first caliph of the Umayyad dynasty, transferred the seat of the caliphate from Mecca to Damascus, where it remained until the Abbassids seized power and transferred the Caliphate to Baghdad in 750.

As long as the capital of the empire was in Damascus, Jordan, which lies on the route between Damascus and Arabia, continued to have some importance. The love of the Umayyad for the desert was another reason, as attested to by the ruins of many Umayyad palaces in the Jordan desert.

After the Abbassids transferred the capital to Baghdad, however, Jordan fell into decay. Jordan and Palestine remained part of the Arab Empire until 1099, when the Crusaders created the Latin Kingdom of Jerusalem.

The Crusaders

The Principality of Transjordan (Oultre-Jordain) was the most important fief of the kingdom, and its capital, Le Krak or La Pierre du Desert (ancient Kir Moab, present-day Kerak), was the center of all Crusader activity east of the Jordan. The principality extended from Wadi Zerqa Ma'in to the Gulf of Aqaba. Other fortresses were built at Shobak (Montreal), Wadi Musa (Le Vaux Moyse), and Jeziret Far'on (Isle de Graye). From these fortresses, and often in violation of truces, the Crusaders attacked Moslem caravans plying between Damascus, Mecca, and Egypt. Qal'at el Rabad at Ajlun was built by one of Saladin's generals to protect the caravans against the Crusaders.

In 1187 Jerusalem fell to Saladin (Salah ed-Din) and Palestine was restored to the Arabs. In the early 13th century, Mongol tribes from central Asia seized Jerusalem and with the aid of Egypt under the Mameluks marched on Syria. After a quarrel with the Mameluks, the Mongols withdrew, thus enabling the Mameluks, under Baybars and Qalawun, to capture the remaining Crusader relics in the Levant. By the close of the century the Crusaders had vanished from the Holy Land.

The 14th century opened with another Mongol devastation, this time at the hands of Timur (Tamerlane). A century later, all the Middle East fell to the Ottoman Turks, and for the next 400 years Palestine and Jordan were to be an Ottoman province.

The Turks' only concern with Jordan was to guard the pilgrim's road to Mecca. Its precise route changed several times through the centuries, but from the time of the Turks in the 16th century pilgrims took only one road from Damascus to Mecca through Jordan because the Turks built a series of fortified watering places, which they kept garrisoned on the pilgrims' behalf. In Jordan the principal stations were Mafraq, Zerqa, Dab'a, Qatrana, Hasa, Aneiza, Ma'an, Aqaba, and El Mudawwara. Today, the route of the railway and the Desert Highway almost parallel the old pilgrims' route, and ruins of the forts can still be seen.

At Mezerib in the north and at Ma'an in the south the caravans stopped for periods of a week to ten days to make final arrangements and to enable pilgrims from southern Lebanon and west of the Jordan to join.

At the opening of the 19th century, after Napoleon's unsuccessful campaign in Egypt, Palestine was drawn into the affairs of the European powers and became part of the "Eastern Question." Protection of religious shrines in the Holy Land became the pretext for European intervention in the area. Rivalries between the religious communities became so intense that their disputes were one of the immediate causes of the Crimean War.

In 1855, for the first time since the Crusades, a cross was carried through the streets of Jerusalem and Christians were allowed to visit the Dome of the Rock. The next 50 years saw the arrival of many missionary groups from Europe and America.

Also from the early 19th century, European explorers began to uncover the ancient sites so long lost to the western world, and their tales of adventure, such as Charles Doughty's *Travels in Arabia Deserta,* excited all Europe to follow in their path. Among the most famous was the Swiss explorer Burckhardt who discovered Petra in Jordan and Abu Simbel in Egypt.

During World War I Palestine and Jordan, as part of the Otto-man Empire, were garrisoned with Turkish troops. The Sherif of Mecca, Emir Hussein of the Hashemite family of Hejaz, sided with the allies. The Hashemites, the present ruling family of Jordan, trace their ancestry to the Prophet Muhammad, who was a mem-ber of the Hashem clan.

Modern Jordan

The history of modern Jordan begins with the drive to rid the country of the Turkish yoke. Indeed, the desire for independence from the Ottomans became the force that unified the Arabs from Syria to Arabia and from Egypt to Iraq.

In 1914 Hussein, the Sherif of Mecca, and great-grandfather of the present King Hussein of Jordan, assumed leadership of the Arab nationalist movement, and the Arab Revolt was under way by June of 1916. Hussein's son, Emir Faisal, with the aid of the British Colonel T. E. Lawrence—the legendary "Lawrence of Ara-bia"—took charge of the military campaign. The following year the Arab army captured Aqaba, and, almost four centuries to the year after the Ottoman conquest, together with the British troops, they took Jerusalem.

At the end of the war Transjordan and Palestine were placed under British Mandate by the League of Nations. By October 1920, however, Emir Abdullah, the second son of Emir Hussein, arrived in Ma'an in southern Jordan with the aim of liberating the land. In March of 1921 he entered Amman and established the Emirate of Trans-Jordan. He met with Winston Churchill in Jerusalem and secured British recognition of the Emirate. Britain remained as the mandatory power. Concurrently, the French established their mandate over Syria and Lebanon, and Emir Faisal was given the throne of Iraq.

On May 25, 1923, the British formally recognized the indepen-dent government of Trans-Jordan under Emir Abdullah. Five years later the Anglo-Jordanian Treaty was signed.

With a small number of British advisers headed by a British resi-dent, Emir Abdullah ruled as an autocrat until 1939. In that year the power of the British resident was reduced, a cabinet responsible to the Emir was established, and a legislative assembly of 20 mem-bers was elected.

During World War II the Arab Legion aided the British in put-ting down an attempted pro-German coup in Iraq and fought against the Vichy French in Syria.

Following World War II, the British Mandate was ended and on May 25, 1946, the Emirate of Trans-Jordan became a Kingdom with Abdullah as King. (This is the date that is celebrated as Jor-dan's Independence Day.)

In 1947, the United Nations General Assembly recommended the partition of Palestine, and in the following year when the Mandate terminated and the British left, war broke out between Arabs and Jews over the establishment of the state of Israel.

Thousands of Arab refugees who fled the war zone were eventually accommodated in camps in the Jordan Valley and around Amman. Almost overnight Jordan's population doubled. An armistice was signed in 1949, and the following year, in April 1950, Central Arab Palestine (the West Bank) voted to join Trans-Jordan. The two were united into one state called the Hashemite Kingdom of Jordan. From the outset Jordan with its meager resources accepted the refugees, giving them citizenship and allowing them to work and own land.

In 1951, King Abdullah was assassinated while he was attending prayer at the Al Aqsa Mosque in Jerusalem. Hussein, his grandson, who was later to become king, was with him. One of the assassin's bullets was deflected from Hussein by a small metal bar he was wearing on his chest. It was the first of many occasions in the tumultuous history of Jordan over the next quarter-century that Hussein came within a hair's breadth of death. His bravery in the face of danger and through the many crises he has faced has won him worldwide respect and admiration, even from his enemies.

Immediately following King Abdullah's death, his son Talal (Hussein's father) was proclaimed king, but due to ill health he reigned only a short while. Hussein became king in 1952 at the age of 17, while he was still a student at Sandhurst in England. In the interim a Regency Council was appointed by Parliament. Hussein formally ascended the throne in May 1953.

A list of the projects that were undertaken in the first ten years of his reign gives an idea of how basic were the problems of Jordan's development: the construction of the Amman-Aqaba desert highway, now one of the country's main roads; the establishment of the first labor law, the first cement factory, the first college of nursing; the formation of a phosphate mining company, a petroleum refining company, a potash company, and an agricultural cooperative; the construction of a port at Aqaba, an irrigation project on the Yarmuk river, an automatic telephone exchange, and establishment of the University of Jordan and Alia, the national airline.

All the while, Hussein had to prove his leadership over and over by thwarting attempts to unseat him both from within the country and from outside. In 1956, King Hussein dismissed Glubb Pasha, the British soldier who had headed the Arab Legion and had served as Chief of Staff of the Jordan Army. The following year the Anglo-Jordanian Treaty was terminated and the last British soldier left Jordan.

On the bright side was one of the most important archeological events of modern times—the discovery of the Dead Sea Scrolls.

These were copper rolls found by a shepherd in a cave on a desolate cliff high above the Dead Sea at Qumran.

King Hussein's first decade ended on a happy note with the birth of his first son, Prince Abdullah. The second ten years began with another important landmark, the visit of Pope Paul VI to the Holy Land in January 1964—the first visit by a pope in modern times.

The basic development of the country continued with the introduction of compulsory education, the launching of the first seven-year economic development program, and the opening of the country's first deluxe hotel by an international chain—the Jordan Inter-Continental Hotel.

The Central Bank of Jordan was inaugurated, reconstruction of the Hejaz Railway began, several dams were completed, television was introduced, and major reforestation projects were launched.

But once again Jordan suffered a sharp reversal. The June 1967 war with Israel resulted in the loss of the West Bank and Jerusalem and thus Jordan's two principal sources of income—agriculture and tourism. At the same time it received another wave of refugees, numbering more than 400,000. Once again Jordan was strained to its limits. In the following tense years, a confrontation with the Palestinian guerrilla movements became inevitable as they grew in strength and openly defied the government's authority. Many times throughout 1970 fighting broke out between the army and the guerrillas, until the final showdown in 1971 when the army launched a major offensive to drive the guerrillas out of the country. It was a costly, bloody struggle, and alienated the king from his Arab neighbors for several years.

King Hussein's third decade took an upward turn with the granting of the vote to women in 1973 and an amnesty to all political prisoners and exiles. Restrictions were raised on travel to the West Bank.

Although no fighting took place on the Jordan border in the October War of 1973, Jordan sent troops and equipment to assist Syria. The following year a summit conference of the Arab heads of state in Rabat passed a resolution, which Jordan accepted, naming the Palestine Liberation Organization as the sole legitimate representative of the Palestinian people.

Over the past decade, many of Jordan's economic projects begun in the 1960s and early 1970s began to bear fruit, particularly in the expansion of agriculture and the creation of an industrial base. In 1972, a conference that detailed a $555-million three-year development plan drew delegates from 26 countries and a wide variety of international organizations. In 1973, a $120 million-dollar project to irrigate the Jordan Valley and resettle 130,000 people there was announced. A new law to encourage investment was enacted; several more large hotels were opened; Alia launched Arab Wings, the Middle East's first business jet charter service, and Jordan

World Airways, Alia's cargo subsidiary; the railroad line to Aqaba and several major roads were completed.

In 1976, a new $2.3 billion five-year development plan was launched: Yarmuk University in Irbid opened, plans were visualized to open training centers in Aqaba and in Kerak. In 1977, marking King Hussein's 25th Jubilee, the $35 million King Talal Dam was completed; several additional training schools, hospitals, and housing projects were started around the country, Aqaba port was expanded, and Alia started direct airline service between Jordan and the U.S. for the first time.

Jordan, given a period of peace and stability, has impressive results to show. The five-year plan that carried the country through 1980 met and sometimes exceeded projections. The same record of accomplishment continued into the second Five-Year Plan (1981–1985), until the drop in oil prices, the continuing turmoil in Lebanon, and the Iran-Iraq war caused setbacks for the entire region.

Royal Jordanian Airline

It might seem unusual in a book of this kind to include the history of an airline, but Royal Jordanian Airline is so much a part of the history and development of modern Jordan that it deserves special mention.

In 1962 King Hussein, himself an accomplished pilot, asked Ali Ghandour, now Royal Jordanian's chairman, to formulate plans for the new airline. Ghandour, an aeronautical engineer by training, had been with the Civil Aviation Department of Lebanon and a vice president of Lebanon International Airways.

There was a small airport in Amman; Jordan had been a signatory of the Civil Aviation Act of Chicago in 1944 and a member of the International Civil Aviation Organization in 1947; but one might say that aviation in Jordan—indeed, in the Middle East— was barely off the ground.

With the full backing of the King, Ghandour, a man of inexhaustible energy and great imagination, drew up a plan which was accepted immediately. On December 8, 1963, Alia as it was first known was born, with instructions from the King to get the airline into operation within seven days!

"It's hard now to remember the sequence of events during that hectic, sleepless week," Ghandour says. "We had an airline on paper. The name, which is the same as that of the King's eldest daughter, Princess Alia, was a good one for an airline. In Arabic it means 'the high and exalted one.' "

The airline was given two former Royal Air Force Dart Heralds, and within a matter of days $460,000 in private capital was raised to buy a used Super DC-7. Qualified pilots were sought, offices rented, and technical workshops set up, and one week to the day—

December 15, 1963—Alia was airborne. Within a week of the initial flight to Beirut, its DC-7 was flying to Cairo and Kuwait. A month later a second DC-7 was purchased and Jeddah added.

One place and a network covering three Arab countries have grown to a fleet of 18 jets, including 747s, which serve 39 cities on four continents—and, for the past decade, Royal Jordanian, as the airline is now called, has operated at a profit in all but two years.

But Royal Jordanian had more than its share of difficulties—long, hard years of operating in the red and frequent crises, including two crippling wars. The months after the 1967 war with Israel were the worst. In one disastrous June week in 1967, a vital part of Jordan—Jerusalem, Bethlehem, Hebron, Jericho, and the fertile Jordan Valley—was lost. The country's two major sources of income, tourism and agriculture, all but disappeared. For Royal Jordanian, it was a matter of survival and many doubted its ability to stay alive. The energy and determination behind the country's progress, despite all its setbacks, characterized the carrier's response to the 1967 disaster. Perhaps more as a gesture of faith than anything else, the airline opened a new route to Athens at the end of 1967.

During this period Royal Jordanian had trouble raising capital, which led the King to change the carrier's status from private venture to government-owned enterprise, enabling it to buy equipment and expand routes and offices. The most notable expansion was its non-stop service to the U.S.—it was the first regularly scheduled Arab carrier to connect the two destinations with regularly scheduled service, started in 1977. The carrier serves Chicago, Houston, Los Angeles and Miami. It plans to add new cities to its networks in the Far East and North Africa and to expand to South America. Over the past few years, Royal Jordanian has modernized its fleet and undertaken a complete image overhaul.

Another part of Royal Jordanian's success is the related services it has developed. Arab Wings, an air taxi, was established in 1975 as a subsidiary to fill the demand for quick air transportation to different parts of the Middle East, particularly to remote spots lacking frequent service. In 1978 it added a flying ambulance. Another subsidiary created the same year was Jordan World Airways, an all-cargo carrier. In 1981 the subsidiary became Arab Air Cargo, a joint venture with Iraq.

On the ground, Royal Jordanian has a catering service that prepares about 10,000 meals per day and can handle up to 20,000; a duty-free shop at Queen Alia International Airport; a training center; and its own art gallery, Alia Gallery, where works by local and international artists are sold.

Alia also plays a prominent role in the promotion and development of the country's tourism. Each of its sales offices abroad functions as a tourism office for the country. Within Jordan itself, Alia has been involved in strengthening and expanding the country's infrastructure and facilities, particularly in the construction of hotels. It holds financial and management interest in the Holiday Inns of Amman and Aqaba, Amman Marriott, and Arab International Hotels, and in 1985, it opened its own hotel, the Alia Gateway at the international airport. Another subsidiary, Royal Tours, was created to develop directional packages to Jordan which would be competitive in the marketplace.

King Hussein, as well as Ghandour, sees the national airlines as an avenue to raise the technical skills of the Jordanians by providing them with the facilities and training required to operate and maintain a modern airline. To this end, Royal Jordanian established the Air Academy to provide comprehensive training in flight, engineering, maintenance, and computer skills, and began its Engine Overhaul Facility in 1977. It was followed by Arab Air Services, which provides a wide range of technical assistance in the aviation field to others in the Middle East and Africa. As a mark of its achievement, the Air Academy was designated the Regional Technical Center for the Middle East by the International Air Transportation Association in 1985.

Ghandour's greatest dream is to have an Air University, which would train personnel for all the Middle East. It's not an idle dream. The plan has the full backing of the King and the Civil Aviation Authorities in Jordan, and the Air Academy's newly acquired status as an IATA Regional Center brings the dream one step closer to fulfillment.

CHRONOLOGY OF JORDANIAN
AND BIBLICAL HISTORY

Historical	Biblical
Prehistory to Neolithic Period, c. 4000 B.C.	**Genesis**
Traces of prehistoric man, artifacts older than 100,000 B.C.	
Chalcolithic Period, c. 4000–3000 B.C.	
Canaanite settlement along coast, as well as in the interior.	
Early Bronze Age, c. 3000–2000 B.C.	
Settlements at Beisan, Megiddo, Ai, and others. The Jordan Valley prosperous and densely populated. Palestine in close contact with Egypt.	
Middle Bronze Age, c. 2000–1600 B.C.	
c. 1900 Abraham arrived in the Land of Canaan.	**Abraham/** Joseph
Joseph sold by brothers, taken to Egypt.	
Hyksos Empire Hyksos (Shepherd Kings) established empire in Egypt lasting until 1550. Held Palestine until 1479 when defeated by Thothmes III at Megiddo. Palestine became part of Egypt for next 400 years.	
c. 1630 Jacob to Egypt.	**Jacob**
Late Bronze Age, c. 1600–1200 B.C.	
Egyptian Empire 15th–14th centuries, Egypt controlled Palestine.	**Exodus, Numbers, Deuteronomy**

	Historical	Biblical
Hittite Invasion	1280 battle of Kadesh, Ramses II checked Hittites advancing from north.	
	Edomites in south Jordan; Moabites, east of the Dead Sea; and Ammonites, east of Gilead.	
Phœnician Empire	c. 1300 Philistine invasion. Settled coast conquered all Palestine.	**Moses and Exodus**
	c. 1250 Joshua crossed Jordan, captured Jericho, and divided Palestine among the twelve tribes.	**Joshua**

Early Iron Age, c. 1200–950 B.C. — **Judges, Samuel I Samuel II, Kings I**

	Historical	Biblical
	Samson killed c. 1100.	**Rulers**/*Prophets*
	Saul crowned King of all Israel c. 1020.	
	Saul slain and Philistines captured Ark c. 1004.	**Saul**/*Nathan*
	David's reign c. 1004–965.	**David**/*Gad*
	Solomon's reign c. 965–922 B.C. Expanded trade from Phœnicia in north to Sheba in south Arabia.	**Solomon**/*Ahiyah*

Late Iron Age, c. 950–549 B.C.

	Historical	Biblical
	Israel (930–721 B.C.) Omrite Dynasty established. Ahab defeated by Mesha, King of Moab c. 850 B.C. Jehu Dynasty followed.	**Omri**/*Jehul* **Ahab**/*Elijah* **Jehoshaphat**/*Elisha* **Jehu**
Assyrian Empire	883–626 B.C. Assyrian raids on coast intermittent with Egyptian raids. 721 B.C. Sargon II captured Samaria. Judah (930–587 B.C.).	**Jeroboam II**/*Jonah* **Zechariah**/*Amos* **Ahaz**/*Hosea* **Hezekiah**/*Isaiah*

	Historical	Biblical
Neo-Babylonian Invasion	605–562 B.C. Nebuchadnezzar's invasion of Phœnicia. 587 B.C. Babylon Captivity.	**Manasseh**/*Zephaniah* **Amon**/*Jeremiah* **Josiah**/*Nahum*

Persian Period, 549–332 B.C.

Nabataeans prominent in south, established capital at Petra. 539 B.C. Jews allowed by Cyrus to return to Palestine.	**Zedekiah**/*Ezekiel*

Hellenistic Period, 332–63 B.C.

332 B.C. conquest by Alexander the Great. After this death Syria and Palestine were divided by Seleucid (north) and Ptolemy (south) until 198 B.C. when Palestine passed to Seleucids.

Revolt against Seleucids led by Judas Maccabaeus (166–160 B.C.), Jonathan (160–143 B.C.), and Simon (142–134 B.C.).

John Hyrcanus I (135–104 B.C.) extended boundaries of Judæa and Samaria.

Decapolis formed in north; Nabataean expansion in south.

Roman Period 63 B.C. – A.D. 330

63 B.C. Roman conquest by Pompey. Hyrcanus II appointed High Priest.

40 B.C. Parthians occupied Palestine. Antigonus made King and High Priest. Herod escaped to Rome, recognized as King of Judæa by Roman Senate.

39 B.C. Herod returned to Palestine, expelled Parthians, and reigned until A.D. 4.   *Birth of Christ*

Historical	Biblical
A.D. 26–36 Pontius Pilate.	*John the Baptist Preaching of Jesus*
A.D. 30 Roman Emperor, Caligula.	*Death of Jesus Conversion of Paul James beheaded, Peter imprisoned, Paul's 1st, 2nd journey*
A.D. 40 Roman Emperor, Claudius. Agrippa I (41–44), ruler in Palestine and Jordan.	
A.D. 50 Roman Emperor, Nero.	*Paul's 3rd journey, Paul captured in Cæsarea, taken to Rome*
A.D. 66 First Jewish revolt.	
A.D. 70 Romans under Titus destroy Jerusalem.	
A.D. 106 Nabataens defeated. Peræa and Petra joined into Roman Province of Arabia.	
A.D. 132 Second Jewish revolt, put down by Hadrian.	
Christianity takes root.	

Byzantine Period, A.D.330–634

Christianity spread rapidly after Constantine conversion.

Reign of Justinian (A.D. 527–565)

A.D. 614 Persian invasion.

Arab Empire, 634–1009

By A.D. 635 all Palestine and Syria under Arab control. Umayyad Dynasty (634–750) established in Damascus, afterwards Caliphate transferred to Baghdad.

Crusader Period, 1099–1268

1098–99 First Crusade, Kingdom of Jerusalem established.

1187 Jerusalem fell to Saladin.

Historical

Mameluk Period, 1263–1516

1263 Mameluk Sultan Baybers of Egypt captured
Crusader strongholds at Kerak and Ajlun. Egyptian
Mameluks held coast intermittently for next 250 years.

1400 Mongol invasion under Tamerlane.

Turkish Period, 1516–1917

1516 Turks conquered Jordan and Palestine. Its
history insignificant for 300 years.

1855 Palestine drawn into affairs of Europe over rights
in the Holy Land. European and American mission-
aries begin to arrive.

1908 Completion of Hejaz Railroad from Damascus
to Medina.

1916 Arab Revolt against the Turks.

1917 Arabs capture Aqaba; Jerusalem taken by Allies.

Modern Jordan 1920–

1920 British Mandate over Palestine and Jordan;
Emir Abdullah arrives in Ma'an.

1921 Abdullah reaches Amman, meets Churchill in
Jerusalem and secures recognition of Emirate.

1923 Emirate of Trans-Jordan established under
Abdullah.

1928 Anglo-Jordanian Treaty signed. British resident
appointed.

1929 First Legislative Council established.

1939 Legislative Council transformed into a regular
cabinet. Arab Legion fights with Allies in World War II.

1946 Mandate ends. Independence achieved
(this date is celebrated as Jordan Independence Day,
May 25). Abdullah becomes King of Trans-Jordan.

1947 U.N. General Assembly recommends the
partition of Palestine.

CHRONOLOGY

Historical

1948 British Mandate of Palestine terminated. Hostilities break out between Jews and Arabs.

1950 Trans-Jordan and Central Palestine combined into the Hashemite Kingdom of Jordan.

1951 King Abdullah assassinated, July 20.

1952 Hussein proclaimed king.

1953 Hussein ascends the throne.

1955 Jordan joins U.N.

1956 Glubb Pasha dismissed as head of Arab Legion.

1957 Termination of Anglo-Jordanian Treaty.

1965 Prince Hassan proclaimed Crown Prince.

1967 War between Israel and Egypt, Syria, Jordan in June. U.N. Resolution 242 calls for Israeli withdrawal from occupied Arab territories.

1972 King Hussein's father Talal dies.

1973 War between Israel and Egypt and Syria in October. U.N. adopts Resolution 338 calling for implementation of Resolution 242.

1974 Arab Summit Conference in Rabat in October names PLO as sole representative of Palestinians.

1977 King Hussein's Silver Jubilee.

1978 Amman Stock Exchange, country's first, opens. Wedding of King Hussein and Queen Noor.

1980 First International Conference on History and Archaeology of Jordan at Oxford University. Jordan National Gallery of Art opens.

1981 Official visit of King Hussein to U.S. New Five-Year Plan to increase GDP 64% by 1985.

1983 Opening of Queen Alya International Airport.

1985 Official visit of King Hussein to U.S. King Hussein delivers landmark speech for peace at 40th Anniversary of U.N. King Hussein's 50th Birthday.

1986 40th Anniversary of Modern Jordan.

THE JORDANIAN WAY OF LIFE

Customs and Culture

Local residents of Amman are accustomed to foreign visitors and are helpful to them. In smaller towns and villages the people are courteous, but they appear more curious and are certainly more conservative.

Jordanians of all stations are formal in their greetings to friends and strangers. If you respect their customs and formality and are polite and smiling in manner, your attitude will be reciprocated.

Jordan is predominantly Moslem, and whether you are in Amman or in a village, you will hear the call to prayer five times a day from a minaret and will see many Jordanians stop their work to pray. Moslems are not self-conscious about praying in public, and often you will see a person on a side street, in front of a shop, in a field, or almost anywhere saying his prayers.

Strict Moslems do not drink alcoholic beverages at any time, nor eat foods prepared with wine. Even modern Moslems who are not so strict about alcohol abstain from eating pork.

During the Moslem month of fasting, known as Ramadan, Moslems do not eat from sunrise to sunset, nor do they smoke or drink. A new law, reflecting the growing influence of Moslem conservatism in the Middle East, prohibits anyone, including non-Moslems and visitors, from drinking or smoking in public during Ramadan; nor can restaurants, except those in hotels, serve food before the hour of breaking the fast. Alcohol cannot be sold except by hotels to registered guests in their rooms.

Women Traveling Alone

Jordan is a male-dominated society, and you will be aware of it from the moment you arrive. However, women can and do travel alone with ease and safety in Jordan. The author has never encountered anything but the most pleasant and courteous treatment.

Unless you are a seasoned traveler, your first trip to Jordan will be more fun and less costly if you join a group—even a small group of three or four. However, you need not hesitate to strike out alone. Jordanians have become accustomed to foreign women traveling on their own. It is only fair to add that your behavior should be circumspect and your dress modest. For example, bareback dresses and shorts absolutely must not be worn on the street.

Coffeehouses and sidewalk cafés in certain areas of town are frequented by men only. While no one is likely to ask you to leave, you will probably not feel comfortable there, since all eyes will be fixed upon you. Also, at traditional dinners and weddings the men may be separated from the women to enjoy separate music and entertainment.

Dress

The traditional Arab male headdress—a checkered cloth of red or black and white—is seen throughout the country, even on men wearing western garb. The woman's traditional costume is a long dress with designs usually representative of a particular area.

By contrast, Jordanians of the younger generation wear slacks and jeans or stylish European fashions. You can see almost all styles and wear almost all, too, except shorts. Even teenagers do not wear shorts anywhere in Jordan. As a visitor you should not, either. Visitors should be aware that the new conservatism is reflected in an increasing number of women wearing very conservative dress, covering all of their body except their face and hands.

A Jordanian Welcome

Jordanians are good-natured, friendly and accommodating to visitors, but they are more reserved than Americans. Highly educated Jordanians are quite sophisticated.

Throughout the Mediterranean world there is an unconcern for time which to westerners, and especially Americans, is frustrating and sometimes irritating. Yet it is precisely the Jordanians' relaxed manner that accounts for much of their charm. They are patient and gracious, and you should try to be likewise. Relax. You will enjoy your visit many times more if you adjust to the system rather than fight it.

Jordan is a country enriched by many cultures—Arab, Circassian, Armenian, Kurdish, and European—all with their own customs and food. Entertaining in the home is still the traditional way of Arab hospitality. You will always be offered coffee or tea in a home, no matter how short your visit. Women are famous for their cooking and take great pride in the preparation and presentation of food.

Feasts are the time to exchange family visits and to give gifts. For a visitor, candy or flowers are customary—Arabs consider it necessary to reciprocate, so you should be careful not to embarrass someone with an expensive gift.

If at any time you encounter a problem, you should report it immediately to the Tourism Authority or to any policeman. Jordan is making a sincere effort to provide comfort and service to her visitors. Your criticism is welcomed, and the authorities work diligently to correct complaints.

Cuisine

Jordanians usually eat a light breakfast, the main meal at lunch, and a light supper. Restaurants and hotel dining rooms serve lunch from 1 to 3 P.M. and dinner after 8 P.M. You will have your greatest treat if you are invited to a Jordanian house for a meal.

Most hotels serve European as well as Jordanian dishes, which are similar to Lebanese and Syrian ones. Those which are traditionally Jordanian are described below:

Mensef: Roast lamb stuffed with rice, highly spiced with cinnamon, sprinkled with pine nuts and almonds, and served with *makheedh* (beaten yogurt combined with the fat of mutton). A mensaf is not just a dish, it's a feast and a ritual—the traditional feast of the Bedouin when a lamb is slaughtered for a guest or a special occasion. For such a ceremony, the whole lamb is served atop a huge tray of rice, and the honored guest may be presented with the eye of the lamb. (But don't fear, this won't happen to you in a restaurant!) If you want to try eating it with your hand the Bedouin way, remember to use only your right hand.

Musakhan: Chicken, previously steamed in a sauce of olive oil, onions, and sumak, is baked on specially prepared bread and covered with a layer of onions marinated in oil and sumak. This is a specialty of Tulkarem (on the West Bank) and was borrowed by Ramallah and Jericho. Several restaurants in Amman specialize in it. The dish is very rich, highly seasoned, and one of the most delicious in the Middle East.

Maqlouba (literally, "upside down"): A stewlike dish of vegetables, usually cauliflower or eggplant, and meat served on rice.

Leban (yogurt) is sometimes added on top. This is a specialty of Jerusalem.

Daud Pasha: Arab stew of meatballs, whole onions, and pine nuts cooked with tomatoes, and served with rice.

Kidreh bil-Furn (pot-in-oven): Cubed meat, rice, chickpeas, and spices are placed in an earthen jar and baked in the oven. This is a specialty of Hebron.

Kubbeh: A dish found in all the Arab countries of the Middle East, but the Jordanians give it a slightly different flavor and preparation. It is cracked wheat and ground meat with spices blended to the consistency of meatloaf, shaped into large egg-shaped pieces, and stuffed with ground meat that has been sauteed with onions. The "egg" is fried in deep oil to give it a lightly crisp outer surface. It can be eaten hot or cold.

Bateenjan Battiri: A miniature light-purple eggplant (grown in Bittir, south of Jerusalem) is stuffed with meat and rice and cooked in tomato sauce.

Fattet el-Hummos: Bed of Arab bread chips covered with chickpeas and their juice and topped with yogurt, garlic, and roasted pine nuts.

Salata bi-Tahini: Finely chopped tossed salad seasoned with the paste of sesame oil.

Fatayir Zalatimo: A pastry to be eaten at Zalatimo's in the Old City of Jerusalem. Mr. Zalatimo called it *mutabaq* rather than *fatayir.* It is a paper-thin dough folded corners-in and filled with cheese or walnuts. The pastry is baked in a brick oven situated in the original wall of ancient Jerusalem. The pastry is made prior to 10 A.M. and should be eaten in the morning. It is served with powdered sugar and syrup and is very rich.

Kanafa: A sweet cake filled with white cheese and served with hot, clear syrup. Often eaten for breakfast as well as dessert. This is the specialty of Nablus.

Khubiz: To Arabs perhaps more than most people, bread is the staff of life. They call it *khubiz* or *eish* (meaning "life"), and there is no meal, even one with a main dish of rice or potatoes, that is not accompanied by a generous serving of it. Lunch for a laborer, for instance, often consists of a loaf of *khubiz,* a tomato, some olives, and a piece of cheese. It fills the stomach and, Arabs insist, nurtures the soul.

Looked upon as a gift from God, assuring that no man will go hungry, bread is treated with reverence. A piece of it fallen on the ground is picked up, kissed, and replaced on the table. Leftover pieces of bread are not thrown away but put upon a window sill or building ledge for whatever hungry soul may pass. Old or dried bread is used in several dishes.

The shape of the bread is always as round as the eternal circle, sometimes thick and dense, sometimes hollow inside, and sometimes even paper thin . . . but always round and flat. It's made usually with white flour, yeast, water, and salt, and preparing it, too, is a ritual.

Qahwa: Coffee, too, is a tradition and a ritual. The true Arab or Bedouin coffee is bitter, rather thin, and heavily flavored with cardamom seed. It is poured from a metal pot with a long spout into tiny cups with no handles. The server (for this type, always a male) shows his skill by raising and lowering the pot in quick motions as he pours. He will continue refilling your cup as often as you hand it to him until you make the proper gesture to stop—a quick side-to-side roll of the hand. In traditional circles a guest takes three cups (each holds only a swallow) before giving the sign. You may stop after the first cup without offending anyone.

The other type of coffee is called Turkish and is thick with as much sugar as one likes. Jordanians tend to drink it very sweet, so if you want it medium or lightly sweetened ask for *sukar aleel* or *areeha.*

Coffee always completes a meal, as a gesture of welcome.

Wine: Red, rose and white wines from Latroun can be purchased at restaurants and groceries. Price ranges from JD 900–1,250 a bottle in shops. *Cremisan,* another local wine (red and white), comes from Bethlehem.

Beer: The local brewery bottles Amstel. The price in restaurants is 1,000 fils for a large, 600 for a small one. At deluxe hotel bars, the price is likely to be double or more.

The *Sahtain Cookbook,* by the American Women's Club of Amman, is a book on Arab cooking that contains recipes for most of the dishes mentioned above. Recipes also appear in each issue of *Jordan,* the magazine of the Jordan Information Office in Washington.

The following series of articles by authorities on different aspects of Jordanian life and traditions has been adapted from articles which appeared in Jordan, *a magazine published by the Ministry of Information.*

CLASSICAL MUSIC

Adapted from an article by the late Adif Alvarez Bulos, *a Lebanese scholar, who studied in London and received his Ph.D. at Harvard University. An authority on the music of the Middle East, he has lectured on Arab music throughout Great Britain and the United States, and has made several recordings.*

When Westerners visit the Middle East for the first time their senses are assailed by new impressions. Perhaps most different of all is the music of the Arabs, which can be heard day and night from every taxi radio, transistor, television set, and record player in town.

Those unfamiliar with the music usually have the impression that the singer—man or woman—is mourning. "Wailing" is a description often used by the uninitiated; and they also quickly note the repetition in Arab songs—going over and over the same words, with the same tune, at the same tempo. Undulating, with an up-and-down quavering of the voice, the tune seems never to end, to have no beginning and no pauses.

Arab music is mainly vocal, often unaccompanied, and strongly influenced by simple folk songs. Uninitiated listeners can be put off by the unfamiliar sound of the Arabic language as used in a song they do not understand. If they were to hear purely instrumental renditions of these melodies, without human voices, probably the sound would not seem so foreign to them; generally speaking, voices change the effect. Unfortunately for the Western neophyte, little Arab music is written for instruments alone.

Usually only well-established singers give solo recitals, and these performances are invariably sold out soon after the high-priced tickets go on sale. The great Egyptian singer Um Kulthum, who died some years ago, gave two recitals in her later years at the annual Festival of Baalbek, the impressive Roman ruin in the mountains outside Beirut. For as far as the eye could see, people were packed tightly into the huge amphitheater and even lined the very rims of the ancient battlements and ruins. Everyone wanted to get as close as possible to the great lady of Middle Eastern music and to listen to the legendary velvet voice.

Um Kulthum sang with unimpaired voice for over 50 years. And, it is safe to say, her popularity throughout the Middle East and North Africa exceeded by some considerable degree that of such singers as Bing Crosby or Frank Sinatra in the Western world.

Feyrouz, the pride of Lebanon, is a tremendously popular woman singer; Sabah is another, also from Lebanon. The emphasis on these women singers is not meant to indicate that only Arab women sing in public or that only Arab women sing well. There are also scores of fine Arab men singers.

Arab audiences express enthusiasm by clapping rhythmically and endlessly, and listeners continually give out with loud, appreciative ooh's and aah's.

There was a time, in the tenth century, when a different state of affairs existed concerning performance decorum. In Damascus, for instance, vocal and instrumental concerts were held at the house of a singer called Azza al-Maila, and there the behavior of the audience was impeccable. No one talked or shouted appreciation while the artist was performing. If anyone was tempted to chat with his neighbor, an attendant with a long stick would reach out for the offender's knuckles and administer a disciplinary rap. Today's audiences are not so quiet or respectful of the artist's efforts.

After the foreign visitor has listened for a time to that endless repetition of the same phrases, he may begin to think about going home early. Why is there so much repetition? The answer lies partly in the psychology of the Arabs, who love to hear the same phrase over and over again. (Have you ever seen two friends meet unexpectedly? In Arabic countries such encounters generate a stream of "Ahlan, Ahlan wa Sahlan, Ahlan, Ahlan!")

Um Kulthum, when she felt her audience enjoyed a certain passage, would repeat it over and over again, sometimes eight times in a row. Now, it must be pointed out that there is also repetition in Western music; just think of Bach. But there it is more artfully disguised by rhythmic and harmonic variations. Arab music is much more "exposed."

If our visiting concertgoer stays throughout, he will find that the performance begins with *taqasim* (improvisations) on the *oud,* a sort of lute, or on the *qanun,* a mini-harpsichord. He may find this portion quite pleasant. In the orchestral prelude, if there is one, all the instruments, including violins, play in unison. Then the singer improvises on the *ya-leil* theme, in which the only words, sung over and over, are "O night!" From the rendition of the cadenza an experienced listener can gauge the skill and beauty of voice of the singer.

Finally the singer embarks on the body of the song, which may be in the form of a long ode *(qasida),* a *muwashah,* or a simple lyric *(dawr),* with the full orchestra playing the accompaniment. This is where the Western ear must prepare itself for a disciplined period of acute listening to the interweaving notes, to try to follow the tune. The orchestra plays the same notes.

Westerners often ask, "What is it that gives Arab music its distinctive flavor? Is it merely the strange language used, or is there also a musical difference?"

First of all, Arab tunes are not built on the Western major and minor scales but on more ancient forms known as modes. In Arabic these are called *maqams,* and some of them contain intervals of a quarter-tone. In conventional Western music, of course, the smallest interval is the half-tone; so one can see the reason for the slurring, slithery quality Arab music has for Western ears.

Furthermore, the absence of harmony in Arab music, which develops along horizontal lines, adds to its strangeness for Westerners. In Western music, which is developed vertically, the melody is seldom sounded alone; instead, a harmonic arrangement gives depth and color to the melodic line.

In Arab music, such combinations as duets, trios, or quartets do not exist. All the instruments of the orchestra accompanying the singer play the same melody in unison. Hence, the ear steeped in harmonized music goes into shock at first.

The past 20 years have witnessed considerable European influence on Arab music, both classical and popular. Now, one does hear harmony, and instruments such as the piano and accordion are added to the traditional instruments of the classic Arab orchestra. Many old Arab songs have even been rearranged as rhumbas, sambas, tangos, and so on. Feyrouz is one of the outstanding singers of this genre.

Feyrouz's name has also been linked with the revival of Arab folksongs in Lebanon, Syria, and Jordan. The warmth of her voice and the utter simplicity of her singing have not only endeared her to the Arab public; she is one of the reasons foreigners are now being wooed by Arab music. Sabah is a more traditional singer, and her songs are much less influenced by Western-inspired innovation.

Arab folksongs for the most part tend to be love songs, songs of yearning or nostalgia, songs praising one's beloved, or songs complaining of the beloved's coldness and indifference. But some songs are lively and lend themselves to dance, such as the *dabke*. A village wedding in traditional style is the ideal occasion for hearing the variety of dance songs with their subtly changing rhythms that stir the body to movement. To the Western ear they are in a minor key, seemingly with sad overtones; but to the ear attuned to their special qualities each one has a message.

Now, what instruments play in the *takht,* as the Arab orchestra is called?

First is the *oud,* known from pre-Islamic times, and from which the lute descended. Then there are the *kanun (qanun),* a trapezoidal stringed instrument mentioned in *The Thousand and One Nights* and similar to the harpsichord, with 24 cords; the *buzuq;* the *nay,* a vertical flute that can be traced back to 3000 B.C.; and percussion instruments such as the *riq,* the *daff,* and the *tablah.* Percussion instruments are an absolute must in Arab music because of its pronounced rhythmic structure. Throughout the song a regular, strong pulse beats constantly. In the Western waltz there are three beats to the bar, with the accent falling on the first beat. A similar arrangement occurs in Arab music, except that the bar is much more complicated. The *nawakht* (rhythmical mode), for instance, contains seven beats to every bar, with accents falling on the first and fourth beats; the second and fifth beats are the weakest.

The melodic line of an Arab song has a distinctive pattern, and its cadences fall differently from those of Western music. The melody is, however, structured in a manner similar to the melodies of European composers of the 18th century. The author has often been struck with the similarity between some of Bach's melodies and the classical Arab songs that have descended to us from Moor-

ish Spain. If the foreigner approaches Arab music with Bach or
Vivaldi in mind, some of its apparent strangeness fades away.

FOLK MUSIC AND DANCE

Adapted from a script for the Hashemite Broadcasting Service by
Maaz Shukayr, *former director of programs, English and Arabic
Services.*

In Jordan each man's work, station in life, pastime, or celebration has its traditional accompaniment in song. Day laborers swing
to a work song; construction gangs heave on pulleys or work cement to the strongly accented beats that belong to the building
trades. There is a plowing song, a seeding song, and a harvest song.
The harvest song is slower in tempo than, say, the lilting themes
that the shepherd out in the desert with his flock uses to while away.
the hours. The tattoo that a taxi driver beats on the roof of his car
to accompany the tune he is humming has the urgency of the
crowded city streets, an urban tempo different from his country
cousin's.

The average Jordanian loves to listen to his country's music—on
the lips of a folksinger, on the radio, over television. He probably
knows every note; but each new verse with an added up-to-date
variation, every fresh anecdote delights him. The traditional tunes
are used over and over for current events, much like calypso in
the Caribbean, bringing a new story in a familiar musical package.

Many Jordanian folksongs have for centuries celebrated the
happy events marking village life. The folksinger gives rein to joy
over the birth of a baby boy, expresses the mixed pride and ner-
vousness of a first day at school, and of course becomes lyrical over
betrothals and weddings. A Jordanian wedding is a festivity in
which the whole village joins, dancing and feasting, and in fact people from all the neighboring villages will participate, coming on
foot or by donkey if the family has not yet achieved the status of
a car. The main festivity is making and listening to music, always
with dancing.

Both classical and folk music in Jordan are constructed on the
17-note scale, so different in effect from the Western chromatic
scale. Also, extremely complex rhythms are characteristic, one un-
derlying beat counterpointed by rippling, undulating airs that leap
and frolic extemporaneously at times. At the end of each couplet,
the singer utters a long drawn out "Oooooooof," lasting from 15
to 75 seconds, during which the audience claps and cheers and asks
for a particular verse or theme for the next go-round. The Arab
tradition is that the music acts as a background for the lyrics,

whose content and poetic style occupy the center of attention. Often the poetry is of great beauty, particularly in dealing with love themes, the wonders of nature, patriotic feelings, and loyalty to one's king.

It doesn't take much for a Jordanian to make music—his own beating foot and a short reed flute will set a group to dancing. There are two reed flutes: one five-holed, the *qasaba,* and the other seven-holed, the *nay.* These are very popular—easily carried, ever-handy, and capable of producing the quarter tones and three-quarter tones peculiar to Arab music.

The other oldest and most omnipresent musical instrument in Jordan is the *rababa*—a one-string violin with a square body and straight neck, still widely used by the Bedouins. Its body is stretched goatskin, and the bow elicits a weird keening sound, liquid or scratching according to the skill of the player. The wail of the *rababa* from a black goatskin tent at night is a true echo of centuries of Bedouin nomadic life. Any time one sees a Bedouin family striking camp, hoisting the whole tent and contents on to the backs of camels, the last thing that is carefully hitched on is the *rababa.*

Besides the reed and stringed instruments, the basic dancemaker is, of course, the percussion family. There is the *daff* or *riqq,* the circular tambourine, the most commonly seen and heard invitation to the dance. But also very popular is the *durbakkah,* a long drum with a skin drumhead. The hollow thump of these instruments is the inevitable background to the dancing of the *debkah,* a folk dance that seems to spring spontaneously into life whenever there are talk, coffee, and more than five or six men gathered together. Properly, as in Jordan, it is a man's dance, with the participants lined up side by side, one elbow akimbo, following the intricate forward and backward steps, slides, jumps, and stamps of a leader, who keeps a handkerchief twirling in one upraised hand throughout the dance.

More sophisticated musical instruments are found in the cities and towns—like the *oud,* a fat relative of the western mandolin, perhaps. It is a deeply ovate stringed instrument with a bent back and five double string plucked with a quill of eagle's feather, and is usually quite a work of the wood mosaicist's art in its melon-shaped, inlaid belly. In the hands of a skilled performer the *oud* has a plangent, plaintive tone, and takes part in the intricate interweaving melodic strands that make true Arab music.

Ascending in scale of sophistication, the *qanoon* presents a real challenge to a music maker. It is an Oriental harp with 78 strings mounted on a trapezoidal box, played with two metal plectra worn on the two index fingers. It approximates a lute, and should be listened to for itself, with a good voice accompaniment.

A *rababa* and a *riqq* suffice to keep *debkah* dancers swaying and weaving for hours at a time, but one of the plucked instruments is used for a faster staccato dance with outspread arms called the *tayyara*—which translates literally as "airplane"—in which the dancer suits the movement of his body and arms to the name of the dance. The *dal'ona* is a very popular village dance, always performed at weddings, christenings, and other happy occasions. A curious dance is the *arja*, meaning "lame"—a name derived from the rather off-beat hesitating and syncopated step, not unlike the movement of a lame man. Occasionally among the Bedouin comes the *sahja*, in which a young woman responds to the clapping of the men in a sort of symbolic duel: the girl carries a sword, emblem of her untouchability; the men act out the lyrics of the chanter, pursuing her. This mixing of the young men and women of the desert must be an occasion for surreptitious courting, for there is not a great deal of coeducational play among Bedouin.

Perhaps one of the most exciting dances in Jordan is the sword dance of Circassian origin performed in honor of a *mukhtar*, or head of a tribe, or coming to its peak of intensity for King Hussein himself. This dance becomes a test of steel nerves for the honoree. It involves a series of ever faster and faster lunges and retreats, swords swirling and slashing, as the dancers hail their lord. They work their way closer and closer to the king, who stands arrow-straight, and the swords flick about his head, with each newcomer protesting his allegiance, stamping and shouting in a frenzy of devotional zeal, *"Yah, Sayidneh, Yah, Hussein!"*

THE BEDOUIN

There are about 40,000 Bedouin in Jordan who manage to live as their ancestors have lived for hundreds of years. It is a rugged life, but safe and comforting in its sure design.

Bedouin (Arabic *bedu*, literally "inhabitants of the desert") are still found throughout most of the Arab world. Today's heaviest concentration of the true Bedouin is in eastern Jordan and the surrounding desert areas of Syria, Iraq, Saudi Arabia, and the Naqab (Negev). In southern Jordan alone they number an estimated 70,000, although some 40 percent of these are settled and no longer roam the desert.

The Bedouin of the sands and lonely waterholes can be seen camped in the desert that flanks the north-south highway which runs through Jordan. They travel in groups, with dozens of camels or large flocks of sheep and goats, and pitch their goat-hair tents one next to the other, sometimes two or three, sometimes a score or more if it is a large tribe.

The Bedouin are strictly organized, with major subdivisions that, in turn, encompass a number of smaller groups. Occupationally, they are divided into three classes—camel herders, sheep herders, and goat herders. Of the three, the camel herders are the real aristocrats of the desert, the *Aaiil* (thoroughbreds), and the ones whose way of life has the most romantic appeal to foreign visitors. The three major camel herding and breeding tribes in Jordan are the Beni Sakhr, the Huweitat, and the Sirhan; among them they possess about 10,000 tents, 20,000 camels, and 1,000 horses.

Despite popular belief, the Bedouin does not wander aimlessly about. He knows exactly where he's going, knows where to drive his flocks and set up his tents, knows where to find water and forage for his herds. Some Bedouin families have followed, more or less, the same migratory route year after year for generations. To the Western eye, the desert often appears much the same in whatever direction one looks. The Bedouin, however, has another eye; with some inner sense he can go back again and again to the same spot in the wide sands.

To read about the Bedouin is one thing; to know them is another. Many visitors to Jordan who sought the adventure of the desert have experienced the hospitality of the Bedouin, the repeated smiling greeting: *"Ahlan wa Sahlan,"* or "Welcome, twice welcome." To a Bedouin, hospitality is second only to honor, and the guest enters the tent as he would his own home.

There he will be seated on the softest, richest carpet and will be served freshly brewed coffee and special delicacies reserved for guests and festive occasions. Members of the family scurry about, seeking ways to make the guest feel more welcome.

The lucky guest is the one who is feted with a Bedouin *mensef,* the traditional feast of the desert. In his autobiography King Hussein describes a visit to a Bedouin tribe:

> When I visit one of our tribes, I sit in the tent with the other guests around me. The tent can be 50 yards long with carpets spread their length, and silken cushions to recline against. Members of the tribe gather before the tent and begin their traditional dances— usually the *debke*—with the songs that go with the dancing. Since I am the honored guest, my name occurs frequently in the improvised songs, and when that happens, they shoot off their rifles as a salute.
>
> After we all sit down and coffee is passed, the sheikh makes his welcoming speech, composing it as he goes along. After him appears the tribal poet who recites his verse of welcome and loyalty.
>
> Then comes the *mensef.* This consists of a huge tray piled high with rice surmounted by a whole lamb, and all of it flavored with yogurt sauce *(jameed).* A group of about eight or ten guests stand around each tray and, sometimes with the help of our host, pluck away at the lamb and roll the rice skillfully into a small ball and pop it in our mouths.
>
> Always, of course, with the right hand.

In the Arab world, the left hand is never used to touch food.

Now something of a myth is the tradition that the honored guest is offered the eye of the sheep to eat.

The nomadic life of the desert is, of course, very hard. There are few modern conveniences out there in the blazing summer sun or the freezing winter nights. The wealthy sheikh's tent may be opulent, but any air conditioning he may enjoy is by God's grace. Much of the cooking is done over open fires fed by logs, twigs, and charcoal, although in recent years small kerosene stoves have been making an appearance in the more affluent tents. The women, as in many other societies, do most of the work, though in the Bedouin home they are not often seen by visitors, especially if the visitor is a male. And they work hard, these women—cooking, washing, carrying water, tending to all the needs of their menfolk, and sewing and weaving besides.

Many of the textiles in and out of the tent, the floor coverings and the tent itself, are made or woven by the women, and they begin from scratch. The animal, whether camel, sheep, or goat, is sheared, the wool washed and spun, sometimes dyed, then hand woven. It is in their dresses that the Bedouin women's fine artistry and talent are most evident. Robes of magnificence, they are usually black, dark blue or dark red; embroidered or woven into them are rich, brilliant designs in intricate geometric or flowered patterns. To the knowledgeable eye the design reveals what part of Jordan the woman comes from, what tribe, and even sometimes the wealth of her husband.

Some of these beautiful dresses are displayed in Jordan's Folklore and Costume Museums beneath the Roman Amphitheater in Amman. And recently some have found their way into the cocktail wardrobes of a number of Western women with a taste for the dramatically different in dress.

The male Bedouin's life is equally rugged. He is, in every sense of the word, the "provider" and "protector" of the family. He spends his days in the harsh desert, caring for his herds of camel, sheep, or goats, to provide food, milk, wool, and leather for his family's needs. Surplus products are sold at market and the money used to buy whatever the desert cannot provide—coffee, sugar, flour, household utensils . . . and jewelry for his wife.

But Bedouin life is often relaxed, too, and in the long, unhurried hours of the desert world there is always time for leisure and recreation. Camel and horse racing, falconry, *debke,* and sword dancing are among the more vigorous pastimes. In the evenings there are the quieter social hours, sitting around the brazier, brewing and drinking thick, sweet, cardamom-flavored coffee. This is a time for talk, about daily work and about the past accomplishments and future hopes of the tribe. There is also recitation of poetry, song, and the soft, plaintive sounds of the *rababa.*

To understand the Bedouin one must look beyond his costume and tent, his camel and nomadic existence, to the strict desert code of honor, loyalty, hospitality, and courage that rules his life. In the desert, civil law is unknown. Bedouin have their own legal structure, their own code of ethics and laws that govern every aspect of behavior. Each tribe polices, governs, and defends the rights of its members. Each member, in turn, carries a communal responsibility for the infraction of any law by any other member of the tribe. The code also protects the rights of any guest, even a foreigner, who happens to be visiting the tribe.

If, for instance, a tribe member commits a crime, he implicates and dishonors not only his own family but often the entire tribe. This is particularly serious when the crime is of a *muhlikat* type—premeditated murder, rape and other sex offenses, treason—where the punishment is death.

Thus desert society provides a large measure of law and order, and threats of anarchy or lawlessness are avoided. In actual fact, compared to large Western cities, the desert is extraordinarily safe. A woman need not fear attack; rape is practically unheard of among the Bedouin, who look upon it as a shameful act beneath the honor and dignity of a man. To the Bedouin, there are only three kinds of man—the brave, the hospitable, and the wise. And all must be, first and foremost, honorable. It is his honor above all else that the Bedouin will defend—with his life, if necessary.

Bedouin are people of great strength and conviction, fiercely independent, and bound, out of choice and integrity, to the pattern of life that time and experience in the harsh desert have determined for them. If the word "free" can be applied to any people, it can be applied to the Bedouin. And they remain free—free to follow their own customs, laws, and traditions—thanks to the Jordanian Government. The Government provides an alternative life for the Bedouin, offering him the comfort of a house instead of a tent, schools for his children, and a settled agricultural life instead of desert wandering. But nothing is forced upon him. Sometimes he may accept the house, but will often pitch his tent next to it—wanting, no doubt, the best of two worlds.

In turn, the Bedouin has expressed his gratitude by being the most fiercely loyal subject in the Hashemite Kingdom of Jordan, and has stood staunchly by the King. Bedouin honor would not permit less.

THE CAMEL: THE BEDOUIN'S BEST FRIEND

The camel spits constantly, smells to high heaven, makes rude noises, is arrogant; he is foolish-looking with his bulbous belly and knobby-kneed, spindly legs; he is clumsy, stupid, lazy, gloomy, cantankerous even with himself, downright mean and hardhearted to his best friends, who feed and water him. And he gives you a bumpy, swaying, bucking ride that leaves you sore for a long time.

But don't tell a Bedouin this. He sees the camel differently. The Bedouin believes the camel is a lordly beast sent just to help him. And, in fact, he does.

The Bedouin finds the camel good for meat to eat, a producer of milk to drink and hair to make clothes and tents. His dried dung is excellent as a heating fuel. He drinks little water out in the desert, where water is scarce; he can go for days on a handful of acacia leaves or plain dry straw, can carry tremendous loads without stopping or sleeping or drinking or eating for far greater distances than any human being can; and he is a personnel carrier of inestimable value, even if he does leave you aching and begging for relief.

The Bedouin will tell you that the farther out in the desert you go, the prettier a camel becomes. And most Jordanians know that, despite the invention and development of the Land-Rover, the desert buggy, heavy-duty four-wheel-drive trucks, helicopters, light planes that land and take off short, or any other modern contraption, the camel is necessary for life in the desert. Without him, it is likely that there would be no Bedouin.

While some people call the camel "God's bad joke," the Bedouin calls him *Ata Allah,* which means "God's gift."

Jordan probably has about a million camels, and they are everywhere. They plod along with men or freight on their backs on some of the streets of Amman, are tethered outside mosques in cities and towns, wander about the valley of Petra and among the magnificent ruins of Jerash, form desert caravans for moving goods just as they have for thousands of years, wander freely in the desert, snort and bump each other at hundreds of waterholes, carry cargoes of fruits and vegetables to markets in the Jordan Valley, pull farm plows and platforms that skid across the ground like wagons without wheels, and walk slowly round and round to operate water pumps.

And camels provide the main transportation for several hundred elite troopers of Jordan's Desert Patrol. Out in the far desert the camel is used to chase down smugglers from neighboring states trying to reach Jordan's thriving markets with contraband goods. On those somewhat rare occasions when a Bedouin breaks a law, Desert Patrolmen track down the culprit by camelback.

The camel is a native of North America. His ancestors first appeared about 40 million years ago, and soon developed into several branches. One branch migrated to South America and eventually evolved into the modern vicuña, guanaco, llama, and alpaca. Other branches crossed from North America into eastern Asia by the ancient Alaskan land bridge over the Bering Sea—a reverse movement of man's journey from eastern Asia across the same bridge to populate North and South America.

Over the centuries some camels developed two humps; these are called Bactrian camels. They are quite large—often eight or nine feet high, huge-bodied, heavily haired, and can tolerate intense cold. They are now found mostly in Siberia and China.

Another camel family branch developed only one hump; these are called dromedaries. Once having crossed from North America they did not stop in Siberia or China, but kept going until they reached the hot sands first of Araby and then of Africa.

The Jordanian dromedary, not as thick-bodied as the Bactrian, reaches seven to nine feet in height through the shoulders. The hump takes him up another foot. He weighs up to 1,400 or 1,600 pounds, and his feet look and act like floppy pillows—just what a beast or man needs to walk on hot and shifting sands.

Camels have two rows of eyelashes—just the thing to keep out blowing desert sands and to cut down the glare of the sun. His ears, mouth, and eyes can close as tightly as a Bank of England vault, important when the desert environment gets rough with whistling winds and shifting sand. Camels can and do eat anything they come upon, including cacti and other desert plants with even sharper spines and barbs. The camel simply nibbles away with his pliable, tough lips, and down go the razor-sharp plants. On such nourishment the camel can go for several days without eating again.

The secret of a camel's digestive ability is his four stomachs— four distinct areas in his body through which food passes. By the time the camel has expelled his waste, it is totally dry and tightly packed, excellent to use as fuel in the Bedouin's open fire.

In the Jordanian desert, when the temperature hits 110 to 120 degrees, a dromedary can move smartly along on a big drink of water every four or five days. He can go much, much longer, but that is rarely necessary because many waterholes are maintained out in the wastelands. When a camel does stop for a drink he takes in gallons of water, and he sucks it up with a loud swish.

A camel makes total use of the water he drinks. Little evaporates or is passed off. The body throws off heat through the skin without sweating, thereby leaving the water inside. Heat from the sun is reflected and does not enter the body. And fat is stored in the hump to be used when other nourishment is not available. The camel is visible proof of Charles Darwin's theory that for animals to survive, they must adjust to their environment—the camel is possibly better adjusted to its environment than any other living thing, plant or animal.

Man makes many uses of the camel, but the two main ones are for his own transportation and to carry his baggage. Getting 700 or 800 pounds of freight on a camel's back is no great problem. Camels are lazy and spend much time on the ground, squatting on their legs, which are folded beneath them. Bedouin have only to strap the freight over the top of the hump, make it secure, thump the animal on the rear and the shoulders to get him up, and then take off across the desert.

For a person to mount a camel—well, that's something else again. So is staying on a swaying camel running all-out across rough terrain. And getting off is no small task, either.

How to Ride a Camel

You must mount a camel when he is squatting on the ground. You cannot throw a leg over him as he stands, as you would with a horse; he is too tall for that. The way to get on a camel is to come up on the squatting animal from the left and rear. Quickly reach for and grip tightly the saddle pommel with the left hand. This is the signal for the camel to get up, and from now on you have to act fast.

Get your right leg across the animal quickly, even if you have to brace yourself by putting your left knee in the saddle itself. A camel gets his hindquarters up first, and fast, by straightening out the hind legs. His front legs are still folded on the ground, and this means he is in a diving position. You've got to be in that saddle, holding on and leaning backward as far as you can, or you will pitch headfirst over the camel's head.

As soon as the two back legs are straight, the camel starts raising his front end. He pushes up with those spindly, unlikely-looking legs, and unless you are holding on tight and ready to shift from leaning backward to sharply leaning forward, you are going to get tossed off. The rider is on an even keel only when all four legs are straight.

As soon as those legs are straight the camel takes off. He doesn't have any idea where he is going, but he is going. And he usually moves off fast. You must turn him about and get him heading in the direction you want to go, stay in the swaying and pitching saddle, and try to look as dignified as possible—which isn't easy.

Some camels are guided entirely with long, pencil-thin sticks, or whips. If a Bedouin wants his animal to turn right, he strokes the camel's head or neck on the left side and more or less shoves the head toward the right. Some camels need the pressure of the stick plus a length of rope running from a bridle to the hand of the rider. This rope, or leather strap, can be used to guide the animal. Some other camels need a more standard bridle and rein controlled by the rider.

Most riders sit in the saddle with one leg hooked over the pommel. Some straddle the animal bareback and clamp their knees to his sides. A camel rocks almost violently from side to side, for the simple reason that he extends both his right front and right rear legs forward at the same time, then his two left legs. The ride would be much better if he worked on the diagonal, but the camel doesn't know or care about that, and he would rather you got off anyway.

Procedures for getting off a camel vary from simply jumping off to stopping the animal, then hanging on while he goes through the getting-up process in reverse. Down goes the animal to bended front knees, which pitches you forward precipitously; then he buckles his hind legs, down goes the rear end, and off you go if you don't hang on.

If you have managed to stay on throughout, it is now possible to step off the animal with some degree of dignity.

A warning note must now be sounded. Don't, after your first or second or third camel ride, try to run. Take it easy. Unless you are limber, strong-legged and young, you are going to be unsteady. Your knees might even buckle.

And unless you have recently been riding a horse regularly, playing tennis, walking a couple of miles, jogging, or at least doing a dozen deep knee-bends daily, you are going to be sore. Oh, so sore.

ARABIAN HORSES:
JORDAN'S BLOODED ARISTOCRATS

By
THOMAS C. WEAVER

The author, a longtime resident of Aleppo and Beirut, has ridden, trained, and shown horses for many years. His first Arab horse was the pride of his ten-year-old life in Ohio, and he has always owned one or more Arab horses ever since. He has been President of Aleppo College, where he was the authority on the buying, training, and showing of Arab horses; in Beirut he was Chairman of the Committee on Horse Shows for the Lebanese Federation of Equestrian Sports.

Although unanimity has never for a moment, alas, characterized the views of Arabian horse fanciers throughout the world, in Jordan today the visiting horseman of whatever persuasion will find animals very much to his taste. Roughly, one might identify two basic points of view as the Bedouin and the European. While all agree that the Arabian horse is distinguished by superior beauty, intelligence, and endurance, and further that he is generally recognized as the dominant blood source of all horses of quality, most particularly the English thoroughbred, there is a considerable difference of emphasis in the criteria of evaluation.

The Bedouin places endurance at the top of his list, and the breeder adopting this point of view uses in his stud only those animals that have adequately demonstrated this quality and the capacity to transmit it. The European fancier, on the other hand, puts beauty first, and prefers for his purposes only those animals of exceptional appearance, each one a picture of classical equine perfection. Unsurprisingly, these differing views are clearly reflected in the schooling and use of the horse, the Bedouin breeder concerning himself largely with racing, the European with dressage, saddle classes, and model events.

In Jordan today there are between ten and fifteen thousand horses. The largest private collection is owned by Sherif Nasser bin Jamil (the uncle of King Hussein), a very knowledgeable and devoted horseman who represents the Bedouin view par excellence.

From birth, desert methods are applied to his foals. At six months the colts are placed, several together, in small paddocks where they move about enough to begin development of shoulder muscles. Four or five months later they are transferred to much larger rectangular paddocks. Here gazelles await them, and in the cool of early morning and evening these new companions regularly race each other the length of the paddock, quickly arousing the competitive instincts of the colts, who most enthusiastically join in the fun. Thus the motor of the future race horse—his quarters and hocks—is built up day by day, so that when he is saddled at the age of 18 to 20 months his basic muscling is complete.

At Sherif Nasser's stud I saw two aged matrons, 31 and 34 years old, each with a fine new foal at her side. His horses are all in fine condition, due in part to Jordan's excellent dry climate, with deliciously cool mornings and evenings even in midsummer, and also to the owner's first-rate care, a felicitous combination of modern medicine and traditional Bedouin knowledge and skill. An example of Bedouin practice is to be found in the prudent consideration shown aged mares and their foals: a mare of 15 or more is expected to nurse only three months, and the foal's subsequent milk requirements are provided by a camel.

On this visit to Sherif Nasser's horses, I came away with an extra sense of pleasure deriving from the informal, democratic family atmosphere of the stables, reflecting the manners of the aristocratic Bedouin of the desert: the warmly gracious hospitality, the ready humor, the dignity and the easy relationships of staff, owner and guests.

Sherif Nasser showed me horses of all age groups and of different types—the mountain horse, for example, with his large open nostrils and small hoofs, and the desert horse with his long, relatively closed nostrils and larger hoofs. All of them were beautifully "dry," without an ounce of superfluous flesh, and they all tended to show what in Arabic is called *arih* or streamlining, stemming from a good length of back plus generous depth. In a word, they appeared to combine the speed and strength of the "drinkers of the wind."

Sherif Nasser's stable includes precious mares of ancient lineage long owned by members of his family—Sherif Hussein, King Abdullah, King Feisal I, and other royal figures. These mares are blood treasures comparable to the most precious heirlooms handed down through the successive generations of an old family. One of them, now a sound and cheerful 31 years, is a fine old desert animal of the Hamadani Simri strain, taken into Syria and Iraq by King Feisal I. She is appropriately named Um Dahab—Mother of Gold.

Among the horses one finds example after example of the Bedouin taste and view in the dry, strong, fast animals. I was reminded of a frequent experience from my years as an amateur trainer of a large stable of Arabians: whenever the genuine Bedouin connoisseur came to call, a man from a recognized horse-breeding tribe, he was invariably attracted to just this kind of horse—the doer. He expressed his appreciation in glances rather than words, lest an articulate compliment bring misfortune.

When I asked Sherif Nasser about his hopes for the future, quite apart from his regular involvement with racing in Amman, Beirut, Egypt, and Greece, he replied promptly and precisely: first, to improve the quality of the horse; second, to encourage a new generation of owners and breeders; and third, to guide a new generation of racing jockeys.

Throughout the summer there are five races every Sunday in Amman, three of which are reserved for the Bedouin horses, whose owners and breeders are to be seen camping nearby in their black tents. Although he is a sophisticated and widely experienced horseman, Sherif Nasser holds fast to Bedouin traditions as the basis of his extensive efforts, with which the future of the horse in Jordan is very closely bound.

Another rewarding visit involves a drive of about 30 minutes from Amman to the royal stud of King Hussein, located in a pleasant hollow surrounded by gentle, thickly-wooded hills where the air is so light and dry it fairly sparkles. The stables are of white stucco, with generous stalls surrounding a large patio with a mosaic fountain at the center—altogether a handsome setting that is both Arab and Spanish. Here one meets the European tradition of the Arabian horse, which is itself an ancient line of taste arising from the Golden Age of Islam when the Arabs ruled the Iberian Peninsula, among other places, and involving also the central role of the Arabian horse in the early European schools of equitation.

His Majesty's stud, albeit small when compared to a large racing stable, contains a number of beautiful animals, which the most discriminating European specialist would find it hard to fault. Here one sees the dashing of the head, the large, widely spaced and expressive eyes, the long, lightly curved, beautifully planed neck, the rounded delineation of the jaw, and the generous pointed ears—all the hallmarks of the classical style of beauty one sees in old prints and paintings. One does not expect quite the lean dryness of the desert horse. These horses show their superior blood miles away and remind one of the best specimens of the Arabians' most distinguished offshoot, the English thoroughbred. That the royal stud contains breeding stock with the capacity to dominate and transmit fine quality is evident in the foals and youngsters to be seen.

There is an attractive outdoor school for the use of the royal family and for basic training and dressage exercises. Show jumping today depends in a large degree on thorough basic dressage, for modern courses require not only scope and the ability to jump large obstacles but also great precision, which is itself dependent on the harmony of horse and rider that results in a powerful, submitted and balanced horse, trained to accept his rider's direction in order to do his very best over an exacting course. The higher levels of dressage are to be found in European national and international events and, ultimately, in the *haute école* of the Spanische Hofreitschule of Vienna.

The museum here is an excellent beginning of a collection of saddlery of historic interest.

One leaves Jordan with the hope that conditions will one day permit the expansion of all activities related to the horse: breeding, racing, polo, dressage, trekking, and export. An extensive effort is needed to register each individual horse to reveal his origins clearly and precisely in line with the understandable and legitimate requirements of potential buyers. Climatic conditions are nearly perfect.

THE FACE OF JORDAN

AMMAN

A Modern Capital 3,000 Years Old

Amman, the capital of the Hashemite Kingdom of Jordan, is a modern city spread across seven steep hills. It was only a village when King Abdullah moved the seat of his newly formed government there in the 1920s. Now broad streets lined with modern shops and buildings have replaced the simple little town, and hilltops abound with spacious villas, gardens, government ministries, school, and hospitals. The city's growth has been spectacular in the last decade, jumping from a population of 300,000 to 900,000—and still growing.

Recent excavations reveal that Amman was inhabited in the early Bronze Age. The Bible mentions "Rabbath of Ammon" as the capital of the Ammonites about 1200 B.C. Two hundred years later David stormed the town. It was here that he sent Uriah the Hittite to his certain death in order to take Uriah's beautiful wife, Bathsheba. The city gained a reputation for pride, wealth, and wickedness, and the prophets Amos, Jeremiah, and Ezekiel foretold its destruction.

After the Babylonian captivity the Bible speaks no more of Rabbath-Ammon. Only after the general Ptolemy Philadelphus II (285–247 B.C.) took the town from the Greeks and renamed it for himself can its history be taken up again.

After the Roman conquest of the East, Philadelphia joined the Decapolis and was later captured by Herod the Great. As part of the Roman Province of Arabia the city was rebuilt *a la romana,* and flourished because of its location along the caravan trail. Amman's great Roman theater, seating 5,000 people, is still used today.

In the early Byzantine period the city became the seat of the Christian Bishopric of Petra and Philadelphia. Then, after a brief period of prominence under the Umayyads during the 8th century, it sank into obscurity.

Today Amman is the seat of government and the hub of the country's cultural and commercial activity. Indeed, its present growth is due in part to enormous business expansion, particularly with foreign investment and as headquarters for international business firms. Amman is one of the cleanest cities in the Middle East, and street crime is almost unheard of, making it especially pleasant as a place for families to live.

Amman is now the center of a network of new roads, which greatly facilitate travel. Northward, a new highway runs through the hills of Gilead to Jerash, called the Pompeii of the East, and continues to Irbid, the second largest city, or to Ramtha on the Syrian border. Westward, another highway swings down through the hills of Moab to the Dead Sea, across the Jordan River, and onward to Jericho and Jerusalem.

Southward, the network offers two roads—the King's Highway, the well-trod route of antiquity, which goes to Madaba and Mt. Nebo, Kerak, and Petra, or the new Desert Road, which leads directly to Aqaba. Eastward, a new road crosses the desert to Azraq, making what was once an all-day journey by jeep an easy two-hour drive by car.

Newcomers may find Amman confusing at first because at ground level it is hard to grasp the city's layout. The best place for an overall view of the city is the summit of a hill known as the Citadel, situated in the center of town. It is also the best place to start one's sightseeing. In the panorama the seven major hills *Jebel* plus several minor knolls and valleys can be spotted.

Beginning on the south side, where the promontory overlooks the Roman amphitheater, you face the oldest part of the city, with Jebel Ashrafiyah in the background, distinguished by the Abu Darwish Mosque, a stately structure of white and black stone. Moving clockwise, the next hill is Jebel Nadif, and further to the south and southeast is Jebel Nazal.

On the west and north—areas of most interest to tourists—lie Jebel Amman and Jebel Hussein, with El Webdeh and the new residential district of Shmeisani between them. These areas are the most affluent parts of town where most of the hotels, embassies, restaurants, modern shops, and attractive houses and apartments are located.

Between Jebel Hussein and Jebel al Taj on the east are sections known as Nuzha, Qusur and Wadi Hadadieh. There are the poorer and older sections of the town, some completely filled with communities of refugees and other displaced persons.

EXPLORING AMMAN

The important sites of antiquity in Amman can be visited in half a day. The main ones date from the Roman period. The city's museums and places of interest pertaining to the modern aspects of Jordan may be seen in another half or full day, depending upon one's interests. Entrance to many antiquity sites and museums throughout Jordan is free of charge; others charge a nominal fee.

Ancient Amman lies in Wadi Amman, a ravine through which a stream known as Seil Amman flows from west to east. It is a tributary of the Zerqa River, the Jabbok of the Bible. In ancient times the city consisted of a lower and an upper section. The latter was built on the hill now known as Jebel Qala'at, or the Citadel, and constituted the city's acropolis.

The Citadel

The hill is a strategically located, oblong-shaped plateau that overlooks the forum area of the lower city on the south. From very early times it was an important fortress. It is surrounded by valleys on all sides except the north, where an escarpment was cut to complete its isolation.

The upper section of the hill is in the shape of two rectangles of unequal dimensions. The first, with an east-west orientation, is about 2,700 feet long and about 180 feet wide. The second, with a north-south orientation, is about 1,200 feet long and 240 feet wide. The latter contains the ruins of a temple, a church, a Byzantine-Arab building, and other ancient remnants.

The Romans rebuilt what was apparently an ancient fortress and surrounded it with massive walls, which are among the finest of ancient fortifications to have survived to the present day. The walls consist of lower courses that incline inward in steps of heavy, well-jointed stonework overlaid by a wall of smooth square stones. The fortress' walls were fortified by towers at each corner.

The entrance to the Citadel leads into a spacious court, in the middle of which stand the ruins of a temple dedicated to Hercules, built during the reign of Marcus Aurelius (A.D. 161–180). A fragmentary inscription discovered in the debris around the temple indicated its date. It is situated close to the south wall of the acropolis. Only part of its podium and the bases of the entrance columns

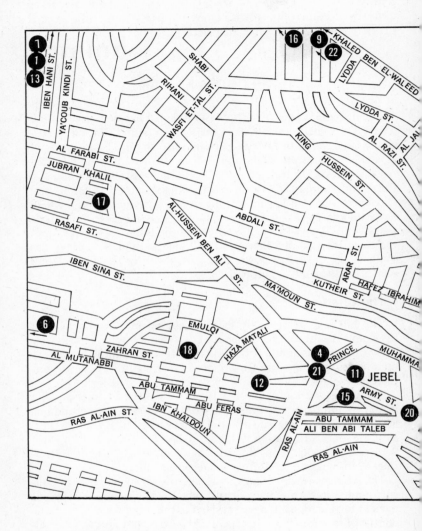

Points of Interest

1) Royal Jordanian Head Office
2) Antiquities Museum
3) Roman Amphitheater and
   Folklore Museum
4) British Embassy

5) Citadel
6) Amra Forum Hotel
7) Amman Marriott Hotel
8) Gold Market
9) Regency and Grand Palace
   hotels
10) Hussein Mosque

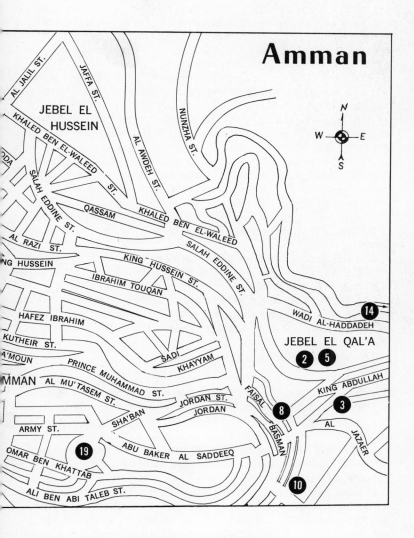

11) Jordan Inter-Continental
12) Ministry of Tourism and
    Antiquities
13) Amman Plaza Hotel
14) Royal Palace
15) U.S. Embassy
16) University of Jordan

17) Holiday Inn
18) Housing Bank Building
19) First Circle
20) Second Circle
21) Third Circle
22) Hussein Sports City

are still in place. Apparently the temple was once a magnificent monument towering above the lower city.

A joint British-Jordanian team headed by the well-known British archeologist Crystal Bennett has carried out excavations at the Citadel every other year since 1972. The aim is to establish a chronology of occupation of the site from earliest times.

Partial excavation near the temple shows that it was built on the site of a sacred rock that archeologists date to the early Bronze Age, c. 3000 B.C.

The Byzantine gate of the Citadel is still standing, and outside the Roman walls is a rock-carved cistern that supplied water to the fortress in times of siege.

On the north side of the Citadel lies *El-Qasr,* the castle, dating from the Umayyad period. It is built in the form of a square enclosing a cross, and its interior is decorated with stone carvings.

From the Citadel there is a good view of Raghdan, the Royal Palace offices across the way, used for official functions. The Palace is guarded by Circassian soldiers in colorful black and red uniforms.

The King's residence recently moved from Hashemiiya Palace on the road to the University to Basman Palace near Raghdan. It is not open to the public.

You should also take a drive around Amman to get oriented to the city. Another good panoramic view can be seen from the top of Jebel Ashrafiyah near the Abu Darivish Mosque.

The Amman Archeological Museum

Hours: 9 A.M.–**4** P.M. **Closed Tuesdays. Tel. 638795.**

Exhibits in the museum are arranged chronologically, beginning at the right after you enter the front door and proceeding counterclockwise. A book describing the displays is available at the entrance.

Prehistoric Times (180,000 B.C. to the Neolithic Period): A skull discovered in Jerusalem reveals that man knew medicine and head surgery thousands of years ago.

Bronze Age (3000–1200 B.C.): The exhibits include pieces found in Jericho: copper lamps, coins, earrings, and decorated pottery. A group of early Bronze Age artifacts were found in a tomb alongside the Amman-Suweileh highway. Middle Bronze Age scarabs and pottery were found at the Citadel, and late Bronze Age utensils come from a temple uncovered during the construction of Amman airport.

Iron Age (1200–500 B.C.): Exhibits of pottery, statues, implements, bronze and iron bracelets, gold ornaments, Egyptian scarabs, and Assyrian seals. A group of pottery coffins imitating Egyptian ones were discovered in Jebel el-Qusur in 1968. (These will be found in a room on the north side of the main hall.) Most of the pottery of this period comes from Sahab, on the east side of Amman. Further excavations are planned here, since evidence shows the site was occupied in the Chalcolithic period.

Nabataean Objects: The Nabataeans are thought to have migrated into southern Jordan about the 5th century B.C. and established their capital at Petra. The objects here were found in Jebel Amman. (For the most part, objects found in the excavations at Petra are retained by the museum there.) The Amman museum's collection of Nabataean pottery is especially important as it contains excellent samples to show the fineness and decoration which made Nabataean pottery outstanding.

Hellenistic Age (330–64 B.C.): Pottery, glassware, jewelry, and marble statues.

Roman Age (64 B.C.–A.D. 330): Marble statues representing gods and heroes, including a statue of Aphrodite found at Jawa, south of Amman; ornaments, glass, and jewelry.

The museum also houses a collection of Byzantine, Moslem, and Crusader items, and a display of the Dead Sea Scrolls.

The museum's collection has outgrown its space, and a great deal of the most recent finds are in storage. Through a joint project financed by the British and Jordanian governments a new museum is being planned.

The Ancient Town

The ravine below the acropolis on the south is divided by the Seil Amman, a stream, into two long, narrow strips of land on which were built streets, public buildings, and the forum. A colonnaded street ran along the north bank of the stream and at its eastern end there was a monumental gate, which probably led up to the temple on the hill.

The hills on both sides of the forum area have a sharp slope, causing a considerable amount of water to be carried down the hills to the forum, so that the stream overflows when the rains are heavy. The Romans solved the problem by covering the stream with a series of arches and vaults as well as installing a network of underground channels and conduits. Most of these have been damaged, either by natural causes or as a result of modern expansion, and some have completely disappeared.

It has been said that nowhere in the Roman Empire did the Roman legionnaires feel more at home than in Amman-Philadelphia. Like Rome, it was built on seven hills, and the city was embellished with fine paved streets, colonnaded plaza, baths, temples, and theaters. Even the climate is similar to that of Rome.

Although the development of the town was restricted by the nature of the site, the traditional Roman city plan was used. Two great streets were the bases of the plan. The longest street, *decumanus maximus,* was a colonnaded street running along a northwest axis and ending at the foot of the acropolis. The *decumanus maximus* eventually led to a Roman road outside town that continued southward to Petra and Aila on the Gulf of Aqaba.

The *cardo,* a shorter street, ran from north to south and was lined with Corinthian columns. The two streets met at a right angle near the point where the Wadi Amman branches north.

Facing the Philadelphia Hotel today, in what is still the heart of the city, there is the large Roman theater built against the slope of a hill. It seats 5,000 spectators. Originally built in the 2nd or 3rd century A.D., it is still used for concerts and other outdoor events. The columns surrounding the forum have been partially reconstructed. The theater's orientation is said to be almost perfect, providing a minimum of sunlight in the spectators' eyes. Considerable restoration has already been done to the theater, and more is scheduled.

East of the hotel are the ruins of a small theater, commonly named the Odeum. To the west is the Nymphaeum, which has not been restored. No inscriptions have been found on the monuments, but the architecture suggests that they, too, were built in the second century A.D.

On either side of the large theater, inside the iron gates, are two museums.

Jordan Museum of Popular Traditions

Hours: 9 A.M.–5 P.M. daily. Tel. 651760.

In the west wing of the Roman theater a museum has been created to display the rich variety of Jordan's traditional dress, jewelry, and utensils.

If you do no other sightseeing in Amman, you should not miss a visit to this museum. The collection is fabulous, and it has been displayed with great taste and charm. A brochure describing the exhibits is available at the museum.

The museum is the creation of Saadiyeh Tell, widow of one of Jordan's most famous prime ministers, Wasfi Tell. Each item in the museum can be considered an heirloom. It is to Mrs. Tell's credit that she had the foresight to preserve this important national heritage and to present it in such an attractive way.

Upon entering the museum, the first hall has four standing figures on the right and two seated ones on the left. The seated lady nearest the door is from Nablus and is wearing a costume called Heaven (green) and Hell (red).

To the trained eye, the cut, color, and patterns of the embroidery on a woman's dress indicate her village or tribe, wealth and status—wife, widow, virgin. According to local tradition, the embroidery was carefully studied by young men seeking brides, for it was a good indication of a woman's skill and talent. Wherever you go in Jordan, you will see some women in embroidered native cos-

tume, but the really fine work is disappearing, and so is the beautiful old handworked silver jewelry, both of which are abundant in
the museum.

In the group of standing figures (from right to left), the first
wears a costume from Bethlehem made in the late 19th century.
On her head she wears what looks like an inverted flowerpot, called
a *shatweh*. It is a cut-off version of the medieval wimple cap or
Camelot hat, which was in vogue at the time of the Crusaders. The
cap is made of heavy padding and decorated with embroidery and
gold and silver coins on the front. From the side of the cap seven
strands of a silver necklace, known as the Seven Souls, are suspended and fall under the chin and across the chest. A waist-length jacket is worn over the dress. It is called a *taksireh*, but is often referred
to as a Crusader's jacket. Both the dress and jacket are encrusted
with silk and gilt-cord embroidery in free-style motifs of flowers,
leaves, and birds—a feature that distinguishes it from the geometric cross-stitch designs that are found in most of the other dresses.
Another distinguishing feature is the color—delicate pink, coral,
blue, and beige—in contrast to the predominantly bright red and
blue of the cross-stitch.

The second figure is from Souf, a village near Ajlun. She wears
a loosely fitted one-piece black dress with a narrow V-neckline. A
soft black veil, caught to the sides of her turban, folds under the
chin and fills in the neckline. This is bordered with blocks of color
appliquéd on by a lace stitch called "daughter of the needle," which
is also found on the hem and sleeves. Her whole figure is draped
with chains, Koran holders, Turkish coins, and bobbles; tassels
hang down her back and cascades of fringe and knots of beads and
shells from her waist.

The third figure is from Beersheba. She looks tough, and is; the
tribes of Beersheba are considered the toughest of the lot. The dress
is voluminous and loaded with jewelry. A triangular face mask is
suspended from her skullcap and spreads like wings across her
cheeks, leaving only her eyes showing. The noseguard is covered
with beads, shells, coins, and embroidery. Around her waist a donkey belt is wound several times, ending in tassels and fringe, with
seashells for good luck and the telling of fortunes. Little bells hang
on swinging straps and move with her, so that she makes the sound
of camel bells as she walks.

Resting at the side of the road, with her donkey's saddle bags
hung on the wall behind her, is a woman from Salt. Her pipe is
a good five feet long, painted all the way down to its end. Her costume, a *khalaga*, makes up in volume what it lacks in embroidery.
Her dress is a triple length of black cotton, hiked up by a belt of
two bands to blouse over almost to the hem.

More costumes, fabrics, utensils, and a magnificent collection of
Bedouin jewelry are displayed in several other rooms.

Folklore Museum

Hours: 9 A.M.–5 P.M. daily except Tuesday. Tel. 651742.
The east wing of the theater houses another folklore museum.
Its aim is to show traditional life—a Bedouin tent, a camel and
rider in full regalia, cooking utensils, weaving, musical instruments, and a collection of old guns and swords.

Ain Ghazal

Several years ago, during the construction of a new highway at
the northern entrance to Amman, an ancient site dating from the
Stone Age was uncovered. After three years of excavation, begun
in 1982 by an American team, some archaeologists say it may be
the most important discovery of the Neolithic Period, 8000–4500
B.C., yet found in the entire Middle East.

Ain Ghazal, which covers 27 acres, is unusually large and well
preserved. It covers the pivotal period of history when man shifted
from nomadic hunting to settled life.

Swafieh

While Ali Erar was digging in his garden one day on the western
edge of Amman, he uncovered part of a beautiful mosaic floor,
measuring about six by nine feet, in a good state of preservation
and containing well-executed designs of birds, animals, and human
figures.

The mosaic, now covered by a protective metal hut, had been
the floor of a church erected during the Byzantine era. The outside
measurements are more than 30 feet by 15 feet. Part of the floor
was destroyed when the south wall of the church collapsed. It consists of a large rectangular field of figures surrounded by a border
about two feet wide.

Outside the border there is a band of white mosaics with geometric designs and fragments of an inscription in Greek: "in the time
of the holy Thomas, bishop . . . of the holy church, with zeal and
labors. . . . " Mention of a bishopric in the area, along with the
designs and technique, which closely resemble those in Madaba,
place this church in the sixth century A.D., a time when the area
was part of the See of Madaba.

The discovery provided new insights into the art and life of early
Christians. It is one of the most beautiful and best preserved mosaic
floors in the area. There is a wide range of color and figures, and
the intricate designs and details reveal a high quality of workmanship. There was an apparent attempt to portray ordinary activities
rather than theological themes. This, scholars believe, reflects the
early Christians' close integration of religion with everyday life.

The four corners of the border held faces representing the four seasons, similar to a design in a mosaic found in one of the Madaba churches. In the border on the north side were pairs of birds or animals facing each other. Vines extend from a colorful amphora in a symmetrical circular pattern to enclose the various figures. To the left of the amphora is a large animal with a remarkable blending of colors, and above it is a human figure leading a donkey. There are two other human figures represented, a camel girl leaning on a staff and a boy wearing shoes and holding a bow. Outside the border are two peasants facing a tree.

Swafieh is a bit difficult to find. It is nothing more than a cluster of houses on a small hill west of the highway about halfway between the sixth and seventh circles on Jebel Amman. There is a small road sign which is easy to miss.

Iraq el Amir

This antiquity site dates back to 4000 B.C., and is located 15 miles southwest of Amman in Wadi es-Seer, an area that is rapidly becoming a city suburb.

Interest in the site began in the 19th century with published reports on ruins that British and French explorers had observed. In 1904–5 an architectural survey was made by H.C. Butler of Princeton University. However, excavation did not occur until the 1960s. It began with Paul Lapp on behalf of the American Schools of Oriental Research and was continued in the 1970s by the French Archaeological Institute in conjunction with the Jordan Department of Antiquities.

The name of the site means "cave of the prince" and comes from a local legend regarding the ancient inhabitants of the caves. The caves—11 in all—are aligned in two rows across the face of a cliff at the site and are believed to have been carved by hand into the rock.

The word "Tobiah" is written in Aramaic on the fascade of one of the caverns. Tobiah was the governor of Ammon (the northern region of Jordan) and a member of an influential clan which established itself here as early as the 8th century B.C. Descendants of the same clan are mentioned in the Bible.

Among the important ruins undercover here is part of a monumental gate, which originally stood about 15 feet high and 10 feet wide, bearing the carving of a lion with its right forepaw raised in heraldic fashion.

The largest structure, known as Qasr el 'Abd, is a two story building, probably dating from the second century B.C. Its lower story has seven windows and two large cats (panthers or leopards) cut into red and white spotted dolomite stone that gives the real life look of animal fur. One animal was placed at an angle with its head turned outward and mouth opened, indicating it served as the waterspout of a fountain.

During the 1979–81 excavation season a large water cistern, wine press and a wall seven feet thick, believed to be from the 6th century, were uncovered in an area near the modern mosque of the present day village. Other discoveries indicate that the site was occupied as late as the 12th century A.D.

Sports City

Hussein Sports City is a large complex on the road to the University. It is operated by the Al Hussein Youth and Sports Organization established in 1966.

The complex has a stadium, seating 25,000 spectators, which is used for soccer games, track and field meets, and various kinds of festivals. The oval-shaped building is circled by a sidewalk of hand-cut red stone; seats are made of white and rose stone. A covered pavilion along the west side shelters a special seating section which holds 2,500 people. A reserved section has a private entrance for King Hussein and his guests and a soundproof press room.

In addition to the main stadium, the complex contains two other soccer and track fields used for minor competition and training. There are three large swimming pools—a main pool for competition, a diving pool with five boards, and a smaller pool for training and for children. There is a spectator stand for 1,500 people. The poolside restaurant is one of Amman's most popular summer lunching spots.

The main tennis courts, which are used for international tournaments, have a seating section for 1,000 spectators. There are six practice courts and an adjoining section for badminton, six volleyball courts, and six basketball courts, Jordan's second favorite sport after soccer. A separate clubhouse has a gymnasium, four squash courts, recreation hall, cafeteria, conference room, and dormitory for visiting teams.

The complex is dominated by the Palace of Culture, a dramatic structure designed to resemble a Bedouin tent. Its auditorium can seat up to 2,500 and is used for dramatic, musical, and social entertainment. It is also suitable for conferences and conventions.

Other facilities of the building include a small auditorium for art exhibitions and other cultural presentations, dressing rooms, press and radio rooms, and a restaurant area. It is centrally heated, air conditioned, and soundproofed.

Hussein Sports City also has its own public gardens where approximately 30,000 trees of different varieties have been planted. The National Martyrs Memorial to the Unknown Soldier includes a small military museum, which contains mementos of the Hashemite family and Jordan's contemporary history. It is open to the public.

PRACTICAL INFORMATION FOR AMMAN

HOTELS. Like other Middle East capitals, a decade ago Amman found itself short of hotel rooms in the midst of a business and travel boom. The problem has disappeared with the opening of hotels in different categories and extensions of existing properties.

Hotel rates and categories are established by the Ministry of Tourism. The government has been examining all hotels with a view to reclassifying them, as many of them have been overrated by international standards. For this reason we do not include the old categories here but rather describe those properties that we have examined in person and can recommend. Prices for single and double are for the room only unless otherwise indicated.

Amman Plaza, Queen Noor St., P.O. Box 950629, tel. 665912. 303 rooms. Price: JD 33 single; JD 36 double. As the newest addition to Amman's roster, the Plaza lives up to its reputation as a luxury hotel, with each spacious guest room having a private bathroom, direct-dial phone, radio, color television with in-house video, and mini-bar. Facilities include 24-hour room service, laundry, and valet; large outdoor swimming pool and well-equpped health club; bars, nightclub, and disco.

Restaurants include the Andalusia, featuring international cuisine, and the Fujiyama, for Japanese specialities; also coffee shop, and streetside cafe. The shopping arcade has a car rental, business service center, barber shop, beauty salon, art gallery, and newsstand. Additionally, the hotel is conveniently situated next to the corporate headquarters of Royal Jordanian Airlines which is based in the Housing Bank Centre where trendy boutiques, jewelers, and a cinema are located.

Amman Marriott, Omar Ben Abu Rabiah St., Shmeisani, P.O. Box 926333; tel. 660100. 296 Rooms. Price: JD 28 single; 31 double.

The modern hotel has large, cheerfully decorated rooms, fitted with 1 double, 2 twin, or 2 double beds; junior suites; and business suites with 1 double bed, a desk, sofa, and chair. All have television with in-house movies, mini-bar, direct-dial phones, private bath, and air conditioning.

The hotel's moderately priced restaurant features a Middle Eastern buffet on Fridays and Sundays. There is a gourmet restaurant, bar and cocktail lounge, disco and nightclub with live entertainment. There is a ballroom, meeting rooms with audio-visual facilities, and a business service center.

The hotel's shopping arcade has a bank, pastry shop, gift and souvenir shops, hair salon, and travel agency. Sports facilities include indoor and outdoor swimming pools, 2 tennis courts, and health club, Jacuzzi, exercise gym with Universal equipment, sauna, and steambaths. The club has local membership for JD 300 for men and women. A 45-minute massage costs JD 5.

Holiday Inn, Al Hussein Ben Ali St., Shmeisani, P.O. Box 6399, tel. 663100. 218 Rooms. Price: JD 28 single; 32 double.

When it opened in 1980, it was the first deluxe hotel to be built in the Jordanian capital since the Inter-Continental opened 2 decades ago. The

Holiday Inn was a joint venture of the Nazzal family, well-known Jordanian innkeepers; Alia, and the Jordan government. It has recently been totally renovated.

The 10-story tower has rooms on 9 floors and a nightclub on the 10th. Each floor has 4 suites and 4 studios in addition to the standard room with 2 double beds. Each enjoys an unobstructed view of the city.

Facilities include restaurants; a 24-hour coffee shop adjacent to the main dining room; Churchill Restaurant and bar; a steakhouse; the Oasis, a lounge patisserie; a French restaurant, and a ballroom that can seat 400 for dinner. The Ambassador nightclub has a cabaret, dinner and dancing. There is a swimming pool with cabanas and a modern health club, plus tennis courts. The shopping arcade includes a curio shop, bank, newsstand, business office, hairdresser, and barber, telex center, and travel agency.

Jordan Inter-Continental, Zahran St., 3rd Circle, Jebel Amman, P.O. Box 35014; tel. 641361. 396 Rooms. Price: JD 27–32 single; 30–35 double.

Located across the street from the American Embassy on Jebel Amman with a commanding view of the city, the modern structure is mellowed by the warmth of its attractive interior design. Guest rooms are large, comfortable, and nicely furnished. Almost all are fitted with twin beds, and most have balconies; all have private bath, direct dial telephone, mini bars, air conditioning, and television with in-house movies. Same day laundry and cleaning service is available.

Facilities include a swimming pool, rooftop restaurant, coffee shop, beauty salon, barber shop, newsstand, airline and car rental, bank, travel agency offices, telex, taxi service, and several shops. Another nice feature: there's a laundry/dry cleaning shop that gives quick service. The bar off the main lobby is a favorite meeting place for businessmen from around the world. The hotel has meeting and banquet facilities, ballroom, and a disco.

There is also a health club with sauna, massage, solarium, gym with Universal equipment, and 2 tennis courts. A business service center provides secretarial and other services. There is a daily buffet luncheon in the coffee shop.

Adjacent to the rear of the hotel is an office and shopping center, known as the Plaza Tower. When the hotel was first built there was almost nothing else in the neighborhood; but the city has grown to such an extent that it is now centrally located.

Alia Gateway Hotel, one mile from Queen Alya International Airport, P.O. Box 39158, tel. 08–51000. 316 rooms. Price: JD 19 single; 24 double.

Alia's most recent project and an affiliate of Inter-Continental's Forum hotels, this tall, modern structure has a large, attractive lobby faced in white Italian marble and brightly lit with crystal chandeliers.

The lobby has a comfortable bar that has become a popular waiting place for transit or delayed passengers. The 24-hour coffee shop is built around an atrium and waterfall and there's an international gourmet restaurant.

Nearly all rooms are fitted with twin beds that can be converted to doubles; there are 10 executive suites. Rooms have bath, international direct-dial phone, TV with in-house movies in English and Arabic, and four-channel radio. Facilities include shops, hairdressers for men and women, Alia ticket office, Avis car rental, Royal Tours agency, outdoor pool and snack bar, 24-hour room service, same-day laundry and dry cleaning, clinic, and house doctor. Secretarial, telex, and other business services and babysitters can also be provided.

Shuttle service between the airport and hotel is available; a direct-line telephone to the hotel is being installed so passengers can request accommodation and transportation. Shuttles runs four times daily between the hotel and Abdali Station in town.

Regency Palace, Queen Alya St., Sports City Rd., P.O. Box 927000, tel. 660000. 300 rooms. Price: JD 28 single; 31 double.

This 22-story building was originally built as an addition to the Grand Palace, but was later made into a separate hotel. It has several restaurants, bars, panoramic rooftop, nightclub, shops, and meeting facilities. Most of the rooms are furnished with twin beds and have air conditioning, direct-dial phone, and television. There is a hair salon, newsstand, bank, and travel agency. The hotel has a health club with sauna, massage, sundeck, and a year-round swimming pool.

Ambassador, Shmeisani, P.O. Box 19014, tel. 665161. 97 rooms. Price: JD 12.500 single; 15.500 double.

Rooms in this modern, 7-story structure are a comfortable size and simply furnished, mostly with twin beds; all have private bathrooms. The hotel is used a great deal by groups. Nicest part of the hotel is its pleasant dining room and bar.

Amra Forum, Sixth Circle, Wadi al Seer, P.O. Box 292, tel. 815071. 300 rooms. Price: JD 21 single; 27 double.

This modern hotel, managed by Inter-Continental Hotels' medium-priced Forum chain, offers good value. It is situated in a suburb near the main road to the new airport. Guest rooms are large and comfortable, though a little drab in decor. All have air conditioning, mini-bar, private bath, direct-dial phone, radio, color television, and in-house movies.

Darotel, P.O. Box 9403, Shmeisani; tel. 668193. 24 rooms. Price: JD 13.200 single; JD 15.400 double. Near the Shmeisani business center, this small hotel is best suited for long-term guests. All rooms have private bath, phone, color television with in-house video, mini-bar, and kitchenette. There is a small restaurant, bar, and a basic health club.

The hotel has a coffee shop and a French restaurant. The lobby bar is one of the liveliest in the city. There is a disco, a swimming pool, and a shopping center.

Grand Palace, Queen Alya St., Sports City Rd., P.O. Box 6916, telex 1292, tel. 661127. 160 rooms. Price: JD 12 single; 15 double.

Most rooms are doubles; all have private bath and balcony. There are a restaurant, cocktail lounge, tearoom, lobby lounge, meeting rooms, shops, hairdresser, newsstand, airline desk, travel agency, and free parking.

Jerusalem International, University Rd., Shmeisani. P.O. Box 926265; tel.: 665121. 187 Rooms. JD 22 single; 29 double.

The hotel is popular with the foreign community and their guests. The decor is perhaps the most opulent in the city.

Hisham, Fourth Circle, Jebel Amman, P.O. Box 5398, tel. 642720. Price: JD 7.700 – 10.230 single; 9.900 – 13.130 double.

Located in a pleasant residential area, the hotel has 23 rooms on 3 floors, in a family atmosphere. Rooms are unusually large, and all are fitted with twin beds plus a couch which can be made into another bed for 2. Rooms have bath (6 with shower only), phone, mini-bar, TV with in-house video, 24-hour room service, heat/air conditioning. Facilities include a restaurant and outdoor terrace for dining and barbeques. It's unequivocally Amman's most popular small hotel. The hotel has its own bakery, which also does catering.

Manar, Shmeisani, P.O. Box 20730, tel. 662186, telex 1624. Price JD 7.260 single; 10.125 double, including breakfast and 10% service.

A fairly new hotel with 43 doubles and 20 singles plus a few suites, in two 4-story buildings connected by a central building where the public rooms are located. All rooms have private bath, phone, 24-hour room service, air conditioning, central heating and radio. Facilities include restaurant, bar, coffee shop, swimming pool, and an outside café. There is a convenient bus stop near the hotel. The hotel is owned by Suchkhian and Amad, who also have the Holy Land Hotel in Jerusalem.

Shepherds, Al Khattab Street, Jebel Amman, P.O. Box 2020, telex: 1410 Shepherd Jo; tel. 639197. Price: JD 7 single; 9 double.

A modest hotel with 44 rooms on 4 floors, conveniently located to downtown. All rooms have private bath (some with shower only), phone, and 24-hour room service. There is a bar/lounge, a dining room, and an outside terrace for drinks and snacks. National Car Rental's office is in the hotel.

Ammon, Fourth Circle, Jabal Amman, P.O. Box 950271, tel. 671133. 55 rooms. Price: JD 11 single; 14 double. Conveniently located near several government ministries and embassies, and within easy reach of business district, the hotel is operated by international professionals from the Hotel Training School in Europe. There is a swimming pool.

Hala, Jabal Amman near Khalidi Hospital, P.O. Box 182423, tel. 644906. 55 rooms. Price: JD 10 single; 13 double. Situated in a quiet neighborhood, near the 3rd Circle, the small hotel represents good value and convenience. Rooms are simply but adequately furnished and have mini-bar, television, direct dial, air conditioning, and private bath. Most have twin beds; 10 are singles. There is 24-hour room service, a rooftop nightclub, coffeeshop and bar.

San Rock, Om Otaina between Fifth and Sixth Circles, P.O. Box 9032, tel. 813800. 100 rooms. Price: JD 13.50 single; 17.50 double. All rooms are air conditioned and have television, direct-dial phone, and private bath. There are several restaurants, bars, disco, and shops; meeting and banquet facilities and business services can be provided.

Tyche, Shmeisani, P.O. Box 3190, tel. 661115. 184 rooms. Price: JD 13.200 single; 17.600 double with full breakfast. Rooms are fitted with double or twin beds and have mini-bar, television, and private bath. There are shops, hair salon, swimming pool travel agent, restaurant, coffee shop, bar, and disco. The hotel caters to groups.

The **American Center of Oriental Research (ACOR),** university area, tel. 846117. The center has 8 rooms for 16 people at its institute. JD 6, including three meals; JD 5 for students. Write to the director, Dr. David McCreey, P.O. Box 2470, Jebel Amman, Amman, Jordan.

ACOR's new headquarters, located on a hillside overlooking the University of Jordan, was built on land donated by the Jordan government and with a grant from the U.S. government for design and site preparation; the center's construction and furnishings were financed mainly by business and private contributions.

The new center, one of the most spacious and best-equipped research centers in the Middle East, accommodates 34 resident scholars, students, and visitors in dormitories, private rooms, and small apartments, along with access to work/study offices, several lounges, communal dining room, and terraces. The three-story building has a research library, workshops, laboratories, fully equipped darkroom, and lecture hall. A small archaeological museum is planned.

The Hotels and Resthouses Corporation, tel. 813243, operates resthouses at Azraq, Dibbeen, Kerak, and Petra with accommodations for JD 6.600 single, JD 10 double. The resthouses at Jerash, Madaba, Ma'an, Ramtha, and Ras en-Nagib offer meals and refreshments only.

PERSONAL SERVICES. Beauty Shops: Amman appears to have a beauty shop on every corner. These shops are up to European standards and their prices are reasonable. Appointments may be made by phone, but most shops take customers without appointments. A wash and set will range from JD 3; manicure, about JD 1.500. Most leading American and European products for home permanent, rinse, or tint are available locally.

George, Marriott Hotel (tel. 660100), is popular with fashionable Jordanian ladies and those of the foreign community—but he's expensive.

Hans, Jebel Amman, First Circle (tel.: 625279), is a long-established shop patronized by the Queen Mother and many of Amman's leading ladies.

Jordan Inter-Continental Beauty Salon is clean and quick. Wash and set costs JD 5 and up.

Munir, Fourth Circle, Jebel Amman (tel. 633913). Very friendly and capable. The salon recently expanded its quarters and now offers sculptured nails, massage, and facials. Call for appointment.

Raja, Jebel Webdeh, is another popular one, especially good at cutting hair, we are told. We've never tried him. JD 5 for wash and set; JD 4 for cut.

Barbers: Leading hotels have barbers or will call one on request. A haircut costs from JD 2 for short hair, and JD 3 for wash and cut or blow-dry.

Laundry and Dry Cleaning: Hotels have facilities for their clients. Most laundry and cleaning plants are small, hand-labor establishments. Laundry is good and speedy; dry cleaning is adequate. Cost for cleaning and pressing a man's suit is about JD 1.500.

Shoe Repair: Most residential areas have tiny repair shops. Ask your hotel concierge to take care of emergency repairs; language might be a problem with tradesmen of this sort.

Watch Repair: Leading makes of Japanese, American, and European watches are sold in Amman, and jewelers selling them will have repair service. Cost will be reasonable.

Pharmacies: There are always several pharmacies in every neighborhood, and they are well stocked with U.S. and European products. Pharmacies have a weekly rotating system so that at least one is open 24 hours. Its name and phone number is announced daily on the radio and in the local newspaper.

Baby Sitters: There is no organized service in Amman, but your hotel should be able to help you arrange for a sitter. Fee should be about JD 2 per hour.

ARCHEOLOGY. In 1962 two American women living in Jordan formed Friends of Archaeology, a society to promote study and visits to archeological and historical sites throughout the country, to enable members to participate in archeological excavations, and to assist the Department of Antiquities. Within a year the organization's membership had grown to 200 with eleven nationalities represented, and it has continued to attract members through the years. Membership is JD 5 single / JD 10 family, and JD 1 student, per year. Applications may be obtained from the American Center, ACOR, or the Department of Antiquities Registration Center. Regular lectures in English by prominent archeologists and visiting scholars are held for members and are open to the public. Throughout the year field trips, usually led by an archeologist, are arranged for members to places of archeological interest.

In addition, members have volunteered their services to the Department of Antiquities, participated in digs at locations throughout the country and assisted with the inventories of several museums. The Society has published a booklet on visits to archeological sites in the Amman area.

If you have an interest in amateur archeology you might find membership in this group enjoyable and stimulating. Nonmembers may go on one outing prior to joining. Visitors to Amman are welcome on day trips. You can contact the Society directly at P.O. Box 2940 or through the director of the American School for Oriental Research in Amman, P.O. Box 2440, tel. 846117, or through the Department of Antiquities, P.O. Box 88, Amman.

SPORTS. Sports Clubs: Amman has several clubs that offer a variety of sports and are open to international membership.

Arabian Horse Club, Bisharat Estate, New Airport Rd., tel. (09) 801233 is a new sporting club that owns and boards for other owners about 50 horses. It is operated by American-educated Michael Bisharat, an expert horseman who is hoping to develop an equestrian team for international competition. Riding instruction is offered for JD 2 for members; JD 5 for non-members. There is a clubhouse, which has a bar and restaurant and shop; a go-cart track, a tennis court; and plans to add more tennis courts and a swimming pool. Club membership is JD 36 single; JD 80 per family per year.

Al-Hussein Youth City (Sports City) is a large complex on the outskirts of Amman. It offers many sports facilities including tennis, squash, indoor and outdoor swimming, and a gymnasium. Membership is sometimes difficult to obtain and is restricted to families and single women; no single men.

The Orthodox Club is located about 3 miles outside the city. Sports activities include tennis, soccer, and swimming.

The Royal Jordanian Automobile Club, Eighth Circle, Jebel Amman, tel. 815261, is on the Wadi Seer Rd. near the American Community School. Considered Amman's best club with a restricted entrance to members and their guests, it has a wide range of facilities, including two swimming pools (plus one for children), 8 tennis courts, 3 squash courts, bowling alley, billiard parlor, and restaurant/bar.

Many hotels in the city such as the Jordan Inter-Continental, Amman Marriott and Holiday Inn, have membership clubs for use of their sporting facilities.

All these clubs have restaurant facilities that are available for use by tourists, provided proper arrangements are made. Ask your hotel for assistance.

Archery: The Amman Archery Club is a part of the Royal Jordanian Automobile Club. It has practice ranges, and a limited supply of equipment is available.

Backgammon: Off King Feisal Street in an alley leading past an open-air coffee house you will find a group of Jordanian men hunched over upturned crates or boxes. Resting on the makeshift tables will be colorful polished mosaic boards with various geometric designs. From time to time a player at each table will roll a pair of dice and shout out the numbers. The other player will usually be smashing a handful of small discs on the board. There is much clatter. As the men play, they puff on their *nargileh,* or water pipes, or sip from small cups of coffee. They rarely look up from their game; they are just as serious about it as any poker or bridge player.

The game they play has been the single most popular game in the Middle East for thousands of years. To the Westerner it is known as backgammon. Jordanians call it "tric trac." Other Arabs call it *nard* or *towleh.* The ancient Arabs called a variation of the game *tabula.* Medieval Englishmen called it "tables." Romans called another variation "twelve-lined game." Westerners call still another variation "parcheesi."

Archeological digs have turned up a table made for a game very much like tric trac over 5,000 years ago in the ancient city of Ur in southern Iraq. The Iranians claim their ancient king, Nardashir, ordered that a game be developed that would balance luck—the thrown dice—and skill—the knowledge of which discs to move or not to move after each throw.

Camel racing and falconry are popular pastimes in Jordan and throughout the Arab world, but nothing approaches the popularity of backgammon. It is played by men and women, young and old. It is played wherever a playing board can be set up—in homes, classrooms, restaurants, cafés, barber shops, police barracks, and military guard booths. Quick games are played on business desks or shop counters during the noon break.

To understand tric trac, think of it as it relates to the calendar. There are 30 discs, which stand for the days of the month. They are black and white, for night and day. Each playing board has four sections, which represent the seasons. There are 24 positions, representing the hours of the day and night. The 12 months of the year are found in each player's 12 positions. The object of the game is to see who can move his discs around the board—equal to completing the year—the fastest.

Bowling: The Bowling Club is situated at the Royal Racing Club near the airport. It has a 4-lane bowling alley. There are also two new clubs that offer bowling—*H and R* on Jebel Amman, Second Circle (opposite Corfu Restaurant), and the Abu Dahab Center, 41 Rainbow St. (next to the British Council), First Circle. The latter is part of a four-story entertainment complex encompassing roller skating, children's rides, and electronic games.

Camping: Jordan offers 5 totally different camping experiences: the desert in the Wadi Rum; the sea on the coast of Aqaba; the canyon at Petra; the mountains and hot springs at Zerka Ma'in; and the forest in Debbin National Park. Propane and kerosene stoves and lanterns for camping are available at reasonable prices in Amman, but other camping equipment is difficult to find. Camping trips of 2 or 3 days into the desert by camel caravan can be organized by travel agencies in Amman.

Chess: The Chess Club, Wadi Seer Rd., is open daily from 5 P.M. to late evening. Visitors are welcome.

Fishing: A wide variety of colorful and exotic fish is found in the Gulf of Aqaba, where fishing is a year-round sport. A glass-bottom boat and fishing equipment can be rented through the hotels in Aqaba. Freshwater fishing can be enjoyed at Wadi Zerka and Azraq. No Western-style tackle is available in Amman. A fishing license is required, and is available from the Royal Society for the Conservation of Wildlife, Fifth Circle, Jebel Amman.

Flying: The Royal Jordanian Air Academy at the Amman Airport offers instruction and the opportunity for flying.

Horseback Riding: The Arabian Horse Club, New Airport Rd., stables 50 horses that are available for riding and instruction. (See details under *Sports Clubs.*)

Horse Racing: Under the supervision of the Royal Racing Club, weekly horse races are held at Marka in Amman in spring and summer. Camel races are held intermittently at the same tracks. Yes, we said "camel races"; it's a-now-I've-seen-everything-experience. Riders bounce in their wooden saddles 8 feet above the ground while their camels run with outstretched necks, feet flat to the ground. In a short run a good camel runs half as fast as a speedy Arabian horse, but in a long run a camel can overtake him.

Hunting: Wild boar, quail, desert sand grouse, partridge, pigeon, dove, duck, snipe, and migratory birds are hunted in Jordan. The season begins in autumn and ends in spring. Jordan has hunting regulations, and you should inquire about these upon arrival. Shotgun shells may be purchased locally; guns are expensive. If you plan to bring firearms, inquire at the nearest Jordanian Embassy for the necessary papers. Good hunting requires excursions into fairly remote areas. These trips will require time and effort on your part. A hunting license is required, but first a gun license must be obtained. Full details are available from the Royal Society for the Conservation of Wildlife, Fifth Circle, Jebel Amman.

Scuba Diving and Snorkeling: Equipment and instruction are available in Aqaba. Spear-fishing is strictly prohibited. Aquamarina, a diving club, has its own boats and equipment and an 84-room hotel located directly on the beach. (See Aqaba Hotels, later in the book, for details.) The marina has about a dozen boats, and instruction is also available in sailing and water skiing. Information can be obtained by writing Aqua Marina, M.A.S.S., P.O. Box 6951, Amman. Tel. 84938; Aqaba, Tel. 3555. Alia has a dive package for $470 plus airfare that includes 10 dives with instructor/guide, equipment, six nights at the Aquamarine Hotel in Aqaba and one night at the Amra Forum in Amman, and hotel/airport transfers.

Swimming: In Amman swimming pools are available to guests at the Alia Gateway, Amman Plaza, Ammon, Amra Forum, Holiday Inn, Jerusalem International, Jordan Inter-Continental, Manar, Marriott, Middle East, Regency Palace, and Tyche hotels. Annual or seasonal memberships are available and the pools can be used by guests at other hotels on payment of a fee, ranging from about JD 2 to 4 per day. The Hussein Sports City, the Orthodox Club and the Royal Jordanian Automobile Club have pools for members only. In most cases single males are not accepted as members. Pools are open from the beginning of May until the end of September. Sports City has an indoor pool also.

The Dead Sea is less than an hour's drive from Amman. Swimming here is an experience you should not miss. The water contains so much salt you will float more than swim. The high salt content also makes it uncomfortable to stay in the water for more than a few minutes at a time.

The best area for swimming is the Gulf of Aqaba, 4 hours by car from Amman over a good highway, 30 minutes by plane. Air-conditioned hotel facilities are available, and the Al Cazar, Aqua Marina and Aqua Marina II Holiday Inns, and Miramar all have swimming pools. South of the town are crystal-clear seas washing miles of empty white-sand beaches.

Tennis: Courts are available for hotel guests and club members at the Marriott and the Jordan Inter-Continental. Hussein Sports City, Automobile Club, and Orthodox Club have tennis courts, but they are for members and their guests. There are also courts at the YWCA.

Water Skiing: At Aqaba, you may rent boats and skis. Cost: JD 2 per person for a quarter-hour, including boat.

GALLERIES. The *Jordan National Gallery,* Jebel Luweibdeh, tel. 630128, opened in 1982 and is one of the country's most ambitious undertakings. In its first two years, it held 24 exhibits of local and foreign artists and acquired a collection of contemporary art that represents a cross-section of the leading artists in Jordan and other Middle East countries. The gallery is under the patronage of the King but it has been Princess Wijdan, the king's sister-in-law, who has been the moving force behind the effort. Hours: 10 A.M. to 1:30 P.M.; 3:30 to 6 P.M. daily except Tuesday.

The number of artists in Jordan has grown considerably during the past decade. There are over 50 painters and sculptors, both men and women, concentrated in the Amman area. Most are members of the Jordanian Artists Association, which serves as a cooperative body through which the artists receive governmental support in their activities. The Ministry of Culture has an exhibition center where the works of Jordanian artists are displayed.

Several commercial galleries stock paintings and prints by local artists. One of the best is located in the Jordan Inter-Continental Hotel. The owner of the shop is very knowledgeable and can give you information on any of the artists whose work she shows. Prices range from JD 40 to JD 500. Two of the gallery's latest talents are Rima Farah, whose work lovingly reflects Arabia, and Kamal Boullata, who specializes in silk-screens, water colors, and seriographs. The gallery also has a nice collection of 18th- and 19th-century prints of Jordan and other Middle East locales. Another gallery, *Alia Art Gallery,* operated by Alia Airlines, is located in the Insurance Bldg., First Circle, Jebel Amman, tel. 639303. Open daily 10 A.M.–1:30 P.M.; 4–7 P.M.

Many exhibitions are held throughout the year in the various cultural centers, clubs, and institutions of Amman. All are open to the public.

Those interested in learning more about Jordan's art scene and perhaps meeting a few of the younger artists might pay a visit to the Royal Institute of Fine Arts, the government art school, on Jebel Amman, opposite the Holiday Inn.

CLUBS. Social and service clubs in Amman offer activities and programs for residents. Foreigners who expect to live here for a time will find them an easy way to make new friends.

The *American Women of Amman Club* is open to all American women and wives of Americans. Other nationals may join as associate members. (Currently, the club has 15 nationalities.) Membership fee is JD 7.50 for one year. It meets on the first Monday of every month at the Marriott Hotel; guests and visitors are welcome.

British Ladies of Amman, tel. 813–129, meets twice a month at the Amra Hotel—mornings of the first Wednesday and evenings of the second Wednesday. Trips are conducted to local places of interest, including welfare centers and factories.

The *Home and Garden Club* is made up of Jordanites and foreigners living in Amman. It meets monthly. Membership is JD 5 per year.

Lions Amman Club meets at 1:30 P.M. on the first and the third Wednesday of every month at the Tyche Hotel. *Lions Philadelphia Club* meets at 1:30 P.M. on the second and fourth Wednesday at the Amman Marriott Hotel. *Philadelphia Rotary Club* meets every Wednesday at the Holiday Inn, at 1:30 P.M. *Rotary Club* holds weekly luncheon meetings each Tuesday at the Jordan Inter-Continental Hotel, at 2 P.M.

YWCA, Third Circle, Jebel Amman, offers cooking, exercise, and tennis classes for a fee. It also has tennis courts available for both men and women members.

Haya Arts Center, Shmeisani, opposite Alia Art Gallery, tel. 665195, is an arts and recreational club for children ages 6 to 14; younger children can use the playgrounds. It has 2 "adventure" playgrounds, a private road system to teach safety with go-carts and bicycles, a library, an arts room, a kiln, and 2 theaters for puppet and magician shows. Membership is JD 12; non-members pay 10 fils per day.

SCHOOLS AND UNIVERSITIES. *American Community School* offers kindergarten through twelfth grade in a 2-semester school year, following the American system. It is accredited to the Middle States Organization. The school year begins in late August and ends in early June.

International Community School offers kindergarten through class nine and follows the British system. *International Baccalaurate School,* for children 6 to 18, also follows the British system. *Abdel Hamid Sharaf Schools,* named for the late prime minister and ambassador to the U.S., is run by the former head mistress of the American School and offers first through tenth grades.

There are several English/Arabic-language kindergartens in Amman run by professionally trained teachers. They accept children from 3 to 5 years.

There are many other schools, but instruction is in the Arabic language with English taught as a second language.

The *University of Jordan,* established in 1962 with 167 students, has grown to an annual enrollment of over 12,000 students in 7 faculties—Arts and Science, Economics and Commerce, Medicine and Nursing, Agriculture, Education, Engineering, Law and *Shari'a* (Moslem jurisprudence). The bachelor's degree is awarded in 29 fields of study and the master's degree in 15 fields of specialization. The faculty numbers about 300.

Women students make up about 38% of the enrollment. All courses in the humanities are taught in Arabic; those in science are taught in English.

The campus, located north of Amman on the road to Jerash, is spread over 300 acres and has 26 buildings. Further expansion is underway. It derives its income from four sources. Two percent of all customs duties collected by the government and fees from certain commercial transactions are earmarked for the University; these make up about 45% of its budget. A second source is an annual government grant, which makes up about 27% of total revenues. Academic fees and tuition account for 13%. The balance of approximately 15% is obtained from aids and contributions from local private industry and individuals, foreign governments, foundations, and international organizations.

The University is unusual in that it is a national institution created by the state but operated independently of any ministry of government.

The University of Yarmouk, created in 1976 in Irbid, is not connected with the University of Jordan. It opened on a 20-acre temporary campus with 4 buildings to house its School of Arts and Sciences and has grown to four faculties—Arts and Sciences, Medical Sciences, Engineering and Agriculture, and Veterinary Medicine—at its permanent site with buildings for classrooms, dormitories, a library, civic and cultural centers, a sports complex, and a medical school with a training hospital of 500 beds. The 2,500-acre campus is located on the Damascus road between Naimeh and Ramtha.

ENTERTAINMENT. Most of the social life in Amman takes place in private homes and at clubs, but there are some activities available to visitors. To learn what is going on in Amman during your visit, consult the *Jordan Times,* the country's daily English-language newspaper. It carries a column listing special events. Notices are sometimes posted at leading hotels and travel agencies.

Movie houses show American and English films as well as Arabic ones. Ask your hotel concierge to check the Arabic newspapers for showtime. Features change every week or so. Tickets are about JD 500.

Bars. Major hotel bars are quite popular with visitors and locals alike. Some offer a daily "happy hour," where patrons get two drinks for the price of one. *Al Yanbou,* the Marriott Hotel bar, is one of the liveliest, with a band from 9 P.M. to 1:30 A.M. The pubs in the Hisham Hotel and Shepherd Hotel are other local favorites.

Discos. Amman's leading discotheque is *El Pasha* in the Jordan Inter-Continental Hotel, but it is expensive. The Amra Hotel disco is a mecca for those wanting to dance to the latest recorded international hits.

H and R Club, off Second Circle, has a disco combined with bowling and a bar and is the current hot nightspot for Amman's trendy set.

Nightclubs. Large hotel nightclubs, such as those in the Amman Plaza, Commodore, Jerusalem International, and Regency Palace, often feature an oriental show.

Cultural Activities. The cultural life of Jordan took on new dimensions when the *Royal Cultural Center* (tel. 661026) opened in 1982. Designed by a British architectural firm that specializes in theater design, the handsome modern center is a multi-purpose building meant to serve the performing as well as the visual arts. It is equipped with exhibition space and meeting facilities. Over the years, the center featured international music stars, theater, ballet groups, and art and sculpture exhibits. It has also been the site of a variety of conferences. Check the local papers or ask your hotel concierge for information on what is being offered during your visit.

The Amman Amateur Theater draws its talent from British and American residents as well as Jordanians, and gives amateur performances throughout the year. The British Council also holds regular lectures and art exhibits, and has library facilities and educational and documentary films. There is a small membership fee.

The French Cultural Center, American Center, Goethe Institute, and Soviet Cultural Center sponsor programs of music and films, art shows, and lectures. Most offer language classes and have libraries open to the public. American and British performers appear occasionally, under the sponsorship of the U.S. Information Service and the British Council.

SHOPPING. The handicrafts of Jordan are interesting, varied, and tempting. You can spend many hours wandering around the *souk,* or bazaar, stopping at shops along the way. Over a cup of coffee you will admire the wares, chat with the shopkeepers, and be persuaded to buy through the innate skill of the merchants, for whom trade has been a tradition for centuries.

One small lane of souk frequented by residents is particularly worth seeking out. It has several shops, such as *Ali Baba and Aladin Bazaar,* that specialize in crafts and—if you're lucky—old bedouin and Yemeni silver jewelry along with antique copper and brassware. Bargain! The lane has no name, but it is behind the Housing Bank, off Saef el Sail Street, beside the fruit market. *Afghani* on Hashemi Street, near the Amphitheater and opposite the Zerka Taxi Terminal, also has an excellent reputation for crafts and antiques. It has branches on Jebel Hussein and Jebel Webdeh.

Modern shops are full of American and European products. If your favorite brand of a particular item is not available, you should be able to find a reasonable substitute. *Al Waha, the Jordan Department Store,* Sixth Circle, resembles a small British department store, selling a variety of personal and household goods under one roof. The ground floor is a super market with escalators to the second floor; there is a pleasant coffeeshop too. There are boutiques and specialty shops in the downtown shopping area and in neighborhoods through the city. In the *souk,* merchants selling similar wares are usually grouped together, as in the Gold Souk.

Fixed prices are becoming widespread, although merchants are still ready to bargain, especially in the Gold Souk and in souvenir shops. Then, too, if you buy a large quantity from any one shop you can expect to get a discount.

For shopping in town it is best to take a taxi or service to the center; parking is not permitted on the main streets of the downtown area.

Store hours: Generally 9 A.M. to 1 or 1:30 P.M. and 3 or 3:30 to 6:30 or 7 P.M. Many shops close on Fridays; others on Sundays. During Ramadan hours are 9 A.M. to 1 P.M. and 4:30 to 8 or 8:30 P.M.

Handicrafts

The cross-culture of the Jordanians is visibly reflected in their handicrafts. Greek and Roman designs evolve into Byzantine and Crusader motifs and mingle with the arabesque. The products are readily available, but the history behind their creation and development is not always so discernible.

Silver Jewelry: Christian and Bedouin symbols prevail in this craft. The most characteristic is the Crusader's cross—5 crosses grouped as one, symbolizing the 5 nations of the crusading armies. The Crusaders' cross is made in many sizes and often set with semiprecious stones. There is also the Jerusalem Cross, the St. James Cross, the Cappadocian, and the Star of Bethlehem. They range in price from JD 1.500 to 5.000. These crosses are also made as brooches, necklaces, earrings, bracelets, and cuff links.

Jewelry still worn by Bedouin women—bracelets, earrings, necklaces, and forehead ornaments—might include the Hand of Fatima (daughter of the Prophet Muhammad), worn as a good-luck charm. The hand is also symbolic to Christians (the hand of Mary) and to Jews (the hand of Esther). Actually, it is a pagan charm predating all three religions; it was used in Jericho in the pre-Hebraic period.

Often silver pieces are inset with blue stones to ward off the evil eye. Others are designed in traditional geometric and arabesque patterns.

The percentage of silver is stamped on most solid silver articles. It is approximately 90% sterling. However, Bedouin silver jewelry is an exception. It is rarely stamped and varies considerably in silver content.

Carved Olivewood: The olivewood industry is comparatively new, but the products reflect centuries of tradition. Bethlehem is known for its skilled craftsmen who make rosaries, album and Bible covers, native-dressed figurines, bases, boxes, crucifixes, creches, and the *masbaha,* which is a string of 33 or 99 beads, often carried by Moslem men. Each bead represents an attribute of Allah. Foreigners have dubbed them "worry beads." A small *masbaha* or a rosary of olivewood with a small glass bubble containing Jordan River water, certified by the Terra Santa, costs JD 1 and up.

A popular gift for children is the caravan of 3 camels led by a donkey. The price is determined by size and carving, and ranges from JD 2 to 10. Another popular item is a spoon-and-fork salad set, which costs JD 1 to 3. There is an olive-wood carving factory located on the road to Madaba which welcomes visitors.

Mother-of-Pearl: Inlaid mother-of-pearl is a specialty of Bethlehem, where many establishments are engaged in the industry. The shell is imported from abroad, as it might have been in olden days. The mother-of-pearl is worked into intricate designs on crucifixes, picture frames, jewelry boxes, and covers for Bibles, prayer books, and the Koran. The skill of the craftsman, rather than the material, determines the price. Mother-of-pearl rosaries cost JD 1.500–5; crosses from 300 fils to JD 3; jewelry boxes from JD 4 to 35 or more, depending on size and quality of work.

Cross-stitch Embroidery: This craft represents delicate skill and many traditions. Most patterns and colors are copied from those on dresses of peasant women, whose home village or tribe may be identified by their dress. Both the handmade materials and the embroidery have undergone several stages of development and are excellent examples of the women's skills. In the past, the towns best known for their handwork were Ramallah, Bethlehem, and Jerusalem. Nowadays a great deal of it is being done by refugees, especially widows, as a livelihood.

In the cross-stitch design 3 main origins are distinguishable. The Byzantine is geometric in form; the Persian uses plants, leaves, flowers, and fruit, copied from rugs; and the third depicts the daily life of the country in the form of animals, birds, and human figures.

The embroidery has 2 basic styles. One is the cross-stitch on silk, linen, or handwoven cotton, using different colored threads, with red and black predominant. The second type is couching, where gold or silver threads are placed in a pattern on velvet, wool, or silky textiles and oversewn. This is a specialty of Bethlehem and typical of the designs found on Crusaders' jackets. The placing and size of designs are left to the imagination of the creator, but the designs themselves are traditional and stylized and bear names revealing their origin, such as the Star of Bethlehem, the Greek Key, the palm tree, the kohl bottle, and many others.

Several private groups, such as the Arab Development Society and the Family Cooperative of Ramallah, have adapted cross-stitch embroidery to useful products. Table linens, dolls, aprons, guest towels, belts, bookmarks, children's dresses, neckties, baby bibs, handbags, and handkerchiefs are reasonably priced and make lovely gifts to take home. There is an Arab Development Society shop whose sign reads Boys Town at the Jordan Inter-Continental Hotel and the hotel's art gallery has representative samples, but one of the best selections are available at Al-Aydi (the Jordan Craft Center), Second Circle, Jebel Amman. Most souvenir and handicraft shops in Amman and elsewhere have at least a small selection. Local residents often purchase items from Mariam Mahamy, who displays goods in her home (between sixth and seventh Circles). Call her residence, tel. 811–371, for directions.

Another popular item is a short coat or cape known as a Crusader's jacket, made of velvet and corded silk, usually in black, white, wine, or blue and embroidered with gold or silver thread. The old ones are difficult to find and are now collector's items; the new ones are machine-made. Kaftans can be found machine stitched from JD 4 to 12. The handmade ones cost as little as JD 12 or as much as JD 100, depending upon the amount and quality of the workmanship.

Palestine Pottery: The art of ceramics is one of the oldest crafts in the Middle East, although Jerusalem's pottery factory was for many years the only one to keep it alive. Now there are many in Hebron as well, and the products are readily available in gift and souvenir shops. The original factory, known as Palestine Pottery, was started in 1919 by 2 potters who were among those brought from Turkey to restore the 16th-century tiles in the Dome of the Rock in Jerusalem.

The tiles and pottery are painted with designs that follow the traditional Islamic art of geometric patterns, decorative Arabic script, and representations of nature. Other pieces show designs of Christian significance, such as the cross, the fish, and scenes from the life of Christ. Another popular motif is a reproduction of the ancient mosaics found in the area. The most notable of these is a mosaic called the Tree of Life, found in the Hisham Palace in Jericho. Copies of ancient tiles in the great mosques of Iran and Turkey and the Dome of the Rock are also available. Prices are reasonable. Tiles, plates, small vases, beer mugs, wall plaques, hors d'oeuvre dishes are priced from JD 1.500 and up. A coffee set with pot, tray, and 6 cups is about JD 8.

Hebron Glass: There are many places now producing glass in Hebron, but for years it was the tradition of one family, handed down for many generations. Ancient techniques are used to produce jugs, bowls, plates, vases, glasses, and mugs that are charming for their primitive qualities—and very fragile. Chunky beads with symbols to ward off the evil eye are made into inexpensive necklaces and bracelets. The most popular color for the glass is deep blue, but it is also made in green, purple, amber, and white. One of the most attractive items is a ceiling lamp made of different pieces of colored glass and costing about JD 12. Four members of the Hebron family have settled in Naur, 20 minutes from Amman, where they have set up a glass factory and showroom. The shop is open daily. On Fridays visitors can watch the glassblowers working at their ovens.

Bedouin Rugs: Brightly colored rugs in traditional tribal designs are handwoven by the Bedouin today as they were in Biblical times and are easily distinguished by their designs. A 9 x 4 rug costs from JD 14 and up. The best are made in Shobak, Kerak, and Tafileh. The Kerak rugs are predominately red and combine design and horizontal strips. Madaba rugs have a geometric pattern and cost about JD 45 for one or one and a half meter. These are not available in the market; they must be bought directly from the weaver.

The genuine Bedouin rugs are half a meter in width, grey and black in color, and have strips that run lengthwise. They cost about JD 40.

To determine that a rug is a "genuine Bedouin," be sure the tassels are a continuation of the rug threads and not sewn on separately. If hemp and cotton are used and the colors are not fast, the rug is a fake.

Aqaba Sand: Decorative patterns in different colors of sand in a bottle are popular souvenirs. Prices are 500 fils to JD 3.

Coral: The bottom of the Gulf of Aqaba is one of the world's most beautiful underwater gardens; coral was fished here until laws were passed to prohibit it. There is still coral in the marketplace but it's expensive. A real coral *masbaha,* or necklace, costs JD 80 and up, but be very careful with fakes. A substance that looks like black coral, and known as *usor* in Arabic, is made into inexpensive jewelry.

Candles: On Christian Street in the Old City of Jerusalem near the Church of the Holy Sepulchre are many candlemakers' shops. There are numerous types, but one in particular is unique to the Holy Land. It is shaped like flat, elongated bells, with a gold tracery design on one side and religious symbols on the other. It is decorative for any season and especially attractive at Christmas. Originally this candle was called *Al Kaff,* which means "the palm." Traditionally a bride held one of these candles in each hand and danced before the bridegroom on the evening of the wedding day.

Huge encrusted candles and bunches of votive tapers are also on sale. You may have candles (and rosaries) blessed in the Church of the Holy Sepulchre.

Fleece-lined Jackets and Slippers: Nothing could be warmer, and the slippers are wonderful for house or after-ski wear. Several shops in Amman specialize in sheepskin jackets. Prices start at JD 15.

Gold: Amman is one of the best places in the world to buy gold, because it is sold by weight, and the price is based on the world-market rate. The price of an item will be the cost of the gold plus the workmanship. If you are planning to buy a valuable gold product you should know the current market rate of gold. You are then in a position to bargain for the finished product and to know if you are getting a fair price. The market in gold is closely supervised by the government, and all items must be marked for their gold content.

Some of the work is done in Jordan by hand. Shops sell rings, bracelets, chains, necklaces, earrings, pins, broaches, pendants, picture frames, charms, watches, clocks, and many other small items.

About 50 shops make up the main gold market, Souk Ad-Dahhab, in the heart of downtown between King Feisal and Shab Sough streets and several tiny lanes in between.

Some shops not in the souk are jewelry shops in the Western sense. They are exclusive, elegant, and high priced, selling only high-quality jewelry, much of it imported. *Jabasini* is located directly on the Second Circle, Jebel Amman, tel. 622228. *Kuzbar,* Fifth Circle, has beautiful and expensive imported jewelry including antique Turkish pieces set with white diamonds. In Shmeisani, jewelry shops include *Bashoura* (in the Jordan Islamic Bank Building) for original designs of precious stones; *Walid Jabasini* in the Housing Bank Centre (next to Amman Plaza Hotel); and *Toros H. Tokajian & Sons* for imported gold chains, rings, and necklaces set with colored zircons.

Al-Aydi, the Jordan Craft Center, in a villa one block from the Second Circle, Jebel Amman. (A sign of a large hand points the way.) Here, you can find some of the best silver, copper, and brass jewelry plus household items, hand-embroidered linens, pillow covers, dresses, and kaftans in traditional designs. There are also handloomed carpets, glass, ceramics, and leatherwork, greeting cards and stationery, and gifts. Some are old, some new but with traditional forms and designs, and some are modern adaptions.

In 1972, a group of women concerned about the dying state of the nation's traditional crafts, opened a craft center where they could display, sell, and draw attention to the works of talented crafts people.

A design by one of the workers—a silver filigree hand with a turqoise eye—(the ancient amulet to ward off the evil eye) won an international prize. This encouraged the women to turn their goodwill, voluntary effort into a commercial enterprise to help the workers make a real living at their craft. The hand also became the group's logo.

With backing from the Jordan Industrial Development Bank and 16 private companies, the women established the Jordan Craft Development Center Company, employed 35 artisans, moved to their present location, and changed the name to Al Aydi, the hands.

From the outset, the women sought true folklore items and avoided cheap imitiations made strictly for the tourist trade. At intervals throughout the year, weavers and other craftsmen demonstrate their work. Manager Abla Kawar is usually on hand to explain the crafts to those who are interested.

Prices at Al-Ayli may seem higher than those in souvenir shops, but when you compare the workmanship you can see the difference. Some of the cross-stitch pillow covers, which range in price from JD 20 to 150 depending on the size and intricacy of the design, are of the quality of fine Persian rugs.

Rabbath Ammon Oriental Bazaar on Jebel Hussein, located on Khaled Ibn Al Waleed Street, specializes in Crusader jackets and caps, scarfs,

blouses, native costumes, gold and silver items, rugs, greeting cards, and
picture slides. Tel.: 663636.

Antiquities: According to the Director of Antiquities, it is prohibited
to sell or buy antiquities older than 18th century and to export them from
the country. Items from the 18th and 19th centuries are available for purchase.

House of Old Arts, Jebel Webdeh, P.O. Box 5050, tel. 621379. For those
who are truly interested in buying old jewelry and objets d'art, they can
do no better than visit this small, unprepossessing shop. You will have
to find it first and that could be a real test of your perseverance! Phone
the store in advance for directions.

Owner Lutfi George Sayegh, who is in his 80's, has been a collector all
his life and has a detailed knowledge of Arab and Middle Eastern art. On
a recent visit, we saw old jewelry of museum quality, which is becoming
increasingly difficult to find. Prices run JD 100 and up. A selection of old
wood framed mirrors and chests with inlaid pearl cost from JD 350 to
700, depending on their size and condition.

If you are contemplating an investment in valuable old jewelry or costumes, a visit to the Folklore Museum adjacent to the Roman amphitheater will help you better evaluate and appreciate Mr. Sayegh's collection.

Miscellaneous

Art Supplies: Basic art supplies can be purchased at the *Art Supply Center,* Second Circle, Jebel Amman. It is operated by Samia Zaru, who is
one of Jordan's well-known artists. You may not always find it open. Tel.
642741.

Bookshops: There are many small stores throughout the city. Stocks
appeared to be limited to popular, fast-selling books. For books on Jordan
and the Middle East try Amman Bookshop, Third Circle, Jebel Amman;
Istaklal in Shmeisani; and the newsstand of the Jordan Inter-Continental.

Clothing: Selections of ready-to-wear clothing is improving all the time
as many new stores open with the latest high-fashion styles. Some of the
best, especially the smart boutiques, are situated on or near the Third and
Fifth Circles on Jebel Amman, near the Khalaf Circle on Jebel Webdeh
and the business centers of Shmeisani. Less expensive clothes are found
in stores on King Feisal Street and other nearby streets in the downtown
area.

Cosmetics and Toiletries: Most well-known brands of European and
American cosmetics and toiletries are available at pharmacies and specialty stores throughout the city. Such shops are often in or near hotels, so
if you forgot to pack something, you should have no difficulty finding it
or an adequate substitute in Amman.

Florists: Flowers can no longer be imported to Jordan, so cut-flower
selection is limited. However, potted flowering plants flourish. There are
neighborhood shops, and your hotel can direct you to one nearby. It is
appropriate to thank a host and hostess for a lunch or dinner invitation
with flowers, a plant, or box of candy.

Food Products: A wide variety of fresh vegetables is available most of
the year, but quality and price will depend on the season. Grocery stores
carry imported canned goods, but prices will be double to triple the U.S.
cost. Local fruit, especially citrus fruit, is excellent.

Local fresh and imported frozen meat and poultry are available on the local market. The lamb and mutton are of better quality than the beef, but are also more expensive.

Liquor is readily available. Grocery stores sell wine, liquor and beer. Cost of liquor in a store begins at JD 4.750 for Scotch.

Export of Local Items: Ask the store where you buy your gifts and souvenirs to ship your purchase to the U.S. or Europe. Generally, oriental stores in Jordan have a reputation for reliability in mailing or shipping parcels.

DINING OUT. The newness of Amman's big-city sophistication can be seen in the limited number of good restaurants. Some of the best ones are at hotels; others are in newly developing residential areas. Then, too, Jordanians prefer to entertain at home. Inviting someone to dine in one's home is the most basic expression of Arab hospitality.

Jordanians do not take lunch until 1 or 2 P.M. Restaurants begin serving lunch after 12 and will serve as late as 3 or 3:30 P.M. In the evening, dinner is served after 8 P.M., and by 10:30 P.M. most of the guests will have finished their meal and begun to leave.

Recently restaurants, like hotels, were classifed with 1- to 5-star ratings. A typical meal for 2 at a 5-star restaurant should cost JD 15–25 and at a 3-star JD 8–12, plus 10% service charge.

Prices in 5- and some 4-star hotel restaurants seem high compared to others; hotel managers say this offsets the relatively low price of hotel rooms in these categories. Friday and Sunday buffets at 5-star hotels range from JD 6.000–7.500.

There are a few restaurants that serve good European dishes and even more that offer American snacks, but the best food is in restaurants that serve Jordanian specialties. Happily, Jordanians are better cooks than they are interior decorators. If you were to judge a restaurant by its decor, you might possibly stop cold at the door. There's a five-and-dime tackiness about even the best ones, although attempts are being made by newer ones to improve decor and ambience. Restaurants are listed here by their locations.

City Center

Jabri, King Hussein St., tel. 624108, and **Jordan Restaurant,** Post Office Square, tel. 638333, are run by the same family. Both offer Jordanian specialties at medium prices. The latter has mounds of *baklawi* and other sweets.

Jerusalem Restaurant (known by its Arabic name, *Al Quds*) is similar to the 2 named above. It is located on King Hussein St., tel. 630168. Moderate.

First Circle, Jebel Amman

Amigo Nabeel, tel. 622617. Both Jordanians and visitors favor this cozy restaurant (somewhat Austrian in atmosphere) that offers exceptionally good value. Continental fare, with excellent lasagna. Granada Hotel.

Diplomat, facing the Circle, tel. 625592. Restaurant and sidewalk café with a large menu of sandwiches, snacks, steaks, and desserts. Prices are moderate, food mediocre.

Restaurant China, tel. 648968. Amman's first Chinese restaurant still retains its reputation for consistently good Oriental food. Housed in a large villa, convenient to city. Very moderate prices.

Second Circle, Jebel Amman

Corfu, one block west of Circle, tel 641585. An attractive indoor/outdoor taverna of rustic decor and moderate price. Traditional Greek dishes, as well as some standard Jordanian and European fare, accompanied by Greek music.

La Creperie, Shepard Hotel, tel. 639197. Super crepes, either as a main course or for desert. A favorite with Amman youngsters. Moderate.

Rheem's, on the Circle. The sign is in Arabic only; look for a large Pepsi sign, just north of Jordan Inter-Continental Hotel and across from University Pharmacy). The best shawarma in Amman. Inexpensive.

Swiss Chalet, Shepard Hotel, tel. 639–197. In a traditional Swiss setting, you will find beef fondue and other Swiss specialities. Open for dinner only. Moderate.

Western-style fast food outlets—**Burger King, McBurger, Omar Snack** and **Queen Burger**—are clustered west of the Circle, perhaps because of the proximity of the American Embassy.

Third Circle, Jebel Amman

Jordan Inter-Continental, tel. 641361. The hotel's rooftop dining room is popular for dinner. Spectacular views. The coffee shop is on the main floor. Both are expensive.

Kashmir, near Holiday Inn, tel. 659520. This highly praised and relatively new Indian restaurant is considered the best in town.

Maatouk, facing Circle, tel. 841337. Menu in Arabic only, but waiters and owners speak English. At the entrance there is a rotisserie for *shawarma,* roast lamb cut in slivers and served in loaves of Arabic or pita bread with onions, mint, and sumak. Just inside the door are piles of sweets and meat- or cheese-filled pastries from which to choose. It's a carry-out place as well as a restaurant.

New Orient Restaurant (also known as **Abu Ahmad**), on a side street one block below the Circle, tel. 841879. The restaurant is in a house with a large outdoor garden. Every year the restaurant is enlarged and improved to accommodate its steadily growing clientele. Now the garden is enclosed by a wall of trees and the earthen floor has been tiled. Unfortunately the service is no faster, but customers leisurely enjoy Jordanian dishes that are not found elsewhere, such as *musakhan,* chicken smothered in onions and sumak. Prices are moderate.

Romero, on a side street across the street from the Jordan Inter-Continental Hotel, tel. 644227. European cuisine; popular with the foreign community. The restaurant makes its own pasta and offers specials created by the owner. Lovely outdoor garden. *Moderate.*

Tower Restaurant, Tower Building, Prince Mohamed Street (directly behind Jordan Inter-Continental Hotel), tel. 634034. Housed on the 23rd floor of a office/shopping complex, the Tower is best for cocktails or coffee while taking in the 360° view of Amman. Open daily.

Uncle Sam's, next to Jordan Inter-Continental Hotel. Reasonably priced American-style breakfasts plus basic fare ranging from cheeseburgers and hotdogs to steak and chicken. Moderate.

Turkish Restaurant, Sixth Circle, tel. 816880. Good Turkish favorites at moderate prices.

University Road Area

El Bustan (The Garden), near the offices of the *Jordan Times,* tel. 661555. Good for mezzah and other Middle Eastern specialities. This restaurant is especially popular in summer, when it moves to its outdoor garden.

Shmeisani

New restaurants are constantly opening in Shmeisani, one of the city's most fashionable business and residential districts, and the area now has some of the most distinguished dining in Amman. Yet in keeping with its cosmopolitan character, many fast-food restaurants have also opened. These include **New York, New York, Tom and Jerry, Kentucky Fried Chicken,** and **Pizza Hut.**

Amman Plaza, Queen Noor Street, tel. 665912. The hotel's three restaurants include *Fujiyama,* the city's only Japanese restaurant, with authentic cuisine in nice surroundings; *Andalusia* for international fare; and a brightly lit coffee shop, open daily from 7 A.M. to midnight.

La Terrasse, on the second floor of an apartment building, tel. 662831. The menu is French; the food is ample but undistinguished. There is a pleasant outdoor terrace. The restaurant is hard to find on one's own, so take a taxi.

Leonardo da Vinci, tel. 662441. A favorite with Amman residents; good Italian and Continental specialities in gracious ambience. Live music most evenings.

Marriott Hotel, tel. 660100. The hotel's restaurant's include *Al Walima,* which serv Continental and Middle Eastern cuisine in an elegant surrounding for dinner only (expensive); and the coffee shop, open daily 6:30 A.M. to midnight, which offers a wide variety of food, including Mexican specialties.

Peking, tel. 681205, This is the city's newest Chinese restaurant. Elegant interior with marvelous dishes ranging from spicy Szechuan to chop suey.

Jebel Webdeh

Two places favored by Amman residents are **Elite,** Jebel Webdeh, tel.: 622130, and **Le Cesar,** Jebel Webdeh, tel. 624421. Both offer European selections.

Mecca Road Area

Alfredo, tel. 821705. Very popular with local people. Fine homemade pasta plus other Italian specialities.

Chen's, tel. 818214. A spacious family-style Chinese restaurant with a large classic menu the generous portions. Reasonably priced.

Steakhouse, Jaber Centre, tel. 826666. Recommended for a variety of fine U.S.-imported beef. Closed Mondays.

Wadi Es Seer

L'Olivier, Jebel Abdoun, in a new fashionable area near the Orthodox Club, was once the city's most chic restaurant but has not held its popularity, although it is still expensive.

Royal Automobile Club, Wadi es Seer Road, tel. 815261, and **Orthodox Club,** Jebel Abdoun, tel. 810491, are private clubs; however, they accept individual nonmembers for dinner. Ask your hotel to make the arrangements.

Beyond Amman

One of Jordan's best restaurants, **The Lebanese Restaurant,** also known as *Im Khalili,* is situated on the south side of Jerash and worth the 30-minute drive. Another is **Ya Hella,** in Jerash. Both specialize in Lebanese dishes.

Arabian Horse Club, Airport Highway. Pub of the riding club is popular with families.

National Amman Park. Brand new restaurant with very good Middle Eastern cuisine, that opened to the accolades of local residents. It has a park setting that is especially pleasant at night.

Pine Palace, Queen Alia International Airport Highway, tel. 714809. On a hill in a garden setting of pine trees, this relatively new restaurant has a nice view and fine Jordanian cuisine. Popular venue for weekend luncheon outings.

NEWSPAPERS. In addition to the English-language daily *Jordan Times,* the *International Herald-Tribune* and British newspapers are available, usually a day late. Bookshops stock American and European periodicals and major Middle East ones.

NORTH OF AMMAN

Jerash: 29 miles

A 45-minute drive over an excellent new highway through the lovely hills of Gilead takes one to Jerash, the best and most complete ruins of a provincial Roman city in the world. Jerash was buried under sand and rubble for centuries, until 1806, when the German traveler Seetzen discovered the site. Excavations were begun in 1925.

Five miles before reaching the site, the road crosses the Zerqa River, the Jabbok of the Bible. On the northwest you will see a lovely wooded area—this is one of the greenest parts of the country.

Most authorities agree that Jerash (Gerasa) was founded by the soldiers of Alexander the Great about 332 B.C., although the site was occupied from Neolithic times. After the Roman conquest in 63 B.C., the city joined the Decapolis and established trade with the Nabataeans of Petra. Jesus may have passed through Jerash on a trip to Jerusalem, following the eastern highlands route through the Decapolis.

In A.D. 90, Jerash was absorbed into the Roman Province of Arabia. In the following two centuries the city reached the height of its prosperity. Afterward, the rise of Palmyra and a shift in trade routes caused its steady decline.

By the Byzantine period—from which most of its church ruins date—Jerash had deteriorated. The invasions of the Persians and later the Arabs in the seventh century added further to its decline. Finally, in the twelfth century, when the Crusaders attempted to take the city, it was practically demolished and later abandoned.

In 1878 under the Turks the east bank of the stream that flows through Jerash was settled by Circassians. Today the little town is a modern counterpoint to the ruins of the ancient city.

As one approaches Jerash from the south, one's first sight is the triple-arched gateway built in A.D. 129 to celebrate Emperor Hadrian's visit to the city. On the west a road leads to Ajlun. Beyond the arch is the ancient Hippodrome.

A quick tour of the main ruins of Jerash takes a half-day. Those who are especially interested in Roman and Byzantine ruins should allow a full day. A government resthouse, operated by the Jordan Hotels and Resthouses Corporation, is located at the entrance to the ruins, on a rise of ground that offers a good overview of the site. Refreshments and toilet facilities are available at the resthouse. There is an illuminated map and a plan of the town broken down into numbered walks for exploring a particular section. A member of the Jordan Tourist Police is on duty.

The present entrance to ancient Jerash is on the east side of the site. There is a guide in residence, but if you can carry along Harding's *The Antiquities of Jordan* you will find it is better than a guide.

On the south side of the site is the enormous oval-shaped Forum, encircled by 56 columns with Ionic capitals standing in their original position. Many have been restored. The forum, which was used as a market and assembly place, is in a remarkable state of preservation. It is the only oval-shaped Roman forum ever uncovered.

On the hill above the Forum is the Temple of Zeus, built in the 1st century A.D. on the site of an earlier sanctuary. Next to it is the large theater, where extensive restoration has been done. It originally contained 32 tiers of seats and accommodated 5,000 spectators. Today the theater is used for plays and festivals.

From the highest level of this area there is a spectacular view, with ancient Jerash in the foreground and the modern town in the distance. It is also a good vantage point from which to take pictures of the forum.

Beyond the forum leading to the North Gate is the Street of Columns, the main thoroughfare of Jerash. Many of the columns were found in their original position; others have been restored. Their capitals are Corinthian. An aqueduct ran across the top of the columns, carrying fresh water to all parts of the city. Crossing the main street at right angles are two other streets, running east-west. At each crossroads was a tetrapylon, consisting of four piers, each supporting four columns, and probably surmounted by a statue.

On the west side of the Street of Columns about 180 yards beyond the South Tetrapylon is the Nymphaeum, a semicircular structure that was both a fountain and a temple of the nymphs. Its walls are elaborately carved. From the large urns held by the statues, water once cascaded over the face of the temple into a pool. The façade of the pool was decorated with lion's heads; the water passed through the lion's mouths into drains along the street below.

Immediately after the Nymphaeum, on the same side of the street, stands the Temple of Artemis. The temple, built in the 2nd century A.D. for the patron goddess of Jerash, is the most imposing building on the site. From the massive Propylaeum a flight of stairs leads to a platform (now restored). Beyond, a second flight of stairs (also restored) running the width of the courtyard leads to the outer porch of the temple. This porch consists of the outer wall of the courtyard with a row of columns in front. Five doors lead from the outer porch into the courtyard, a rectangular enclosure lined with columns on all sides. The columns and the outer walls formed a kind of portico, lined with rooms or recesses.

In the middle of the courtyard stands the temple proper, originally approached by a flight of stairs. The *cella,* or holy part of the temple, was built on a platform and was surrounded on all sides by 45-foot columns with Corinthian capitals. Under the platform of the *cella* were vaults, one of which now houses a museum.

Facing the Temple of Artemis are the remains of the Viaduct Church, which was built over the forecourt of the Temple of Artemis.

Standing at the nave of the church, with a view of the Temple in the background and a panorama of the hills and valleys of Gilead in the foreground, you can easily envisage the spectacular sight the Temple must have been to travelers approaching Jerash in ancient days.

A few steps further along the Street of Columns on the right are the Baths, dating from the 2nd century A.D. The dome is the oldest known example built on pendentives.

Across the street from the Baths is the North Theater, with a seating capacity of 1,200. Two hundred yards farther along the same street is the North Gate, the north limit of the city.

Thirteen churches have been uncovered in Jerash, and authorities say that probably many more lie buried under the ground. All the known ones have been dated except one.

The Cathedral, dated A.D. 350, is the earliest known Christian building in Jerash. It lies south of the Nymphaeum, and consists of a central nave with north and south aisles. Most of the stones and architectural details were taken from the Temple of Dionysos. West of the Cathedral is the large Church of St. Theodore, built about A.D. 496. Farther west are the ruins of three other churches. The plan of the middle church, dedicated to St. John, consists of a circle set in a square. The one on the north, dedicated to Saints Cosmos and Damianus, and the other on the south, dedicated to St. George, are of the usual basilica type, as is the Cathedral. The three churches had communicating doors and a common atrium, and were paved with mosaics.

The church west of the Temple of Artemis was originally a synagogue. It was converted into a church in A.D. 530.

The ruins of the other churches are not important enough to warrant description here. Yet, in general, one might say the churches in Jerash are some of the best examples of Byzantine architecture at its worst.

About a half-mile north of the city walls lies the principal cemetery of the ancient city. Nearby is a spring called *Birketain* ("two pools"), which supplied some of the city's water, and a small theater. According to an inscription on the latter, the licentious water festival of Maiumas was held here as late as the 6th century A.D.

Dr. Assem Bargouthi, professor of archeology at the University of Jordan, has headed three recent digs at Jerash that revealed a new residential area, exposing houses on a side street running off the Street of Columns. A minor drainage system connects each house with the drainage system of the main avenue.

Three types of water system also were uncovered. One consists of pieces of stone carved in a semicircular shape and fitted end to end, in the style of Roman aqueducts. Another type is lined with plaster and covered with slabs of stone. The third is constructed of round pottery pipes lined with plaster, resembling our present-day underground water pipes.

Further along the Street of Columns, excavations revealed a monumental structure 150 feet in length. Dr. Bargouthi believes that this could have had great public significance and may turn out to be the real forum of Jerash.

Because of the vastness of the ancient site—an estimated 90 percent of ancient Jerash still lies buried—Jordan has encouraged scholars from around the world to participate in the excavations. Many more new areas are being uncovered. In the past few years, 25 different groups—several of them American—were at work on the site.

AMMAN

Peddlers of ancient coins and oil lamps are frequent visitors to
sites of antiquity in Jordan, especially Jerash. Sometimes their
wares are genuine, more often they are not; so let the buyer beware.

Sound and Light Performance: A *Son et Lumière* was inaugurated at Jerash in the summer of 1983. Guests are seated near the entrance at a site that overlooks the Temple of Artemis and the main street of the ancient city.

The performance begins at sunset with a 25 minute segment on
the history of Jerash. Afterwards, the group walks south on the
main street to the Forum for a ten-minute narrative and to hear
the sounds of the market as it might have been in Roman times.
Finally, they take their seats at the Theater for another ten-minute
segment, an imaginery reenactment of Roman Emperor Hadrian's
arrival in Jerash in the 2nd century A.D.

Performances run once daily and twice on Thursday and Sunday, and are in English and Arabic three times per week, and in
German and French twice weekly. Check locally for the exact
nights. Admission is JD 1. JETT operates special buses to the performance for JD 1 round-trip.

A restaurant and a new resthouse with offices for the Ministry
of Tourism and Department of Antiquities opened in 1983 as part
of the on-going project to upgrade Jerash and expand its facilities.

The Jerash Festival: The idea for an arts festival that would utilize the extensive and dramatic ruins of Jerash was first conceived
in the 1950s. But until 1981, when the first Jerash Festival was
staged, nothing more than a few special events were held here.

The main purpose of the first effort was to assess the country's
ability to stage an international event of this nature and to gauge
the response of the public. In addition, the organizers hoped to gain
experience in management, administration, and technology.

When the idea of the festival was first discussed at Yarmouk University, Queen Noor, the present Queen of Jordan, defined the purpose of the Festival. She suggested that it serve as a center for the
arts, promoting and encouraging talent. A committee of 12 faculty
members from the University and an administrative staff was created to plan, prepare, and execute the project.

When the first festival attracted 100,000 people in three days,
the organizers knew they had a winner. Immediately, they decided
to make it an annual national festival which would appeal to a wide
age group. It was developed along the broadest possible lines—art,
books, crafts, folklore, local and international song, music, theater
and drama, as well as a children's segment. The stress was on Jordan's heritage, with contributions from Arab and international cultures; international participation would come from the four corners of the world.

The Festival committee, headed by the Queen, was reorganized
and various private, commercial, and governmental bodies were

asked to participate. The government has contributed about JD 150,000 to the Festival, but its organizers hope to make it self-sustaining in the future. It has also received a great deal of support that has saved it a considerable amount of expense. Alia under-writes the cost of transporting foreign artists; the army constructs stages, booths, and other on-site requirements; and dozens of people donate their services.

The Festival has hosted many foreign troupes, including the ballet from Spain and London; Turkish, Soviet, and American-Indian folk dancers; China's famous acrobatic team; a theater group from Tunis; Ferouz, the famous Lebanese vocalist; the Reda dance group from Egypt; plus eight local Arabic and English-speaking theater groups. The Empire State Institute of the Performing Arts staged a children's program of *Sleeping Beauty* in 1984 and The Red Clay Ramblers from the United States appeared in 1985.

An entrance fee of JD 1 covers all but special performances which range from JD 2 to 5. Motorcoach transportation from Amman is available from morning to midnight, throughout the ten-day event.

Ajlun: 41 miles; 14 miles west of Jerash

Ajlun is not often visited by foreign tourists, probably because they think it is difficult to reach, or because they are not aware of its attractions. It is only a short drive from Jerash, and in the past few years has been developed as a weekend resort with sports facilities, restaurant, and overnight sleeping accommodations at a resthouse.

Ajlun's main attraction is a twelfth-century Arab castle, often mistaken for a Crusader fortification. Qala'at al-Rabad was built as a defense against—not for—the Crusaders.

Qala'at al-Rabad is perched on top of a 4,068-foot mountain, with a spectacular view of the Jordan Valley and the Biblical land of Gilead. It is claimed that on a clear day one can see from Mt. Hermon in the north to the Dead Sea 90 miles away to the south.

The fortress is one of the best examples of Arab military architecture in Jordan. It was built in 1184 by Izzeddin Usama, one of the generals of Saladin, specifically to protect the caravan and pilgrimage route and to stem the advance of the Crusader armies spreading out from Jerusalem and Damascus.

The castle was destroyed in 1260 by the Mongols and rebuilt by the Mameluks, who took it over later in the same century. The Mameluks considered it too vulnerable, and reinforced it by doubling its walls and by constructing a second bastion outside the existing ones.

After you climb to the top, you will welcome a rest. Sit for a while and enjoy the view—a 360-degree sweep over half of ancient Palestine. To the west, verdant hills disappear into the haze over the Jordan River; nearby the Zerqa River rolls southward in a broad, green snakelike pattern. Eastward, Jerash's green shows up against the barren mountains of Gilead on the horizon; and far to the east, beyond the National Park's edge, the endless desert begins again.

Another point of interest in Ajlun is an old mosque built during the Middle Ages on the site of a church.

The Debbin National Park, reached by the old road to Jerash north of the Zerqa River, was opened in 1972. For a country which is 80 percent desert, a national forest is a source of considerable pride, and Jordanians enjoy taking their families here to picnic and pass the day among the pines and oaks and, in the spring, to gather wildflowers. The Park stretches about 30 miles from Ajlun to the village of Debbin, and is part of the watershed whose rivers feed the Jordan River from the east. Snow run-off from the mountains of Gilead makes it one of the country's richest regions.

En route to Ajlun, there is the American Hospital of the Southern Baptist Church, which gives medical care to about 50 villages in the vicinity. Throughout the Ajlun area there are ancient sites which have only been partially investigated. Deir Abu Said is said to be the place of Absalom's death; Listib, the birthplace of the prophet Elijah. There are many old churches and ruins of ancient buildings in the vicinity.

Irbid: 53 miles; 24 miles northwest of Jerash

Irbid is one of Jordan's fastest growing industrial areas, and the administrative center of the country's most fertile region. A new university was opened here last year on a temporary 20-acre campus. Planned for a capacity of 20,000 students by 1985, the University of Yarmuk has a School of Arts and Sciences and expects to add studies in medical sciences, engineering, agriculture, and veterinary medicine.

The town is built on the site of an early Bronze Age settlement. It is Beth Arbel of the Bible and Arbila of the Decapolis. Some authorities claim it is the burial place of Moses's mother and four of his sons.

South of Irbid is Tell al-Husn, another early Bronze Age site, usually identified as Dion of the Decapolis.

Umm Qais: 95 miles; 19 miles northwest of Irbid near the Syrian border

Ancient Gadara, one of the important cities of the Decapolis, was the capital of the Roman district of Gadarites. The remains of three theaters, a temple, a colonnaded street, and an aqueduct give an idea of the city's former grandeur. Situated at an altitude of 1,700 feet, it commands a magnificent view of the Sea of Galilee, the Yarmuk River Valley, and the Golan Heights. Its strategic position must have been responsible for the development of the city, first mentioned in ancient records from about the 3rd century B.C. as "an inexpungible stronghold" during the wars between the Ptolemies of Egypt and the Seleucides of Syria.

In 218 B.C., the Seleucid king Antiochus III, after a decisive victory near Sidon, overran Galilee, crossed the Jordan River, captured the city of Pella (Tabaqat Fahl in the Jordan Valley), and laid siege to Gadara. The inhabitants did not resist, being apparently eager to throw off the Egyptian yoke. Immediately after the fall of Gadara, Philadelphia (Amman) was also conquered.

The penetration of Hellenism was feared by the Jews as a challenge to their religious traditions, and led to a revolt during the reign of Antiochus Epophanes (174–175 B.C.). Judas, son of the priest Mathathias, defeated the Seleucids in 165 B.C. Under John Hyrcanus in 100 B.C. Gadara was captured and destroyed after a six-month siege.

The city recovered its independence in 65 B.C. when the Roman general Pompey conquered the East. A new era began for Gadara, which continued until the Arab conquest. Under Pompey, the Decapolis, a commonwealth of ten cities—most of them situated on the East Bank of the Jordan—was created. Each city was a free city-state *(polis)* and governed a large, intensively cultivated territory with many small villages. Commercial activity increased the wealth of the ten cities, and building was undertaken on a large scale. The layout of each town was similar to those of Greek and Roman cities—colonnaded streets, temples, theaters, public fountains, marketplaces, and stadiums. A Greek inscription found in the Gadara forum tells us that wealthy citizens shared in paying the expenses of public buildings.

One reason the Decapolis was created was to stop the Nabataean advance to the north. The Nabataeans controlled most of Transjordan and the Negev; hence they controlled the trade and caravan route. Under Aretas III (87–62 B.C.) the Nabataeans had pushed their northern frontiers to Damascus.

During the time of Mark Antony part of the Nabataean territories east of the Dead Sea were presented to Cleopatra. The Nabataean king, Malichos I (47–30 B.C.), was allowed to rule his territories but had to pay tribute to the queen. Apparently the Nabataean king was averse to paying these taxes, causing Mark Antony to send Herod against him. After many battles, Malichos was defeated near Philadelphia in 31 B.C. Later Herod the Great was granted the cities of Gadara and Hippos by Octavius after the latter's naval victory at Actium. When Herod died in 4 B.C., Gadara recovered its independence.

According to the Bible (St. Matthew 8:28), Jesus visited the territory of Gadara and here exorcised two men possessed by devils.

He ordered the demons to go out from the men and to enter into a herd of pigs. When news spread of this miracle, the whole town turned out to meet Jesus and "besought Him to remove Himself from their country." Hoade's *Guide to Jordan* maintains that the incident took place at Kursi on the east shore of the Sea of Galilee, rather than at Umm Qais.

In A.D. 68 the first Jewish revolt broke out. Vespasian captured the cities on the East Bank in order to destroy the Jewish colonies; he was welcomed in Gadara, apparently as a liberator.

When Trajan annexed the Nabataean kingdom into the Province of Arabia in A.D. 106, Gadara remained independent. Like many cities of the Decapolis, Gadara reached its golden age in the second century. It is from this period that most of its buildings date. In the 4th century it became an episcopal seat and flourished until the 7th century.

Apparently, Gadara was famous in ancient times for its hot springs. According to the Roman geographer Strabo, who lived in the time of Augustus, the pleasure-loving Romans came here "after having enjoyed the restorative effects of the hot springs of Amatha [el Hammi], retired for refreshments, enjoying the cooler heights of the city, and solacing their leisure with the plays performed in the theaters." This helps explain why three theaters were built in the city and why many poets and philosophers came from it. One of the natives of the city had written on his tomb, "I am from Gadara, fond of the muses."

In the 2nd century A.D., Josephus described Gadara as a wealthy city, and wrote that "villas and small cities lay round about it." Gadara controlled a large area, extending to Lake Tiberias. After the Byzantine period it slowly declined, and by the Arab period was a small village.

Only limited excavations have been undertaken. Our earlier knowledge of the ruins is based mainly on the short account published by the archeologist Schumacher in 1880. In 1973, an archeological expedition began excavations under the German Evangelic School of Jerusalem. The group is continuing its work, and is undertaking restorations as well. The institute has a workshop near the University in Amman.

The city is approached from the east, where the acropolis is now covered with modern houses. On this side, a strong wall reinforced with towers once protected the city. Entering from the eastern gate, the visitor comes to the northern theater, badly damaged by earthquakes and vandalism. In front of the theater, there is an open area, most probably a forum. From here a colonnaded street, bordered by columns and shops, runs westward. It was paved with basalt slabs, and the marks of chariot wheels are visible.

The colonnaded street leads to the western gate. On the right a few feet before the gate are the ruins of a nymphaeum, and to the left the remains of a large basilica. A street running southward leads to the western theater. On the way, one can see the vaults which supported the basilica. A massive wall behind the basilica may have belonged to a temple.

The western theater is smaller than the northern one but is in better condition. Built of black basalt, the two-storied auditorium consists of 14 tiers on the first level and ten on the upper one. A horizontal gangway separates the two tiers; vaults support the seats, most of which are in good condition. The orchestra, now covered with stones, is more than a half-circle. At the lowest tier of the first story, near the central stairway, is a headless white marble statue, contrasting with the black basalt, representing a seated goddess holding a cornucopia in her left hand. The legs of her chair are adorned with lion heads, a symbol of Astarte. A similar goddess in a standing position is represented on the coins of Gadara.

From the western theater there is a sweeping view of the lake and the Golan Heights.

East of the city on the road to Tiberias, a large mausoleum was discovered in 1968 and excavated the following year. A stairway with 18 steps leads to a rectangular courtyard, which was probably covered by a roof. Some columns crowned by Corinthian capitals are still standing in the middle of the court. Later on a smaller portico, semicircular in shape, was added. Four steps lead to the funeral chamber, which was closed by a heavy, pivoted stone door. There are small chambers on three sides, six on each side arranged in two stories. This family mausoleum is one of the largest ever found in Jordan.

North of the mausoleum is a circular podium, 21 feet in diameter, perhaps belonging to another tomb. It is approached by a flight of steps, and scattered about in the surrounding fields are Ionic capitals, which presumably once topped the columns. A third mausoleum, situated on the northern slopes near the Baths, is in ruins. In the Baths, mosaics in the floor and four basins can be seen. Greek inscriptions in the mosaic read "Health to Heraclides the founder and to the bathers." Heraclides is thought to have been a rich citizen of Gadara who financed the building of the Baths.

The East Ghor Canal, Jordan's most ambitious irrigation project, begins near Umm Qais and continues south through the Jordan Valley. A road south of Umm Qais and another west of Irbid lead to Pella, one of the major cities of the Decapolis and the city to which the earliest Christians fled from persecution in Jerusalem in the 2nd century A.D. Pella can also be reached from Salt by a road along the Jordan Valley.

In January 1979, a joint project of Wooster College, the University of Sydney, and the Department of Antiquities began a ten-year excavation to uncover the ruins of Pella, which are expected to be as extensive as those of Jerash. The site is important for its early

Bronze Age settlement as well as for the Roman one. The name of Pella comes from the birthplace of Alexander the Great in Greece. The site is known locally in Arabic as Tabaqat Fahil.

Ramtha: 64 miles; 35 miles north of Jerash

Ramtha is the northern frontier post where the visitor enters Jordan from Syria. Here papers and cars must be checked, customs passed, and visas obtained if necessary. The restaurant provides hot and cold food and drinks. Postcards and small souvenirs are on sale, and restroom facilities are available.

Four miles further is Dera'a in Syria, the Edrei of the Bible.

Umm el Jimal: 12 miles east of Mafraq, off the Baghdad Highway

Northeast of Amman, another good highway leads to Ruseifa (8 miles), situated in a lovely green valley. It is one of the main centers for the mining of phosphates, Jordan's main export.

Further along, the road passes through Zerqa (14 miles), which is the administrative center of the district by the same name. Once only a small Circassian village and headquarters of the Arab Legion, the town has grown into one of the main industrial centers of the country. Throughout the area there are many sites of antiquity which have been identified but never studied closely or excavated extensively. These date from Nabataean, Roman, and Byzantine times, although several go back to the Chalcolithic period.

Approximately nine miles north of Zerqa the highway divides, and a new road on the east leads to Azraq and the Umayyad Palace of Qasr el Hallabat.

Continuing north, the road comes to Mafraq (43 miles), the administrative center of the area. Its development started with the building of the oil pipeline from Iraq to Haifa in the 1930s. Mafraq is surrounded by a desert of black basalt (a volcanic lava stone), which stretches from the Jebel Druze in Syria south through eastern Jordan. Outside of Mafraq the area is sparsely populated today, but at one time it is believed to have supported a large population. One ancient center is Umm el Jimal, meaning "mother of the camel." Known as the black oasis, this curious place has extensive ruins of a Roman-Byzantine-Umayyad town built on an earlier Nabataean settlement, and constructed entirely of black and steel-gray basalt. From a distance it has the appearance of a bombed or burned-out city. As one writer has said, it would make a good setting for *Macbeth*. It is thought to have been a caravan staging post. The many open spaces within the town are assumed to have been for the accommodation of the caravans; hence its name.

Umm el Jimal is believed to have been founded in the early Roman period at a time when the area enjoyed considerable Nabataean influence. It flourished as a frontier city of the Roman and Byzantine Empires and continued to prosper in the Umayyad period. It was destroyed by earthquake at the end of the Umayyad period, and was not rebuilt because the region of the Hauran lost its preeminence when the seat of government shifted to Baghdad under the Abbassids.

The builders, using the hard rock as though it were wood—an architectural style known as corbeling—shaped the basalt into shingles and beams and constructed ceilings and roofs by laying the stone beams, six to nine feet long, on cantilevered supports protruding from the walls. They carved doors out of the basalt and balanced them on sockets in diamond-hard door jambs, and barred them shut with crossbars of basalt. They hollowed out drinking basins, still used today, and cut deep into the solid rock to make cisterns. Visitors will be able to appreciate the success of these methods. Numerous buildings are still standing two and three stories high, with some of their ceilings intact after 1500 years.

Perhaps even more impressive than the building skill of the first settlers was their excellent hydraulic engineering. Neither spring nor stream has ever been found in Umm el Jimal. Rainfall, minimal and sporadic, had to be collected and every drop stored to see the population of five to ten thousand through the long dry season.

They constructed a dam across the Wadi running west of the city to provide irrigation water for the surrounding fields, and a ground-level aquaduct many miles long to collect the runoff from the sloping terrain to the north. A number of branch channels were cut to direct the water into large open pools throughout the city as well as to smaller, roofed-over cisterns adjacent to nearly every house and public building. The supply of water thus created should have been ample for the people and their domestic animals, except perhaps in a succession of extremely dry winters.

The study of this ancient water system has inspired present-day engineers to consider the possibility of similar systems to support Jordan's growing population and to increase agriculture in village settlements.

The ruins of Umm el Jimal cover an area of about 200 acres and appear as one great tumbled mass. The houses follow the typical eastern style: a central courtyard with rooms around it and an external stairway leading to the upper stories.

A small temple inside the South Gate on the west side has been called the Nabataean temple because of a Nabataean carved lintel over the door. Otherwise, no Nabataean remains have been uncovered.

Numerous gravestones with Latin and Greek inscriptions have given archaeologists a catalogue of names of the inhabitants that indicates that the residents were local Arab nomads who settled in the region and who are believed to have built Umm el Jimal under the security of the Roman Empire.

Early in the 2nd century A.D. the Romans appear to have taken over and may have called the site "Thantia"; there was a town by this name in the vicinity.

Nothing is known of the town during the early Christian period, but judging from the 15 churches on the site it must have been some kind of religious center. Furthermore, Christianity came here early; the church of Julianus, built in 345, is the earliest dated church east of the Jordan so far documented.

The city was enclosed by a wall with six gates, two each on the west, south, and east sides. The walls were constructed about the 2nd century A.D. and rebuilt in the 4th century. The only monumental gate is on the west side, but one gate on the south and one on the east are flanked by towers.

The Gate of Commodus (A.D. 176–180) on the west side consists of two towers projecting outside the city walls and connected by two arches. An inscription dates it to the joint reign of Marcus Aurelius and his son Commodus. The gate was named by H.C. Butler, who made the first detailed plan of Umm el Jimal in 1905.

The Praetorium (dated A.D. 371) lies in a large open space between the two gates on the west side. It is the second grandest house in town, with a ceiling coming together to make a sort of dome, surrounded by a simple but well-defined moulding in a whiter stone. It consists of two buildings constructed along the north and west sides of an open court. The north building is rectangular. The door is in the middle of the south side and opens onto an atrium with four columns. The atrium is flanked by two large halls, while to the north are five rooms. There is evidence of another floor.

The Barracks, which dominate the town as one approaches, date from the 5th century. The building is located near the middle of the south wall, and is also known as the *Deir,* or monastery. The building is rectangular, with a chapel of three aisles on the east side. Around an open court are single and double rows of rooms. At the southwest corner is a six-story tower with a balcony on each side. Around an open court are single and double rows of rooms. At the southwest corner is a six-story tower with a balcony on each side. The stonecutting is Roman, but by Byzantine times it is thought to have become a monastery. The inscription running round the tower has numerous crude crosses, and gives, in Greek, the names of the archangels Michael, Gabriel, Raphael and Uriel.

As in the houses, there is an outside staircase made of cantilevered corbels, and windows over which machicolations were hung for the purpose of pouring down hot oil or lead on attackers. The top floor of the tower has narrow slot windows with machicolations over the lower ones.

Churches

It seems strange that Christianity took such a grip on this town, although many other such improbable sites of early Christianity are found in the Syrian desert as well. As noted earlier, the church of Saint Julianus was built here in A.D. 345. It is located between the Gate of Commodus and the northwest corner of the city, and consists of ten transverse bays with a semicircular apse ending at the eastern end, as churches were then oriented. Everywhere amid the fallen stones large and small crosses, ornate and simple, are scratched in the surface.

Philip Hitti in his *History of Syria* says, "The one-nave church of Umm el Jimal illustrates the primitive type of Christian church . . . an elongated room, favored because of its simplicity and relation to the prevailing type of structure."

The other type of architecture used at Umm el Jimal is the basilica, which has a central nave and two side aisles separated by arches that run parallel to the axis of the church and end in circular apses.

The Cathedral (dated A.D. 557) is in the basilica style, and stands in the middle of the town, between the two gates on the west side.

The West Church, the best-preserved church, lies outside the north gate of the east wall. Four arches have survived and support a second story with high windows. There is a well-defined Jerusalem cross cut deep into an arch. The entrance is dignified and imposing with a high arched window over the door. Near it are the underground tombs, on which some names survive. These are large chambers entered by subterranean tunnels, with a series of arches supporting the main chamber's roof, and niches cut out all around them for the sarcophagi.

Other churches deserving mention are the Numerianos Church, situated north of the barracks in the open space; Klondianos Church, opposite the Gate of Commodus, and the Double Church, one basilica and one hall, situated between the two gates on the east side. Between the South Gate and the southwest corner there is a church called the Governorate.

In 1972, Dr. Bert DeVries, professor of history and archeology at Calvin College in Grand Rapids, Michigan, began extensive work at Umm el Jimal with an aerial and ground survey to map out the entire city, its numerous buildings, defensive walls, and water reservoirs. Two years later he and Dr. James Sauer, director of the American Center for Oriental Research, conducted a preliminary excavation to verify the periods of occupation of the city. This excavation, carried out in cooperation with the Department of Antiquities and the American Center for Oriental Research, yielded Roman, Byzantine, and Umayyad pottery in successive strata of occupation. This pottery is the first systematically studied collection from the Southern Hauran region.

Dr. DeVries has also excavated some specific buildings at Umm el Jimal, including the Barracks, the Praetorium, a private house, and the city wall, all located in the southern half of the city. In general, the dates of construction and occupation of these buildings proved to be later than previously thought.

The so-called Nabataean Temple was founded on Byzantine materials; the 5th century A.D. date for the Barracks was confirmed, and both the Praetorium and the private house contained good Byzantine and Umayyad occupation levels. Although pottery from these cultures was found mixed in with later materials, no Roman or Nabataean occupation levels were found anywhere in the excavation.

Perhaps the most surprising result of this excavation is the discovery that Umm el Jimal was a significant Umayyad city, whereas previously it had been thought of only as a Nabataean, Roman, and Byzantine city. Because several Umayyad occupation levels were found, a study of the pottery from these levels is expected to contribute significantly to refining the distinction between the early and late Umayyad periods.

Dr. DeVries has been working with the Department of Antiquities to consolidate the buildings that were excavated. This phase of the project includes strengthening walls to prevent further collapse, clearing debris and posting signs to make the buildings more accessible and understandable to visitors, and the writing of a booklet for the Ministry of Tourism to serve as a guide for visitors.

Dr. DeVries is writing a book describing the results of his work at Umm el Jimal. He also will excavate the northern half of the city and study the role of Umm el Jimal in the geographic region of the Hauran.

Nearby Sites

In 1944, Nelson Glueck examined other ancient sites in this region between the Iraq Petroleum Company pipeline and the Syrian border, e.g., Ba'ij, Sabha, Sabiyeh, and Umm el Quttein. These are all marked by basalt buildings similar to those of Umm el Jimal. They were occupied in Nabataean, Roman, Byzantine, and medieval Arab times. Each has reservoirs hewn out of the solid rock, and each house had its own cistern. The district must have once had a population of thousands, compared with a few hundred of today.

Wadi Sirhan, which has an extensive supply of underground water, was the lifeline between the Nabataean kingdom in southern Syria and its territory in south Jordan. The Wadi extends from Azraq to within eight miles of Jauf, an oasis and former Nabataean outpost. Wadi Sirhan is 200 miles long and 18 miles wide, and today most of it lies in Saudi Arabia. This long, shallow depression acts as an extensive catchment basin for rain and rain run-offs. The line of the Desert Castles marks the line of the slope of the watershed eastward.

Although rains are infrequent in the Wadi Sirhan and the east desert of Jordan, at times heavy rain can fall for days. The water collects and may remain for months in low-lying lands.

SOUTH OF AMMAN

One of the most historic and scenic roads in the Middle East, the King's Highway runs from Amman to Aqaba through the ancient lands of Ammon, Moab, and Edom. The road passes through Hesban, Madaba, the ancient cities of Dhibon, Kerak, Tafileh, and Shobak, and on to Petra. The route is spectacular when it winds through the gorges of Wadi Mujib and Wadi el Hasa. There are even parts of the ancient Roman road and column markers still visible in several places along the way.

Hisban: 12 miles on the King's Highway

On the road to Madaba west of the modern village of Hisban there is a large site occupied from 1200 B.C. to A.D. 1400, which is believed to be the Heshbon of the Bible. Old Testament references describe it as the capital of the Amorites, who had taken it from the Moabites (Num. 21:26; 32:37). Later Jeremiah assigned it to Ammon, and by Herod's time it was used as a buttress against the Nabataeans. Still later, Saladin occupied it, and in the 19th century a new village grew up in the vicinity.

In 1968, excavations were begun by Andrews University on the hillside covered with half-buried columns and foundation stones. A Byzantine church, Hellenistic and Persian walls and pottery, and a 500 B.C. ostracon inscribed with Egyptian, Babylonian, and West-Semitic names was uncovered. A second season in 1971 produced Roman and Byzantine tombs from three different cemeteries, some with jewelry and gold, skeletons, and an abundance of pottery.

In previous excavations the oldest material that had been found dated only to the 7th century B.C. In 1973, pottery and a small wall dating from the early Ammonite kingdom of the 12th–11th centuries B.C. were found. After a gap of 400 years, people lived here again during the 6th to 7th century B.C. Other aspects of the Ammonite era came to light on the western slope, where a strange complex of Iron Age walls were uncovered. The complex was built in six stages, partly over bedrock and partly over earlier rubble.

In the southwest cemetery, nine more tombs were explored, and some yielded fine Byzantine glass, pottery vessels, and evidence of burial customs and tomb construction.

For the first time, an investigation was made of the buildings that are visible above ground in the southwest village of Hisban. For years they had been called Turkish, but pottery identifies them as Mameluk. Also explored for the first time were the curious underground holes, each as big or bigger than a living room, that had been dug through the rock. They are interconnected with tunnels and ramps and an occasional hole made through the ceiling to the outside surface. They are thought to have been cisterns dug by the Romans or Byzantines.

In addition to the excavations, the Department of Antiquities and the Andrews University team made a detailed survey of the area within a six-mile radius. These included Wadi Hesban almost all the way to Tell er-Rama, ancient Livias in the Jordan Valley, from where, in ancient times, the road led to Jericho and Jerusalem. Hesban was part of a heavily populated region throughout history. Altogether about 103 sites were explored.

Madaba: 19 miles on the King's Highway

Madaba, the city of mosaics, dates from the middle Bronze Age, about 2000 B.C. It is mentioned in the Bible as Medeba, a border town of the Moabites at the time of the Exodus (Num. 21:30; Joshua 13:9).

In the mid-9th century B.C., the Hebrews were driven out by the Moab king, Mesha. Madaba is mentioned on the famous Mesha stele, an inscribed stone left by King Mesha in praise of himself and his mighty conquests. Centuries later Madaba was promised to the Nabataeans in exchange for their helping John Hyrcanus I recover Jerusalem from the Seleucids at the end of the 2nd century B.C.

After the death of Alexander the Great in 323 B.C., his generals held the area. With the peace that Roman rule brought to the area, Madaba became a typical provincial town like Jerash, and its trade helped it develop into one of the main cities of the region.

Under the Byzantines it became the seat of a bishopric; a Bishop Janios represented Madaba at the Council of Chalcedon in A.D. 451. During the Byzantine era Madaba reached its peak, and most of its famous mosaics date from this period.

In 614 the town was destroyed by the Persians, and in 747 it was badly damaged by earthquake and finally abandoned. And so it remained until the early 19th century, when 2,000 Christians from Kerak settled on the ancient site.

As the new settlers dug the foundations of their houses, many discovered ancient Byzantine mosaics. Today many of these are housed in the churches and homes of the town. The best example is in the modern Greek Orthodox Church of St. George. The mosaic, discovered in 1884, is a map picturing Palestine and Jerusalem, Egypt and the Nile at the time of Justinian. Most localities shown on the map were important cities or sites of events in the Old Testament. The map is designed in shadings of red, green, blue, brown, violet, and yellow, and set on a background of white limestone. It depicts the countryside and its landmarks from the northern Jordan River Valley to the branches of the Nile, showing some Mediterranean coast with its cities, the Dead Sea, and the mountains of Moab.

The most important part of the mosaic is a primitive, though clear, city plan of Jerusalem as it was in the 6th century. A street of columns, the walls and the gates of the city can be distinguished. One can also recognize principal buildings such as the Church of the Holy Sepulchre.

The sacred spring of Elisha is shown as a shrine with a red dome; a stream of water flows from it to Jericho, a many-towered city surrounded by palm trees—"a city of fragrance and palm," as in the Bible. The Greek name, "Neapolis," as in the West Bank town of Nablus, appears, and in the Nile the fish are pictured as big as boats, while at the mouth of the Jordan, where the waters enter the Dead Sea, the fish turn away in agony.

The Madaba Museum

Opposite the Police Station. (Entrance fee: 250 fils; hours: 9–5 daily except Tues.)

The museum houses beautiful mosaics, some risque. One of the largest, uncovered in 1960, measures 18 feet by 21 feet and shows Achilles carrying a lyre, with Patroclus on his right and his favorite slave girl, Persis, on his left. Above the latter's head is Eros carrying a crown, and above Eros is a mythical creature, half-man, half-goat. Another mosaic, measuring 15 feet by 15 feet and filled with geometric designs, has exceptionally good color, and the workmanship rivals that of the mosaics of Ravenna.

There are dozens of small mosaics to be seen around town in private houses, and others continue to turn up as foundations are dug for new buildings. Some of the houses are open to the public; at others the mosaics are shown by members of the family for a small fee.

The Madaba Rest House, half a block from St. George's Church, has a small gift shop. It serves refreshments and can provide information on the town.

Madaba can be reached from Amman by regular bus and taxi service, which operate frequently.

Mount Nebo: 6 miles northwest of Madaba

The outer point of the Moab mountain is one of the alleged sites of the tomb of Moses. From here one sees a remarkable panorama across the Jordan Valley and the Dead Sea to the Judean Hills—the scene Moses saw (Num. 23:14). On a clear day the towers of the Mount of Olives in Jerusalem are visible.

For years the Franciscans have been excavating at Mt. Nebo, and on its topmost ridge, at Siyagha (which means "monastery" in Aramaic), they have uncovered the church and monasteries referred to by early pilgrims and travelers. Inside a Byzantine church (which dates from the late 6th century) are many of the mosaics uncovered here and in the immediate area during the last few years. One of the most beautiful and almost perfectly preserved mosaic, 9 by 30 feet, has a large, richly colored pictorial area depicting rural scenes; a Greek inscription that dates the floor and names the artists and pious contributors.

According to M. Piccirillo, who excavated the site, the first Christian communities of the region wanted to perpetuate the memory of the last moments in Moses' life by building a sanctuary on top of Mount Nebo overlooking the Jordan Valley and the Dead Sea. The place may already have been identified by an earlier funeral monument. Etheria, a Roman pilgrim at the end of the 4th century, reported in her memoirs that she had visited a little church, the Memorial of Moses, built on the summit of the mountain and kept by Egyptian monks. In the next century another pilgrim recorded that he had seen the memorial in a large church. The Franciscans' excavations from 1933–1937 and again in the 1960s confirmed these reports. In 1976 work was resumed, and, as Piccirillo notes, when the new discovery was made "the excavation, which was at first thought to be a routine job, became a scientific and artistic adventure that will remain an unforgettable experience for all the members of the expedition."

In front of the church the Franciscans added in 1984 a new iron sculpture of a cross wrapped with a serpent. The cross denotes the Biblical event when God told Moses that if those who had been bitten by the serpent looked upon the cross and believed, they would be saved.

Khirbet el-Mukhaiyat, about two miles southeast of Mt. Nebo, is the site of another sixth-century church with a beautifully preserved mosaic floor. The scenes depicted are anything but pious, and show the lingering influences of paganism—mythical sea beasts and other animals; lyrical dancing figures, and a complicated scene involving bulls, trees, and a fine altar. Archeologists believe that Mukhaiyat is the site of the ancient town of Nebo mentioned in the Bible (Num. 32:3, 38).

On a nearby mountain top southwest of Madaba was Biblical Machaerus (present-day Mukawir), where Herod held court in a palace he built upon an ancient fortress. According to the historian Josephus, this is the place where Salome danced and John the Baptist was beheaded.

Ma'in Spa Village: From Madaba through the tiny village of Ma'in. A new road runs southwest to the mineral springs of Zerka Ma'in, the Callirhoe of classical times, where Herod the Great, among others, came for the cure. It is still used today for the same purpose. In all, there are about 50 springs located along the canyon of Zerka Ma'in, forming small and large pools with temperatures ranging from warm to boiling; a hot waterfall spills into the largest of the pools. Recently, these waters were harnessed for a new health spa. The drive to the spa takes in the magnificent scenery of the Dead Sea and the Jordan Valley.

Ashtar Hotel, P.O. Box 184194, Amman, tel. 667699 (Amman) or 802071 (at the spa). 142 rooms. JD 22 single and JD 24 double with buffet breakfast. The new hotel has a spectacular setting in a valley famous since Biblical times for its therapeutic thermal springs and is said to be the best-equipped spa in the Middle East with a large team of physiotherapists and doctors to treat arthritis, rheumatism, muscular disorders, and other ailments. Guest rooms have private balcony, bath, radio, television, and mini-bar. There is a large outdoor swimming pool, a bar, disco, and giftshop. The pleasant, spacious dining room and coffee shop command views of a cascading thermal waterfall where adventurous guests may scamper under its hot, mineral-rich waters. Two separate pools—for men and women—have water temperature of 38–40 degrees C; specialized massages are also available. The hotel also operates a group of air-conditioned trailers with its own outdoor pool, mineral baths, and restaurant. Day use of the facilities is permitted upon payment of a fee.

Dhiban: 39 miles; 27 miles south of Madaba

Dhiban (Biblical Dibon) (Num. 21:26-30; 32:34), one-time capital of the Moabites, has now been excavated down to 3000 B.C. levels. Here the Mesha stele, a carved stone that records the battles between the Moabites and the kings of Israel around 850 B.C., was found in 1868. The discovery was sensational for many reasons, not the least of which was the fact that at the time of its discovery it was the earliest example of Hebrew writing to be found in the region.

Approximately 10 miles beyond Dhiban the road reaches Wadi Mujib, the Arnon of the Bible (Num. 21:3–15; Deut. 2:24–36). The gorge is over two miles wide and drops approximately 3,600 feet; its river empties into the Dead Sea.

All along the ancient route are magnificent views, famous sites and Biblical battlefields, Roman, Arab, and Byzantine ruins, small villages, shepherds with their flocks, and Bedouin with their tents. On the descent one can make out the old Roman road and the ruins of a Roman bridge. On the ascent one can see the Dead Sea in the distance. Where the present road and the Roman one meet, there is a fort dating from the Roman period which also has Nabataean ruins. It was used as a station for pilgrims and is known as Mahattat el Haj.

Rabbah: 65 miles; 10 miles north of Kerak

On the west side of the road are partial excavations of a large site of Roman and Byzantine ruins. Rabbah has been identified as the City or Moab, which played an important role in the war between King Mesha and the Kingdom of Israel in the 9th century B.C. After the Greek conquest in 331 B.C., the town was renamed Aeropolis. During the Nabataean rule from the 2nd century B.C. to A.D. 2nd century, the town prospered as a caravan station and continued its importance under the Romans. During the Byzantine period it was the See of the Bishop of Petra until the Arab conquest in A.D. 687.

Kerak: 75 miles; 55 miles south of Madaba

Crak des Moabites, or Kir-Moab and Kir Hare-seth of the Bible (2 Kings 3:25; Is. 15:1), rises 3,400 feet above its surrounding plateau and the Dead Sea Valley and crowns a hilltop with enormous walls and battlements.

Kerak was a walled Crusader town, built for defense, not beauty. For 50 years it held out against attack from Moslem armies until finally in 1189 Saladin took it. Inside the walls today there is a predominantly Moslem town.

In the castle, masterful cross-vaulting leads into more and longer galleries, stables, chambers, and lookouts. The total concept of the fortress gives one pause—the colossal task of building on this precipice, maintaining its defense, and supplying the needs of thousands of men and animals staggers the imagination.

To those for whom the Crusaders hold a fascination, the exploration of their castles can be a haunting, melancholy experience. From Turkey to the Gulf of Aqaba, the Crusaders built a chain of hilltop strongholds, carefully planned to be approximately a day's journey apart, sometimes on the foundation and walls of earlier fortresses. Fire signals were sent at night from chateau to chateau, to tell the knights in Jerusalem the news from the See of the day before. Each castle had its distinction, but few matched Kerak for intrigue and chivalry, bravery and betrayal.

The mountaintop fortresses that the Crusaders built east of the Jordan were strategically located on a line between the Dead Sea and the King's Highway. To maintain themselves, the Crusaders cultivated and protected the lands in the nearby valleys, and from there extended their control eastward into the flatlands, where they grew wheat and other grains as the Romans had done before them.

The main commercial caravans moved between Egypt and Syria via Sinai to Aila (Aqaba) before they turned north to Damascus or south to Arabia. This was the route that had also been used by the Biblical kings and later by the Greeks and the Romans. Farther east, there was another lucrative route—the Hajj or pilgrimage track from Damascus to Mecca, with even bigger caravans.

The early kings of Jerusalem extended the Crusaders' domain as far south as the Gulf of Aqaba, where they put a small garrison on an offshore island to extort tolls from the trade coming by sea. From Aqaba the goods were transhipped over Sinai by caravan to Gaza or Egypt and thence to Europe. The Crusaders also had a garrison in Aqaba. Further north, to watch over the caravans in and out of Petra and to control their supply lines, they had built a fortress at Shobak.

In 1132 Baldwin I, King of Jerusalem, ordered the Lord of Transjordan, Payem the Butler, to build a fortress at Kerak to help strengthen his communication lines and defenses. Kerak was strategically situated halfway along the great stretch from Shobak to Jerusalem. From Kerak, Baldwin could receive warnings of an approaching enemy or respond to cries for help. From Kerak, the military route to Askalon—a favorite Egyptian attacking point—could be controlled. From here, the lines south could be kept open to Petra and Aqaba, and the caravans coming from Arabia could be made to pay tribute. Baldwin was right, and for him and his three successors, the money poured into the coffers of Jerusalem.

When Baldwin III died his son was not yet thirteen and a leper. For a time Miles de Plancy, Lord of Trans-Jordan and Kerak, was regent for the young heir; but he was assassinated, leaving his wife, Stephanie, mistress of the Crak de Chevalier. Reynald, or Reginald de Chatillon, a knight who arrived in the Holy Land with the Second Crusade and who was anything but a flower of chivalry, upon hearing of the death of the regent, rushed to the widow Stephanie, one of the richest women in the Holy Land. He succeeded in winning her hand and with it her powerful domain.

By feudal law, the young heir had to be named Baldwin IV. As he reached 16, the Leper King grew worse and realized that he must die without an heir. With the affairs of the kingdom torn by infighting among the feudal nobles, he decided to sue for peace with the Moslems. He made a truce with Saladin, which granted safe passage to the caravans of both the Moslems and Christians through each other's lands.

After Baldwin's truce the caravan trade increased along the routes via Kerak. Reynald, unable to resist the temptation, broke the truce and his king's pledge and seized a rich caravan headed for Mecca. Saladin responded by capturing 1,500 pilgrims on their way to Jerusalem, and the long battle was on.

Although Saladin withdrew when Stephanie's fire signals brought help from Jersualem, the Moslem warrior would come back.

According to legend, one of the chivalrous events of the Crusades took place at Kerak. During the wedding feast of Humphrey of Toron and Isabel, the sister of Baldwin, Saladin made a surprise attack on the castle. The Christian governor sent a gift of meat and wine to Saladin, informing him of the wedding. Saladin gracefully acknowledged the gift and sent a message asking which was the bridal suite so that his soldiers could avoid bombarding it.

Soon after the first incident, Reynald broke the truce again, whereupon Saladin crossed the Jordan with an enormous army. Reynald unfortunately persuaded King Guy of Jerusalem to attack, leading to a disastrous defeat for the Crusaders at the battle of the Horns of Hittin. When the slaughter ended, only King Guy and a few knights were left to surrender. Saladin received them in his tent and gave them water. But when he discovered Reynald among them, he upbraided him for his treachery, received a rude answer, and with one swing of his sword cut off Reynald's head.

That was July 3, 1187. King Guy and the other knights, with the True Cross, were sent to Damascus as prisoners. Stephanie held out at Kerak for another year, but finally Saladin cut off all supplies, threatened the local villagers against helping the Crusaders, and simply waited.

Saladin needed Kerak. For 50 years it had dominated the caravan routes to Arabia, Egypt, and the pilgrimage route to Mecca. Moreover, it had stuck like a bone in the Arab's throat. It had sent fire signals nightly to Jerusalem, keeping in touch with Crusader leaders; it had supplied its armies from the rich valleys at its feet; and it had made vassals of the local inhabitants.

More Crusades and many battles followed, but by the close of the 12th century the Christian knights had begun a slow retreat to the sea, and Moslem rule rolled in like a tide to replace them. Kerak became an administrative post of the Arabs, and in 1263 the Egyptian ruler Baybars is reported to have destroyed its Crusader church.

When the Turks conquered the Middle East, they used the castle for some time. The town prospered and grew to fill the area enclosed by the walls; but the castle itself was neglected.

Today many of its battlements have been shored up and its passages opened. One passage has been made into the *Kerak Museum.* (Entrance: 250 fils, hours: 9–5 daily, Wed. to 1.) Artifacts from Buseira, Bab el Dhra, and other excavation sites in the Kerak region are on display. Beyond the entrance gate one enters the medieval world. There are remains of the reservoir where water had been stored, the chapel, and a little round enclosure where the only efforts toward decoration appear in rows of carvings around its dome.

The castle is open from sunup to sundown. Guides are available through the museum or the Government Rest House next to the castle.

The Rest House, built from native stone to blend with the castle, sits on the crest of the mountain overlooking the valley and the Dead Sea. It has 13 twin-bedded rooms, each with a shower and toilet, warm water, and heat in winter. The hostel's dining room has a terrace overlooking a magnificent view. Arabic food and international dishes are available; or the restaurant will pack picnic lunches.

The drive to Kerak from Amman takes about two hours, and you can see Kerak in its entirety in two to three hours. An excellent picnicking area is located by a spring in the valley below. Ask at the police post for directions.

There are many Christian families in Kerak with very old names that go back to and beyond the Crusaders to the Byzantine period, when Kerak was an important bishopric. On a hill below Kerak there is a village still called Franj—from "Franks."

Among the Moslems, too, some old Christian terms remain. For example, one of the tribes is called "Bawareesh"—probably from parish, since in Arabic "p" becomes "b." One of the families of this tribe is named Matraneh, which in Arabic means "bishop."

Below Kerak, an interesting side trip can be taken down to the Dead Sea to the place where the Crusaders built a port—their nearest escape route to Jerusalem from Kerak.

Continuing south on the King's Highway to Tafila there are two villages that are significant in the history of early Islam. It was on these plains that the first army of Islam suffered its first defeat against the Byzantines in 632. It was to be the Arabs' Dunkirk. Afterwards, the battered army returned to Arabia to regroup and plan. When they charged north again against the Byzantines a few years later, they did not stop until they took Damascus. Today, in the villages of Mauta and Mazar, there are two mosques that commemorate the Moslem leaders who were killed here in the first battle.

Khirbet el-Tannur is a Nabataean temple from the 1st century B.C. located in the vicinity on a mountain peak.

Qasr Tafila: 118 miles; 40 miles south of Kerak

After crossing Wadi Hasa, the road reaches Tafila, much of which is built from or into and around Crusader ruins. There is an enormous keep or donjon built in the early 12th century. A custodian has the key to this medieval relic and will also give you a tour of the other remaining Crusader and Mameluk structures, if requested. Tafila is set in a valley with abundant water and surrounded by olive groves.

Qasr Buseira, nine miles south of Tafila, at the village of Buseira, is a huge pile of roughly fitted stones with an occasional arch or retaining wall still standing, on a cliff above Wadi Khanzira, a valley which extends to the Dead Sea. Buseira is thought to have been one of the main towns of the Edomite Kingdom.

The area that lies west of Tafila and Shobak is among the most important lands of ancient history. It was a mining and smelting center from the Bronze Age down through the Arab conquest. Khirbet Nahas, 21 miles south of the Dead Sea, is the site of copper mines that were in use during and after the reign of Solomon. The land was also part of the caravan route that led through the Wadi Araba to Aqaba. In Biblical times it was the land of the Edomites. Down through history control of this land ensured its owners great wealth. It was also the reason so many battles were fought here in ancient times. Just before reaching Shobak, the road crosses Wadi Fidan, which marks the north boundary of the Ma'an district that extends all the way to the Gulf of Aqaba. The main towns of the district are Ma'an, located on the Desert Highway, and Aqaba at the head of the Gulf.

Shobak: 154 miles on the King's Highway; 117 on the Desert Highway; 19 miles north of Petra

The ancient Crusader fortress of Montreal stands alone, crowning a mountain of rock overlooking the most barren, weatherworn, windswept, and desolate land one can imagine. There is a good view of the fortress as one approaches from the south on a road that climbs up directly to the castle.

Mons Reglais, the Montreal Castle of Shobak, was the parent of the chain of Crusader castles built between the 11th and 13th centuries. It is situated about halfway between Kerak and Petra. Built by Baldwin I about 1115, it was besieged several times by Saladin and finally captured in 1189. The Mameluks restored it in the 14th century. Today, the castle is little more than a pile of stone except for its outside walls, a square keep and a donjon beautifully carved with Arabic inscriptions. It is built on a hill surrounded by a natural moat, and contains a rock-cut well shaft of 375 steps leading down to an underground water supply—one of the deepest well shafts ever dug by the Crusaders. As with all mountaintop castles, the view is magnificent.

From Shobak the road passes through rolling highlands on which there is snow as late as mid-March, and leads to Wadi Musa, a picturesque village near the entrance to Petra. Wadi Musa ("the springs of Moses") was apparently named in the belief that it was the site where Moses struck the rocks that brought forth water.

About one mile before the village there is a magnificent view of Wadi Musa in the foreground and the mountains of the Petra canyon in the background. It is an excellent spot to take photographs. A small, domed, white-stone building was built over the spring in 1985 to protect the water. You are allowed to take water from the spring.

Petra: 160 miles

> Match me such marvel save in Eastern clime,
> A rose-red city half as old as time.—*Dean Burgon*

These words were written decades ago by a traveler who rode camel and horse over mountains, through valleys, across streams, and into desert to reach a site hidden in the mountain vastness of southern Jordan. After its rediscovery in the early 19th century, ancient Petra, capital of the Nabataean Arabs, became a goal of adventurers, globe-trotters, explorers, historians, and archeologists.

Over the century, the way to Petra became easier and safer, but even as late as 1955 the trip from Amman was ten days by horse or a day of rough driving by car, available only to the few who could afford the time and cost of such a trip. Today, the new road from Amman to Petra has changed all this.

Those captivated by the romance of the East may regret the passing of an era when the remoteness of ancient Petra added to its fascination and lure. Now that the long trek is no longer necessary, one could afford to agree with them. Frankly, we enjoyed the comfortable car ride from Amman to the entrance of Petra. The fact that the drive on the Desert Highway takes only three hours need not lessen one's enthusiasm or detract from Petra's wondrousness in the slightest. Petra is still mysterious, formidable, and magnificent.

Petra, which means rock, was a fortress city set in a canyon whose only entrance was a long, narrow passage, the Siq. Inside the canyon the Nabataeans created a city by carving houses and temples out of the variegated rock of the canyon walls. The sunlight plays on the rock, changing its colors from hot yellow at high noon to red in the reflection of the setting sun, to purple in the afterglow of twilight. The changing light casts a mood over Petra—and all the hundreds of words written about it cannot adequately describe its effect.

The story of Petra prior to the Nabataeans is vague in our history books. It was probably the land of the Biblical Horites around 2000 B.C., and later the land of the Edomites, who controlled southern Jordan at the time of Moses and the Exodus. Petra is sometimes identified with Sela, the capital of the Edomites in the Bible (2 Kings

14:7; Is. 16:1). When the Crusaders occupied the site in the 12th century, they called it Sel, recalling its Biblical name. Sela, too, means rock.

The Nabataeans, a Semitic tribe from North Arabia, settled in Petra probably around 800 B.C. By the 4th century B.C. they had occupied the territory astride the main trade route from Arabia to the Fertile Crescent and had become protectors of the caravans that passed through their lands. As payment for this protection, the Nabataeans were able to extract enormous tolls from the caravan traders.

In 312 B.C. the Seleucids, heirs of Alexander the Great's empire in Syria, attempted to dislodge the Nabataeans from their envious position. Instead, the Nabataeans routed their enemy in a night attack and ended conclusively any Seleucid designs on their territory.

For the two centuries that followed, the Nabataeans maintained their independence and carved out an empire that extended as far north as Damascus. With their wealth from the caravans and their expert engineering skills, the Nabataeans enlarged their rose-colored city and embellished it with high temples, houses, and tombs.

After Pompey's conquest of Syria and Palestine in 63 B.C., the Romans gradually extended their control into south Jordan. The Nabataean domain remained autonomous but was dependent upon Rome. Finally, in A.D. 106, Nabataean power gave way and their lands, along with most of Palestine and Jordan, were incorporated into the Roman Province of Arabia.

Under the Romans, Petra reached its height. Many buildings were added, including a rock-carved theater, baths, a colonnaded street, a forum, and a temple (the most complete free-standing building that can be seen there today). Other buildings were carved out of the living rock.

Eventually, when one of its main competitors, Palmyra (Tadmor) in Syria, started to emerge as an important caravan trade center, Petra's prominence began to dwindle. The end came when the Romans began to use ships to bring the merchandise from South Arabia north through the Red Sea, making caravans, already risky, too slow to be profitable. Some inhabitants, of course, stayed in Petra.

Early in the Christian era Petra became part of the Byzantine Empire, and a number of important buildings, alterations of earlier Nabataean ones, date from this period. Later, when the Moslem armies marched north from Arabia, Petra fell to the Arabs. But by this period the main trade routes of the East had shifted, and Petra's source of wealth had vanished. With time, Petra's glories were forgotten, and for hundreds of years even its location was lost to the world, until the early 19th century when the Swiss explorer

John Burckhardt stumbled upon it by chance during a Middle Eastern expedition he had undertaken for an English learned society.

When Burckhardt was traveling from Damascus to Cairo by way of Aqaba, he heard stories from local Bedouin about a strange place with ancient ruins. From the descriptions he thought the site might be the lost city of Petra. Because of his expert knowledge of Arabic and Islam, Burckhardt could pass himself off as a Moslem and move about unexplored areas without being questioned. On the pretext of having vowed to make a sacrifice at the tomb of Aaron, Burckhardt was allowed by local tribes to proceed to Mt. Hor. En route he saw Petra, but unfortunately he could not linger for fear of arousing suspicion. Apparently, however, he made a few stops, for he later described some of the monuments in his writings.

The track into Petra leads down a hill past the ancient dam of the Nabataeans. In olden times the dam dispersed the dangerous floodwaters of the wadi (valley) into channels, and a canal sent a large part of it by a circuitous route outside the canyon walls. Later, the Romans developed a similar system using terra cotta pipes. Both the Nabataean channels and the Roman pipes are clearly visible.

After centuries of neglect the dam collapsed. In 1963, after a group of tourists were caught in a flash flood in the wadi, the dam was reconstructed to ensure the year-round safety of the Siq. In building the new dam, modern engineers followed the basic plan that the Nabataeans had used more than twenty centuries earlier.

Beyond the dam one enters the Siq. From here, the dreamlike world of Petra begins. The Siq, barely wide enough for a car, hides between sheer rocks towering 200 to 300 feet. In some places the walls are so close they appear to be meeting overhead. In ancient days the Siq was Petra's protection from surprise attack; only a few men were needed to hold the passage against invaders. In Roman times a stone-paved road led through the passage and into the main thoroughfare of the city.

Upon emerging from the path, you will be dazzled by the sight of an imposing tomb in classic Greek style carved out of rose-colored rock on the side of a cliff. This is the *Treasury,* or Khaznat Faron, one of the best preserved monuments in Petra. Its surface appears so smooth it would seem to be covered with a film of rose-colored powder. The Treasury gets its name from an old belief that pirates (perhaps Ali Baba and the Forty Thieves!) hid their stolen treasures here.

Beyond the Treasury the path turns to the right and leads past many of Petra's fine tombs and temples topped with the characteristic crow-step design, the hallmark of Nabataean architecture. Further along, the trail runs by a second-century Roman theater carved from rock at the foot of Mt. Nejr. The theater once seated 3,000 spectators. Behind it a trail and steps lead to the High Place of Sacrifice, a mountain-top sanctuary in the center of Petra canyon.

East of the main road, a cliffside is lined with more of Petra's beautiful tombs and temples—the largest cluster and among the most beautiful groups in the canyon at easy access. Farther ahead on the original Roman road stand the remains of the Nymphaeum, the Roman Triumphal Arch and a structure known as Kasr al-Bint. In front of this Roman temple, excavations of the Jordanian Department of Antiquities continue to probe Petra's hidden past. The entire center area is believed to be the old city—now under centuries of earth. It will take archeologists decades to uncover it.

In order to see the ruins of Petra, one must climb several cliffs and mountains within the canyon. The principal sites are the Monastery and the High Place of Sacrifice. Each is a half-day's excursion at a leisurely pace.

West of the temple a footpath leads up the mountain to the Monastery, or Deir. Along the way one can marvel at the beautiful rock formation and the carvings on the side of the cliffs. Upon arrival at the top one is directly in front of the Monastery, one of the largest and most handsome temples in Petra.

The Monastery was carved about the 3rd century A.D. as a temple to the glory of the Nabataean god Dhu-shara, chief diety of Petra. Crosses carved on the temple walls probably indicate that at some later date the temple was used as a church. The edifice measures 165 feet wide and 148 feet high, but its size is deceiving. Only when you see someone standing in the doorway does the enormous size of the façade become apparent.

The panoramic view from the hill beyond the Monastery is one of the most impressive in the Middle East. Some 4,000 feet below lie Wadi as-Siyagh and Wadi Araba, part of the Great Rift Valley extending from the Jordan Valley in the north to the eastern coast of Africa in the south. Sinai, the Negev, and the Biblical lands of Canaan are on the horizon.

Three hundred meters to the southwest is Jebel Harun (Mt. Hor), site of the tomb of Aaron, the brother of Moses. An annual sacrifice is made on Mt. Hor by local Bedouin during Id al-Adha, the Moslem Feast of Sacrifice. In Moslem tradition the feast is held at the end of the pilgrimage to Mecca, and the sacrifice is symbolic of Abraham's offering of his son.

A trail southeast of the hostel along the Wadi Tarasa leads up the side of Mt. Nejr to the High Place of Sacrifice. Along the way more of Petra's stupendous rock formation, temples, and tombs are in evidence. Especially important are the Tomb of the Soldiers and the inner chamber of the Festival Hall.

At the High Place, the ancient altar, with drains for the blood of the sacrifice, is flanked by two obelisks of solid rock. These were probably meant to mark the limits of the sanctuary. The altar is said to be exactly east-west at the equinox. From the summit of Mt. Nejr, one of the highest peaks in Petra, the entire canyon and surrounding area are in view.

The descent from Mt. Nejr can be made by an ancient rock-cut stairway (restored by the Jordanian Department of Antiquities) on the reverse side of the mountain. The way is lined with houses, temples, and tombs topped with the traditional Nabataean crowstep design. The path ends near the Roman Theater and the main road to Petra.

A third climb—not so steep—can be made east of the theater by way of the old Roman road to a cliffside faced with many amazing structures. These include the dramatic Corinthian Tomb, the Palace Tomb (a three-story edifice thought to be a copy of a Roman palace), and the Urn Tomb, which has a paved and colonnaded courtyard extending over a two-story vault. A Greek inscription inside the Urn Tomb says that the building was used as a church in A.D. 447. The variegated rock on this cliffside is some of the best in Petra. For hearty climbers there are several paths and rock steps that lead to the very top of the cliff. It is worth the climb; the color of the rock is fantastic and the view of the canyon is magnificent.

A small museum of Petra, arranged by the Friends of Archeology and the Department of Antiquities, is located in a cave west of the temple. A ticket to enter Petra costs JD 1, and must be purchased from a kiosk located at the road leading to the Siq.

A last note: At your first sight of Petra you may be confused and even disappointed. It does not have the immediate impact of the colossal Temples of Baalbeck or Ramses' statues at Abu Simbel. Rather, Petra's effect is one of bewilderment and slowly developing fascination. Some temples are visible on the road as you enter but many others are not. The area inside the canyon is two square miles, so you do not get the whole effect until you have examined the temples, houses, and rock at close hand, and climbed the mountains and cliffsides to look down on the sweeping panorama of the canyon. After that, Petra is sure to linger in your mind for years to come.

Aklat and Beida: 5 miles north of Petra

Aklat, a settlement dating back 9,000 years, is one of the oldest sites in the Holy Land and is considered by archeologists to be as important as Jericho for the evidence that has been uncovered from the Neolithic and subsequent periods.

Excavations were started by Diana Kirkbride, one of the best-known archeologists working in the Middle East. She returned every 2 years for a period of 2 to 3 months until 1967. Six main building levels were uncovered and 4 different types of architecture, each with its own individual and significant techniques. Each village of the 6 main levels seems to have lasted an average of 75 years.

The earliest inhabitants of Aklat, circa 7,000 B.C., were a Neolithic people who used stone tools in their daily life, before the invention of pottery. They built houses, developed crafts, and ground grain. Later when Petra became the capital of the Nabataean Kingdom, the Nabataeans terraced the uneven ground for agriculture.

The excavations conducted by Ms. Kirkbride are at about 3,000 feet above sea level. The first level dates from about 6,000 B.C. Proper identification of the top level was difficult due to erosion and the destruction caused by the terracing of the Nabataeans. Small rectangular houses with plastered floors were found.

The second and third levels date from about 6,600 B.C. Houses in these levels were all of the same size except for one large house in the second level, which was a single room measuring 27 by 21 feet, with massive walls still standing to the height of three feet, and with a hearth in the center. Entrance was through doorways in the walls, which were thick enough to accommodate three descending steps to the plastered floor inside. South and west of this house were long rectangular buildings with wide unplastered walls, divided into six rooms by corridors. Artifacts suggest that they were workshops rather than dwellings, and the crafts show a certain degree of specialization even at this early date. One room contained a variety of heavy implements—grinders, polishers, and axes. In another room an oval wooden box holding 114 choice flints was found. The big house was probably the meeting place and eating room for the workers.

Level four dates from about 6,780 B.C. and was much damaged by later building activities. The structures were of circular walls broken by entrances. Walls and floors were plastered, similar to those of Jericho. In Level five there is strong evidence of an architectural evolution.

Level six is from 7,000 B.C. and contains the earliest Neolithic houses yet found. They are unique—circular in plan with stout posts set into the floor at regular intervals and united by beams to a strong central post. The scheme is similar to that of a wigwam. A wide stone wall was then erected around this scaffolding, with its interior face buttressing the posts. Across the upward slanting beams, brush or reeds were laid at right angles, like thatch. This supported a thick clay roof, which was probably given a fresh coat of mud annually. Interior walls, ceiling and floors were plastered. Three of these "clusters" were excavated.

Burial practices at Aklat were somewhat macabre and resemble those of other sites, such as Jericho, Hacilar, and Catal Huyuk in Turkey. Adults were buried without heads, while infants and small children were buried in an undisturbed state under the floors. A cemetery was found outside the village.

Several hundred yards north of the ancient site of Aklat is a narrow passage similar to the Siq of Petra that leads to an area known as **Beida,** which is believed to have been a Nabataean settlement from the 5th century B.C.—predating Petra—with houses and temples carved into the rocky hillside. One of its temples has a magnificent carved façade with columns similar to Greek and Roman ones but with an elegance unlike any others. At the far end of the passage, the remnants of steps (for those who are agile and surefooted) lead to a lookout with a magnificent view of the canyon and valley below.

The road from Petra to Beida passes a new village built by the government to resettle the Bedouin who once inhabited the caves inside the Petra canyon. The village has a school, and medical and administration centers to care for the Bedouin.

Gharandal: South of Wadi Musa a road leads west to Gharandal, where there is one of the most unlikely structures in the whole Middle East—a Chinese pagoda. Gharandal, which is 48 miles north of Aqaba via the new road through the Wadi Araba, is the site of a small village that was once a Nabataean settlement and is thought to have been the capital of the Edomites at one time.

From Petra to Aqaba, you return to the main road to join the Desert Highway north of Ras al Naqab.

PRACTICAL INFORMATION FOR PETRA

HOW TO GET THERE. On the Desert Highway from Amman to Ma'an you can drive to Petra in 3 hours. The old road via Madaba, Kerak and Shobak is an 5-hour drive.

A mile or so beyond Wadi Musa at Al-Ji Police Post, or the Visitors Center in front of the Government Rest House, you can hire a horse or donkey to ride the trail through the Siq into Petra. The horses are docile old souls, and their owners walk alongside holding the reins for timid riders. If you prefer you may walk the trail, which is well worth every step. We recommend the walk; it gives one time to stop and admire the fantastic rock formation. In any case, be sure to wear comfortable, flat, walking shoes (sneakers are perfect). The distance through the Siq is less than 2 miles, and the walk or ride takes about 45 minutes. An occasional truck or jeep makes a trip through the Siq to carry food and supplies to workers at the camp or archeological sites, but there is no regular motor traffic into the Petra canyon.

WHEN TO GO. The best months to visit Petra are September through November and March through May. Many people make the excursion in one day, but to cover Petra adequately one should plan to spend at least 2 days. Petra is one of the few places in the world that can truly be called unique. It deserves a longer stay than most tourists devote to it.

PLANNING YOUR TRIP. In planning your first trip to Petra you should use a good travel agent in Amman, who can arrange for a car and driver for a 1-, 2- or 3-day visit. The fee is approximately JD 40 per person for overnight at the hotel and includes transportation to Petra by 5-passenger car, meals, horses, entrance fee, and guide with stops in Madaba, Mt. Nebo, and Kerak en route.

Even if you decide to make your own arrangements for getting to Petra, you should have a guide to lead you around the ruins on your first tour. At Al-Ji Police Post and the Tourist Center English-speaking guides are available for JD 10 a day. The fee for a horse or donkey ride in and out of Petra is JD 5, and the owner will expect a tip.

Jordan Tours and Transport (JETT) offers bus tours daily for JD 14 round-trip, including horse, guide, lunch, and entrance fee. The bus departs at 6:30 A.M. from Abdali Station and returns at about 7 P.M.

HOTELS: *Petra Forum Hotel,* P.O. Box 30, Wadi Musa, tel. 61246; or 634200 in Amman. Rates: JD 19 single; 22 double; 25 rooms and 55 suites. The 82-room hotel, located outside Petra canyon about a quarter mile from the entrance to the Siq, is the first of international standing in the Petra region, and there are already plans to expand it. The hotel was built with World Bank aid, which matched the government's $6-million investment as part of a project to upgrade the antiquity sites of Jerash and Petra.

Architect-decorator Joe Diviney, engaged as a consultant by the World Bank, has given the hotel its quality. The hotel's management has given it local identity by getting the people of the Petra region involved in all phases of its operation. Most of the Jordanian staff are from the nearby village of Wadi Musa and were trained by the hotel.

Facilities include two restaurants serving international and Middle Eastern cuisine, and a heated swimming pool. Most guest rooms have twin beds, 14 have 2 double beds. The most desirable rooms have a private terrace where one can enjoy the sunset over Petra.

A camping area with showers and toilets is available near the hotel for those who bring sleeping equipment with them. The hotel plans to add 40 tents and more camping facilities. Meals can be taken at the hotel but they tend to be expensive. The hotel also packs picnic lunches.

The hotel operates a snack shop serving sandwiches and beverages inside the canyon where the Government Antiquities Department has its offices.

Government Rest House: 35 rooms. JD 6.600 single; 10 double. Situated near the entrance to the Siq, the guesthouse is built around an ancient tomb carved into the rock; guest rooms are in a modern structure and are large and comfortable with baths and hot water. There is a dining room and bar; the food is good and ample.

CAUTION: If you plan to visit Petra from December through March, be sure to take along warm clothes. It can be very cold at night. The new hotel has heat but the Rest House does not.

ITINERARIES AND PHOTOGRAPHY. If you leave Amman by 8 A.M. you can arrive in Petra for lunch at the hotel. Afterward, climb to the Monastery and return by sunset. This is an excellent time to photograph Petra to the east; the rocks glow in the light of the setting sun.

Early in the morning on the second day climb to the High Place of Sacrifice. This is the best time to take pictures to the west. Upon descending from the High Place continue to the Treasury for more picture-taking. The best hour at the Treasury is about 10 to 11 A.M., when the façade is in full sunlight, or about 4 P.M., when the stone is a deep pink—almost a raspberry color. After an early lunch, climb to the Urn, Palace, and Corinthian Tombs.

You should plan to leave from inside Petra canyon by 4 P.M. in order to walk through the Siq in sunlight and to return to Amman by 8 in the evening.

For a 1-day visit you must leave Amman by 6 A.M. to arrive in Petra by 9 A.M. Moving fast, you could make 2 climbs and leave the Siq an hour before sunset.

SUGGESTED READING. If you want to read up on Petra before your visit, several books offer excellent descriptions: G.L. Harding, *The Antiquities of Jordan;* Julian Huxley, *From an Antique Land;* and Iain Browning, *Petra.*

THE DESERT HIGHWAY

The alternate route from Amman to Aqaba is the Desert Highway, which follows closely the railway line and the old pilgrim and caravan routes established during the Ottoman period. The drive takes about four hours.

The best road out of Amman is the same four-lane highway that leads to the airport. Near the turnoff for the airport another road branches right to Madaba, 8 miles away; Aqaba is a 192-miles distance. The highway is heavily traveled by commercial trucks en route to and from Europe, Lebanon, and Syria to Saudi Arabia and the Gulf.

On both sides of the road in the springtime the fields are green with a new crop of grass, which brings the Bedouin to graze their flocks of camels, sheep, and goats. After 27 miles there is a cutoff on the right to Dhiban, and about one hour after leaving Amman you will be in Qatrana, which is a truck stop. There is also a pilgrims' camp—cement-block houses where pilgrims to Mecca are given lodgings.

On the right of the road there is a small fort, and a turnoff for Kerak, which is about 25 miles away. Noticing these turnoffs and distance, one cannot help but compare them with the road via the King's Highway. In every instance, 10 or 20 miles on the Desert Highway represent two times the driving time on the King's Highway.

After about two hours out of Amman the road reaches Al-Hasa, the country's main center for phosphate mining. A few minutes more and a road on the west leads to Shobak and thence to Wadi Musa and Petra, about 25 miles away.

Approximately three hours from Amman you will reach *Ma'an*, the administrative capital of the region. On the northern outskirts of Ma'an is the government rest house (no overnight accommodations). The road divides just south of here—on the right is the way to Aqaba; the left goes directly to El Mudawwara, the first town on the Jordanian-Saudi border. Ma'an is the major town of south Jordan, a stop on the railway line and a market center for the Bedouin of this region.

Farther on, there is another turnoff on the west for Petra, about 19 miles away. From here Aqaba is about 63 miles further south.

At about 48 miles north of Aqaba the road reaches Ras el Naqab, the most scenic part of the road. From here all the way into Aqaba it is a downhill winding road and takes about one to one and a half hours to drive.

On a hill overlooking Ras al Naqab at the head of the mountain pass there is a rest house where refreshments are served. It is worth the short detour for the view. There is a howling, chilly wind on this mountaintop, but there is also one of the most spectacular views in all Jordan. Here, in a flash, one can understand why in the olden days such high points were strategic to the control of the flow of goods and the march of armies. The location of ancient sites throughout Jordan—be it fort, castle, village, or temple—was always related to survival, situated to take advantage of a water supply or an advantageous location.

This panorama will also tell you a great deal about erosion and what happens to land in the centuries that follow neglect or abuse. As far as the eye can see there are mountains of rock, as at Shobak, but history tells us that at one time there were trees on these mountain sides. The Jordanian government is trying hard to reforest areas where there is enough soil to make it feasible, and has undertaken a "Green Plan" of reforestation in various regions of the kingdom.

On a clear day Wadi Rum, described later in this chapter, can be seen in the distance on the southeast.

Aqaba: 204 miles

At the southernmost tip of Jordan on the Red Sea is the country's only seaport, Aqaba, set in an amphitheater of rugged, stark mountains. The clear blue waters stretching along the Sinai Peninsula on the west and to Saudi Arabia on the east have some of the most beautiful coral reefs and fish to be found anywhere in the world. Scuba enthusiasts come from thousands of miles away, including the United States, to enjoy diving here.

Aqaba is probably the Biblical Eloth (1 Kings 9:26). Excavations at Tell al Khalifa, west of the present town, uncovered what some archeologists believe are King Solomon's copper smelters of Ezion Geber. Others place it on an island, Ile de Graye, three miles offshore, known since antiquity as Pharaoh's Island.

One of the earliest mentions of Aqaba dates from the 10th century B.C., and indicated that there was much sweet water only three or four meters beneath the earth's surface in some places. It is partly because of this water, and the strategic location at the end of the Red Sea, that Aqaba has been important so many times in history.

Aqaba engaged in extensive trade with South Arabia and the land of Sheba, and flourished up to the time of the Arab conquest. The great Roman road from Damascus via Amman and Petra extended south to Aqaba, where it turned west to Egypt.

During most of the 12th century the town of Aqaba and its immediate vicinity were held by the Crusader kingdom of Jerusalem as part of its fiefdom of Oultre-Jourdan. The crusaders built a fortress and placed a small garrison in the town; they made it a bishopric, and the title "Bishop of Aqaba" has survived in the Roman Catholic Church to this day. With the occupation of Aqaba the crusaders hoped to divide militarily the Moslems of Egypt from those of Arabia, and to be in a position strategically to levy tolls on the caravan trade.

Under the Ottoman Empire Aqaba was administratively part of the province of Hejaz, which encompassed Mecca and Medina and thus the western Arabian peninsula, rather than part of the Syrian district, which was geographically closer.

From the retreat of the Crusaders to the 19th century little is known about Aqaba until its sudden prominence in World War I during the Arab Revolt.

During the 19th century Aqaba had become part of Egypt. The Egyptians constructed a road across Sinai during the 1830s and '40s, and Aqaba became a staging and boundary point on the pilgrim route from Egypt to Mecca. However, improvements in navigation on the Red Sea after 1840 reduced the significance of the land route, and Egypt abandoned the town and the head of the Gulf of Aqaba to the Ottomans when the boundary between these two states was demarcated across the Sinai Peninsula in 1906.

Thereafter, Aqaba remained a sleepy oasis until 1917, when the British began using it as a supply route in their military offense against the Turks. After World War I, the southern boundary of Britain's mandate of Trans Jordan was not defined. Leaders of the Arabian peninsula believed that the boundary was located 20 to 50 miles north of the town of Aqaba, since this had been the approximate boundary of the former Ottoman province of Hejaz. This would have allotted the southernmost part of Jordan, as well as Eliat, to the Kingdom of Hejaz, which in 1925 became part of Saudi Arabia.

Subsequently, Britain, through a series of treaties with Saudi Arabia, established the eastern boundaries for its mandate. However, no southern boundary was agreed upon, and Britain unilaterally marked one from a point on the Gulf just south of the town of Aqaba and running approximately east-south-east. This line gave about five miles of shoreline to Jordan. Britain's action was not accepted by Saudi Arabia which, however, agreed to maintain the status quo pending a solution of the matter.

Jordan had traditionally used Haifa and Jaffa on the Mediterranean as its ports. With the establishment of Israel in 1948, access to these ports was cut off. In the 1950s Jordan began developing a port at Aqaba, which had been connected by a paved road to the railroad terminal at Ma'an since 1936. Use of the port increased with the development of Jordan's phosphate and potash exports, and piers were constructed, but with the growth of traffic, land soon became insufficient for port development within Jordan's territory. A treaty with Saudi Arabia in 1965 finally provided a solution for both the 40-year-old boundary question and the land requirements of the port of Aqaba. In exchange for about 4,000 square miles of Jordanian territory in the desert interior of the extreme southeastern corner of the country, Jordan obtained approximately ten miles of additional coastline south of the previous boundary on the Gulf.

The new boundary line on the Gulf of Aqaba is 330 yards north of the Saudi Arabian police post of Al Durra. The additional territory has enabled Jordan to expand both port and urban facilities as well as develop a resort area at Aqaba. Port facilities, however, have been expanded faster than tourist ones. These days about 50 ships a month are unloaded at new docks, compared to two or three 15 years ago. Furthermore, the port handles cargo ships not only for Jordan but also for Syria, Iraq and Saudi Arabia. The reopening of the Suez Canal in 1975 also created new business for the port.

As noted earlier, phosphate is the most important cargo loaded in Aqaba port. It is Jordan's main source of foreign currency. The phosphate comes from mines at Al-Hasa, on the railroad opened only a few years ago and already inadequate to handle the requirements. Trucks are used to help bring the phosphate from the mines to Aqaba.

The phosphate is unloaded from the rails into bins alongside Aqaba docks, located south of the town, and is powered from the bins through the pipes, across the docks, and into open holds of ships.

Aqaba's population has grown from 1,700 at the end of World War II to about 20,000 today. In the old days the only way to reach the tiny fishing village from Amman was over a very bad road or by several days' trek through the desert—neither of which appealed to tourists.

Today, there are daily Alia flights making the 30-minute hop to Aqaba from Amman. By car, the drive is four hours on the Desert Highway, five hours or more via the King's Highway. There is taxi service and regular bus service from Amman.

Maximum day temperatures at Aqaba in December are in the mid-70's F. In March and April they are in the 80's; from June to August the temperature can exceed 100° F. There are 12 hours of sunshine a day in July, 6 in December, and about eight at Eastertime. The humidity, however, is low all through the year.

A trip to Aqaba can easily be combined with one to Petra. The cruise ships that call at Aqaba offer a day's excursion to Petra.

Aqaba is for the most part a new town. The old Crusader fort, Qasr Aqaba, has been made into an office of the Tourism Authority and museum. It was built on the shores of the Gulf of Aqaba under Baldwin I, c. 1116. The Mameluks acquired it in 1320, and an inscription mentions Qansuh El Ghouri, a Mameluk who reigned in 1505. Above the double-arched portal flanked by towers is the Hashemite Coat of Arms, added in the early 20th century by the Sharif of Mecca.

The road west from the hotel cluster leads to King Hussein's villa on the beach, where he is a frequent visitor. It is the last house before the demarcation line. Elath is on the western side of the Gulf.

King Hussein's active interest in sports has had a great deal to do with helping Aqaba develop as a resort. He has often been pictured waterskiing and snorkeling at Aqaba. By leading the way he has made it popular with others.

Aqaba's Undersea Life

The Gulf of Aqaba has an unusual marine environment. Complex water movements, including chilled vertical currents, combine with the removal of warm surface water by the strong north winds. These leave the water surprisingly cool and invigorating—an ideal situation for coral growth and plant life. It also helps produce an incredible variety of fish, so abundant that divers do not need to use tanks; the water is so clear that they can see up to 150 feet away. All one needs is a mask, snorkel tube for breathing, and flippers. The variety includes chicken fish, clown fish, iron fish, crinoid, sea urchin, butterfly fish, sting ray, trigger fish, goby, shrimp, grouper, scorpion fish, stone fish, and more.

In addition to hundreds of species of fish, there are miles of reefs—a magnificent living world under the sea only a few feet from the beach and easily seen by diving or from the comfort of a glass-bottom boat. The boats belong to the hotels, which have jetties so that visitors can step into them easily. Some boats seat up to 12 passengers and have overhead awnings to protect them from the sun. Incidentally, spearfishing and the removal of coral are taboo.

If fish and reefs are not enough, there are shipwrecks to explore—no one knows how many. But when one remembers that the Red Sea has been an avenue of trade since ancient times, it's easy to speculate on the ships that never made their destination and are still lying at the bottom of this sea.

Aqaba has two diving centers. **Aquamarina Club** is fully equipped and can accommodate up to 50 divers. It offers two diving trips for certified divers daily at 9:30 A.M. and 2:30 P.M. with instructor. One dive JD 5; snorkeling JD 2.500. Resort dive course JD 20. Club offers windsurfing, waterskiing, fishing, sailing, rowing, surf sailing, and pedal boating. The club has two annual water-ski festivals: the first week of April and November 14, King Hussein's birthday.

The Aqaba Diving Center, located on the beach next to the Aqaba Beach Hotel, has tanks and belts and its own bus that takes divers to the beach. Cost for transportation and equipment is JD 5 per dive for one person and JD 4 per dive for groups of ten. The bus departs about 8 A.M. and 2:00 P.M., returning three hours later. For non-divers, the center has a glass-bottom boat. Cost is JD 3 for a three-hour trip. Contact Mahmoud Hilawi, who also operates tours to Wadi Rum and Petra.

A Marine Science Station, established by the Jordan Government to study the unusual marine environment of the area, provides facilities for research. The Station is located southeast of town.

SCUBA DIVING IN THE RED SEA

Because of the enormous interest and attraction of Jordan's Red Sea waters for scuba fans, we are including here an article from Jordan Magazine *by Carl Roessler, underwater photographer and author of* The Underwater Wilderness. *Since 1974 Roessler has accompanied American scuba divers to Aqaba on trips organized by See and Sea, Inc. of San Francisco, a travel service specializing in diving programs.*

Regularly since 1974, our scuba diving groups have been traveling to Jordan for the excitement of photographing the hauntingly beautiful world that lies beneath the waters of the Gulf of Aqaba. This long and narrow finger of the Red Sea, which stretches north to Jordan, holds thousands of miles of fabulous coral reefs that house an abundant variety of fish and plant life. The water's transparency—you can see up to 150 feet away—makes it ideal for underwater photography.

From the moment we step aboard our boat, it is as though we embark upon a journey to another planet, so totally is it another world that opens up before our eyes. No more than a few meters out, we see through the clear water the shallow coral reefs along the coast. They are, both in their color and in the incredible variety of marine life that surround them, a dazzling sight.

No more than a snorkel and face mask or a glass-bottomed boat are needed to see intricate thickets of sculptured stony corals punctuated by the delicate branches of fire coral a few feet beneath the surface. Here and there, schools of tiny anchovy hover about, and occasionally a larger fish glides lazily by. All are bathed in the diamond sparkle of sunlight as it pierces through the water in prismatic pattern.

In some areas, the sea floor is an open sandy expanse with scattered coral heads. Here, each coral thicket becomes a sanctuary, sheltering brilliantly colored fish of many species. The fish hover near these free-standing coral heads for protection. The structures, with their many crevices and complexities, offer the smaller fish a handy place to take cover if a barracuda or other predator happens by.

For the photographer, this results in amazing assemblies of beautifully colored reef fish that require no swimming at all to find. Schools of vivid orange fairy basslets with purple eyes capture the sun's brightness in their own flashing dance, drawing the diver again and again to watch them.

Here and there on the coral reefs one may find a variety of unusual species: tiny pink coral clusters, delicate soft coral in rose, violet, and hazy pink, and gaudy red sponges, each of which is decorated with at least one tiny nudibranch (shell-less snail) ringed with blue, white and orange bands.

Each dive reveals new marvels. One pleasant morning we find a hawksbill turtle napping amid the corals. Right next to the turtle, a small moray eel with a yellow mouth snaps this way and that, as if carrying on a conversation with his larger companion.

On other dives we find many examples of the amazing relationship between the clownfish and the anemone. Anemones capture small fish by means of contact-actuated stinging cells lining their snaky tentacles. But the clownfish is exempt. The anemone chemically "recognizes" a mucus the clownfish secretes on his skin, and holds its sting. With this startling immunity the clownfish swims among the armed tentacles with flashing confidence, indeed uses them to protect himself from larger fish!

Other brilliantly hued fish on the Aqaba reefs include butterflyfish of several species, pufferfish, delicate pipefish, angelfish, and a rainbow of others. The colors of the king angelfish are arrayed in vertical slashes of blue, yellow and white. Usually one of the shyest of reef fish, these striking fellows will occasionally surprise the visiting photographer by swimming right up to the camera.

Each day we discover even more splendid undersea sites. One area was so beautiful we returned several times. Its appeal was an extraordinary population of the extravagantly designed lionfish. This is one of the world's most beautiful fish, and nowhere in the world have I seen more than here. In many locations in the Indo-Pacific a visitor may see one or two lionfish in a week of diving. In Aqaba, one will find at least a dozen on every dive. Indeed, on several dives we found as many as a dozen or more at a single coral head! At least six species of these plumed fish are seen regularly in Aqaba's waters. In what ranks as a personal thrill, on two of my trips I have managed to photograph a species that authorities tell me may be new to science. It does not conform to the defined fin structure and color patterns of the known species, and scientists are studying the pictures now to determine whether it is a species unique to Aqaba.

By the end of the two weeks, our divers have made perhaps 30 different excursions into the sea. Their films are carefully packed, and they dream of the photos with which they'll relive these incredibly beautiful days.

As we cruise for a last time along the barren coastline, looking down at the passing reefs, we are silent. We wonder how soon we may return to these serene reefs. Will they escape the damage to which reefs around the world have been subjected? Economic development is slowly spreading down Jordan's coastline as the needs of a busy nation translate into docks, highways, and construction facilities.

To its great credit, the Jordanian government has recognized its marine resources as a national treasure and is moving to protect the reefs. Laws against spearfishing, coral collection, and other damaging activities are already in place. The University of Jordan is carefully monitoring the impact of shipping and construction on the marine life of Aqaba and to date has detected only a minor effect.

Wadi Rum: 35 miles northeast of Aqaba, south of Ma'an

Those who have seen the film *Lawrence of Arabia* will remember the magnificent desert scenery with towering cliffs of weathered stone. The weirdly shaped rocks jutting up from the valley floor, the color of the stone and red sand, and the endless span of sky creates a panorama of strange beauty with an almost ethereal quality—scenery unsurpassed in the Middle East. This is Wadi Rum, a great valley lying northeast to southeast in the desert of southern Jordan; a vast, silent place that has been named the Valley of the Moon.

Wadi Rum was the route that T. E. Lawrence and Sherif Hussein took in World War I to fight the Turks. For those who take the same route it will seem a journey into another world.

Archeologists are certain that the area of Wadi Rum was one of the earliest inhabited sites in Jordan, and a holy site during Nabataean times. Excavations in the south have uncovered a small village dating from 4500 B.C., and on a hill in the center of the valley there are the remains of a small temple, probably Nabataean and probably built about the 1st century B.C. There are also slabs of rock throughout the valley with inscriptions in early Thamudic writing, recording the names of travelers of old who were apparently moved by what Lawrence called "this processional way greater than imagination," and who left their mark before vanishing in the vastness of time and the wadi.

Wadi Rum resulted from a great crack in the surface of the earth caused by an enormous upheaval that shattered mammoth pieces of granite and sandstone and heaved them upward in the form of great cliffs. The weatherworn rocks are like pale purple mountains rising out of infinity. As one gets closer to them, their purple color gives way to the tawny hues of sandstone ridges that tower a thousand feet in the air and are topped with domes worn smooth by a constant wind. Overhead the sky is pale and colorless; underfoot, the sand is rust. All around there is emptiness and silence—a silence so great, one can hear it; space so immense, man is dwarfed to insignificance.

To penetrate the heart of Wadi Rum takes less than an hour from the Desert Highway. It lies in the center of a vast plain between Jebel Ram and Jebel Um Ishrin, almost a mile away. Both are parts of the high cliffs that Lawrence described as being like "gigantic buildings along two sides of their street."

Wadi Rum can be reached by car in about an hour's drive from Aqaba. From the Desert Highway, about halfway between the villages of Qwairah and Khirbet al Khalidi, about 25 miles north of Aqaba, a paved road turns east and crosses the desert for about 18 miles to the fort of the Wadi Rum Desert Patrol. The fort with its crenellated walls, gun towers, slit windows, and swinging gates is itself out of a movie set, but an even greater treat—especially for photographers—are the men of the Desert Patrol, who wear the most handsome uniforms in the Middle East—and they know it! The splendid outfit is a long khaki kilt held by a bright red bandolier, a holster with a dagger around the waist, and a rifle slung over the back. The headdress is the traditional red-and-white checkered *kafiya* worn by the Bedouin of Jordan, but wrapped under the chin and tucked into the *egal* with a slightly cocky tilt. The patrolmen, in Bedouin tradition, are friendly and hospitable to travelers, and will probably offer you coffee and answer questions willingly.

Rum is the home of several Bedouin tribes. At the fort there is a school and two shops to serve the small settlement of Bedouin who set up their black tents in the vicinity. Water is available from the springs. Without it, the valley, whose summer temperatures reach 140°F. and where no more than four inches of rain fall in a year, would be uninhabitable.

To travel beyond the area of the fort one needs a Land-Rover, which can be rented in Aqaba. The driver or owner of the Land-Rover will know the routes and should accompany you. Do not try it alone, because you might lose your way, and in the desert that's a serious matter.

Normally the trip to Wadi Rum is a half-day's excursion from Aqaba and is best made from early fall through spring, although in early spring high winds sometimes create a dust bowl in the valley that obstructs viewing and all but eliminates photography.

Approximately six miles east of Wadi Rum at Disih on the way to El Mudawwara an Italian excavation has uncovered a Nabataean site which was thought to be the capital a century and a half before the Nabataeans moved into Petra.

PRACTICAL INFORMATION FOR AQABA

HOTELS. Along with improvements in roads, airport and port facilities have come hotels, the main ones of which are situated along the water's edge.

Holiday Inn Aqaba, P.O. Box 215, Aqaba, tel. 312426, telex 62263. 173 rooms. JD 28 single; JD 32 double with service and taxes. Facilities include a restaurant, coffee shop, and nightclub. Recently renovated, rooms are furnished in the traditional Holiday Inn style with two double beds. All rooms are air conditioned and equipped with television, radio, telephone, mini-bar, and private bath. Guest rooms are on three floors built around the swimming pool.

Coral Beach Hotel, P.O. Box 71, tel. 313521, telex 62227. 92 rooms. JD 11 single; JD 14 double. The hotel is built in a half-moon shape, with guest rooms facing the sea and overlooking the hotel's private beach. Rooms are attractively furnished, comfortable, and air conditioned, with private bath and phone. There are a large dining room, bar, and night club.

Aqaba Hotel, P.O.B. 43, Aqaba, tel. 314091, telex 62240. 101 rooms. JD 9 single and JD 12 double w/half board, plus 20% service. The hotel has recently been taken over and managed by the government. There are various categories of rooms, ranging from those in the main building by the sea to prefab cottages, which do not face the sea. Adequate for a short stay when budget is a concern.

Aquamarine Hotel, P.O. Box 96, tel. 316250, telex 62249. 71 rooms. JD 26 double, with tax; single supplement JD 5. The hotel began as a diving club, but has grown and expanded and now has the most extensive sports, restaurant, and entertainment facilities in Aqaba. Rooms are nicely appointed. Facilities include large swimming pool, disco, travel agency, beauty salon, gift shop, and sauna. Snorkeling, scuba diving, waterskiing, and squash are available.

Aqua Marina II, P.O. Box 1060, Aqaba, tel. 315165, telex 62308. 64 rooms. JD 26 double, with tax; single supplement JD 5. Located a short distance from the city center, this modest hotel recently became part of the Aqua Marine group. Facilities include a swimming pool and children's pool.

Alcazar Hotel, P.O. Box 392, tel. 314131, telex 62242. 132 rooms. JD 20 double, with half-board, single supplement JD 4. A modern hotel with arabesque decor about two blocks from the beach. Local residents rave over the friendly, accommodating staff. All rooms have air conditioning and private balcony. There is an Olympic-size pool. Transport to out-of-town beaches to view underwater life and fish can be arranged.

Miramar, P.O. Box 60, Aqaba, tel. 314339. telex 62275. 100 rooms. JD 20 double, with half board; single supplement JD 4. This hotel is located between city center and beach, and all rooms have bath, television, radio, and phone. There is a swimming pool and a health club.

AQABA RESTAURANTS. Outside of hotels, the most popular restaurant is *El Far,* a rustic place directly on the beach that specializes in seafood.

Tours to Wadi Rum: *From Aqaba,* Petra Tours, tel. 313574, operates half-day, full-day, and overnight trips to Wadi Rum for groups. During the winter, if you are traveling alone, you can usually join a group that the tour company is handling. On the excursion you go by car or motorcoach as far as the Wadi Rum police station. From there you ride a camel to the Nabataean temple in Wadi Rum and have lunch at a tented camp in the desert. JD 15 includes lunch and beverages. A longer excursion continues after lunch by a land-rover trip south to the Saudi Arabian border, and returns to Aqaba via the desert. JD 15 per person.

The overnight trip is one and half days, JD 50, or 2 days, JD 85, depending on the departure time from Aqaba. Participants sleep in a Bedouin tent about 5 miles inside Wadi Rum. In the evening there is a barbecue dinner, with folklore music and dance. After breakfast the following day, there are camel rides or hiking, and lunch is served before the return trip which is by jeep to the police station and bus back to Aqaba.

From Aqaba, Petra Tours also has excursions to Petra, JD 15.

Ferry. Aqaba is now connected to Sinai in Eygpt by a ferry that carries passengers and cars. It departs daily at 11 A.M. and 4 P.M. for the port of Nuweibah. Tickets must be purchased in advance from the Jordan National Shipping Co., Hammamat St. (opposite Ali Baba Restaurant), tel. 315342. Cost is JD 12.250 first class; JD 8.500 second class. The ferry is used mainly by laborers riding steerage and families in second class. Food is served in first and second class. Toilet facilities are available but not very clean. Most foreigners go first class, some with their car. Cost for a small vehicle is JD 21.500; JD 35.250 for an auto more than 15 feet in length. Reservations and passenger tickets can be obtained in Amman. though Zaatarah Travel, Prince Mohamed Street, Third Circle, next to Citibank, tel. 642332.

EAST OF AMMAN

Arab Palaces in the Desert

In the desert between Amman and Azraq stand the ruins of several seventh- and eighth-century castles (known in Arabic as *Qasr*). These desert retreats were fortresses, pleasure palaces, watch-posts, and hunting lodges of the Umayyad Caliphs in the early days of the Arab Empire. Their ruins have furnished archeologists, historians, architects, and tourists with a frame in which to picture life in the early Islamic era.

To see them all, one must make the trip in a circle, clockwise or counterclockwise from Amman to Azrak. While once a hard day's drive over desert track, new asphalt highways now make it possible to cover the entire circuit in a half day.

The Umayyads were the first of the Arab rulers to set up the capital of their new empire outside Arabia, and they chose Damascus, which had been one of the major cities of the Orient since antiquity. The Umayyads had come from the desert, and their first caliph, Muawiya, fearing that his son and heir might lose the desert virtues, returned with him frequently to the desert away from the crowded and polluted city. First they camped in tents, and then they built palaces where there was game, which they hunted with falcon, saluki dogs, and trained cheetahs, and they raced their fine Arabian horses. In the evening they were entertained by poets, dancers, and musicians.

Today these desert palaces stand lonely and eroded, dotting the landscape of sand and scrub, baking in the hot sun. There are five castles on the circuit, each with its own character, each bearing the mark of its builder or most illustrious occupant. Azraq and Hallabat are of Roman and even earlier construction, with overlays from Umayyad, Crusader and Mameluk usage. Amra, Kharanah and Mushatta are purely Umayyad. The last-named is thought to have been built by none other than Walid II, one of the greatest of the Umayyad caliphs.

About 12 miles southeast of Amman, near the airport, is the ruin of **Qasr el-Mushatta,** the biggest and once the most ornate palace, and today the most despoiled of all. Mushatta was a real palace. It is a large square, 450 feet on each side, with 23 circular towers built into its walls two stories high around an inner court surrounded by archways; a great trefoil hall; vaulting, now fallen—and all built on a grand scale. For some unknown reason the palace was never completed.

Only traces of the lavish carvings that once decorated the walls are left. Just prior to World War I, the Turkish Sultan Abd-Al-

Hamid gave the palace to Kaiser Wilhelm. Subsequently the carvings were stripped from the walls and shipped to a museum in Berlin. Lying about in the field are a few remnants of the elaborate carving and friezes of intricate design. In the south wall of the palace is a niche, thought to indicate the mosque.

From Qasr el-Mushatta the road leads northeast for 10 miles to a large Roman reservoir at **Al-Muwaqqar.** Traces of a palace built by Yazid II are visible. The site now has only a tiny village and a desert patrol post. In one of the ancient cisterns a hydrometer with Kufic lettering was found, suggesting that the area once had a large supply of water.

Qasr Kharana, one of the most interesting of the desert castles, lies east-southeast of Al-Muwaqqar (or nine miles west of Qasr al-Amra). Apparently, it was the only one built for purely defensive purposes. A painted inscription dates the building A.D. 711. It was built of large undressed stone, with rows of smaller stones laid between the courses, and the outside walls were plastered over, emphasizing its solid appearance. This and its strategic position along the ancient caravan route suggests a fortress in the truest sense. It was also used as a caravanserai.

The only entrance to the castle is on the south. The long corridors on each side of the entrance housed the stables. The rooms of the castle were built around an open course in the center. The ruined columns in the courtyard once supported a second-story balcony. Stairways lead to corridors and rooms on the upper floor. Most of these rooms are decorated, domed, and vaulted.

In the wadi about one and a half miles west-southwest of the castle is a site covered with thousands of flints from the Upper Paleolithic-Mesolithic Period, more evidence that the area was once inhabited.

Northeast of Kharana, 42 miles east of Amman, 14 miles west of Azraq, lie the best remains of all the desert castles, **Qasr Amra.** Built as a small hunting lodge early in the eighth century during the reign of Walid I, the building is composed of three parallel halls, each with a windowless room at the end. On the inside walls are examples of some of the earliest known painted frescos. The frescos, which had been badly damaged over the centuries by smoke from the cooking fires of squatters and by the scribbling of careless visitors, were cleaned and restored by a team from the Madrid National Museum under the sponsorship of the Spanish government. The frescos are remarkable, rare examples of art that has survived from the Umayyad period.

The paintings, according to Professor K. A. Creswell, are more representative of the Hellenistic art of Syria than of the art of Byzantium, which prevailed in Syria at the time Islam came to that country. However, the nationality of the artist is recognized by art historians as Syrian rather than Greek. They point out that the desert area between Umm el Jimal and Azraq was inhabited by Arab tribes who were never converted to Christianity and thus were not influenced by Byzantine art. Many of their drawings on basalt stone depict nude women, dancing girls, and hunting scenes similar to the Amra paintings. Hence, historians conclude, the frescos of Amra represent the art of Arab tribes influenced by Greco-Roman civilization.

On the back wall of the middle room the painting shows the Caliph enthroned. On the south wall the enemies of Islam—Chosroes of Persia, the Byzantine emperor, the Negus of Abyssinia, and Roderick the Visigoth—are pictured. Other walls are painted with hunting and pleasure scenes. The Baths, too, are elaborately decorated. On the ceiling of the steam room is one of the earliest zodiac representations in Islamic art. The rooms at the back of the left and right halls have lovely mosaic floors.

Adjacent to the building is a large cistern and well which once supplied water for the lodge.

Azraq: 60 miles east of Amman; about 20 miles east of Qasr Amra

In olden days the oasis of Azraq was strategic: it was the only oasis in the eastern desert, and it guarded the northern end of the caravan route through Wadi Sirhan, lying north-south along the western edge of the Arabian desert.

The castle of Azraq, a somber structure of black basalt, is now no more than the shell of what once must have been an imposing fortress. Its front gate is made of one huge black stone. Inscriptions date the fort to the time of Aziz ed-din Aybaq, who was governor of the area in the early 13th century. Other inscriptions, however, indicate that there were earlier Roman and Byzantine structures on the site. Since the Nabataeans used Wadi Sirhan as their main thoroughfare, authorities suggest that even earlier fortifications existed in the area. Here, as in Umm el Jimal, the use of basalt stone shows how man adapted to the lack of wood in the desert.

Because of its plentiful water from spring-fed pools and marshes, Azraq must have been a favorite of the Umayyads and desert tribes down through the centuries, especially for hunting of birds. It is in the migratory path of hundreds of species of birds traveling between Europe and Africa each spring and summer. The area has been made a National Wildlife Sanctuary by the Jordan government.

Perhaps no one made better use of Azraq than T. E. Lawrence, who in his *Seven Pillars of Wisdom* described it as a "luminous, silky Eden." Modern travelers might find that a bit of an exaggeration, but Lawrence apparently loved the place, and used it as his headquarters during the final assault of the Arabs against the Turks in World War I. The room above the Arabic inscription near the entrance was his headquarters—reached now by a perilous stairway. Like all the castle, it is in a ruinous state, with fallen rafters from the roof and gaping holes in the walls. The upper level looks out on the lava-strewn desert in one direction and marshes in the other.

Azraq is a strange mix. There are two villages, one near the fort, one on the marshes. One is Druze, one is Shishani. The new highway to Saudi Arabia has brought a steady stream of traffic through an area that only a few years ago was a remote corner of the desert; today its character is changing rapidly.

The marshes of Azraq are the only permanent body of water in 12,000 square miles of desert, and hence, draw thousands of birds on migration. An expedition that included Julian Huxley counted 188 different species in one week during the migration season.

Although the Jordan desert has lost almost all its native birds and animals, as late as 1900 there were roe deer, antelope, wild ass, bear, cheetah, ibex, oryx, and herds of gazelle. Today there are only a few foxes and wolves here and there. However, if the scheme instituted by the government is successful, some day the animals natural to this area may roam the land again.

South of Azraq is the Shaumari Wildlife Reserve in the Azraq National Park, watched over by the Royal Jordanian Society for the Conservation of Nature. In the spring of 1978, four young male Arabian oryx, all born at the San Diego Wild Animal Park, were re-introduced here. It was the first return of this rare antelope to the Middle East under a project known as Operation Oryx, begun 20 years ago when international organizations united to save the species from extinction by capturing the few remaining animals in the wild.

About halfway between Amman and Azraq and only a few miles off the main highway is **Qasr Hallabat,** converted by the Umayyads into a defense post and pleasure retreat from earlier buildings of the Nabataeans, Romans and Byzantines. The original structure was probably built by the Nabataeans as a defense tower against desert raiders, and later enlarged by the Romans. After some rebuilding by Emperor Justinian in the sixth century, it served as a monastery. Most of the ruins are Roman, and only scattered carvings remain from the Nabataean period. The Department of Antiquities, under the direction of Dr. Ghazi Bisheh, has been excavating here since 1980 and is attempting partial restorations. Dr. Bisheh has uncovered beautiful mosaics dating from the Ummayyed Period and earlier Greek inscriptions.

The hunting lodge and baths of **Hammam al Sarah** are located two miles east of Hallabat. These have been partially rebuilt. The desert road from Azraq to Amman joins the main highway near Zerqa, about 15 miles north of Amman.

THE BIRDS OF AZRAQ

The following is based on an article by J.B. Nelson *which appeared in the magazine* Jordan. *It is included here for the benefit of amateur birdwatchers, ornithologists, and readers whose interest might be sparked by knowing more about the great variety of birds to be seen at Azraq at certain times of the year.*

Of the three migratory routes between Africa and Europe, the favored one has always been through Jordan, a crossroads for birds and other animals long before it became so for man. In the spring and autumn particularly, hordes of migrant birds flood through the country, stopping to rest and feed in the wide oasis of Azraq. The variety is wonderfully rich, and at the height of a season more than 200 species can be sighted.

Viewed from the top of Jebel Aseikhim, where the ruins of a Roman castle now stand, the landscape is a delicately sculptured, subtly colored desert stretching out on all sides. Distantly, to the southwest, lies the vast Azraq depression—the Qa'. In spring the glint of its pools, the cool green of its meadows and marshes and the security of its trees and bushes beckon the high-flying birds. Here food, water, shelter and rest may spell the difference between life or death, particularly to the smaller creatures, despite their capability for astonishing flights across deserts and oceans.

From March to May, from the continent of Africa, they move north, pausing for hours, days or weeks at Azraq—warblers, swallows, flycatchers, chats, bee-eaters, rollers, wagtails, waders, ibises, storks, cranes, herons, falcons, eagles, hawks, and many others. The ducks, which flock to Azraq in such numbers as to make this one of the world's foremost duck marshes, are also moving back to their Asian breeding haunts. In autumn, from August to November, all this will be reserved. But in spring, the pageantry is remarkable—many of the birds come through in full nuptial dress, the males in glorious plumage.

A list of the birds to be seen in a day at Azraq can hardly begin to describe, much less convey, the feeling of beauty one can experience in this unusual oasis. For those fortunate enough to visit Azraq for more than a quick sightseeing tour, there are three expeditions to make—at the end of April, in June and in January. It is a fascinating drama, full, varied and unforgettable—as much to the amateur birdwatcher as it is to the seasoned ornithologist.

If you can spend an April night in Azraq, strike out in the glorious early morning light, with the marsh glowing behind the Shishan Mosque and the tamarisk groves. Beyond, the brown Qa', beginning to dry, sweeps boldly toward the horizon and in the far distance, rising gradually from southeast to northwest, the barren hills lead on to Jebel Druze and Syria. In the marsh behind the pools, reed, marsh and Savi's warblers are singing and will nest, but the willow warblers, chiffchaffs, lesser whitethroats, blackcaps, garden warblers, and many others feed silently and will move on.

Today happens to be a "shrike day." Hundreds of these "butcher birds" dot the bushes—masked, red-backed, in varied grays. You may see the remains of a willow warbler impaled on a sharp twig, the shrike's larder. Now you realize that, although you cannot see huge flocks of birds anywhere, the whole area is in fact alive with them. Down in the cultivated patches are beautiful ortolan and black-headed buntings, with scores of nondescript tree pipits and a gaudy hoopoe excitedly fanning its crest. A collared flycatcher darts out and returns to its perch, and hundreds of sand martins and swallows hawk for insects. A nightjar, cryptic brown and long in wing and tail, darts up from cover and twists away, while a cuckoo that may later charm an English copse flies off swiftly, reminding one of a hawk. A wryneck, whose English name stems from its habit of twisting its head around, was ringed at Azraq and recovered ten days later in Russia.

Walking along the canal, you approach reed-filled lagoons where squacco herons, egrets, and storks are feeding on the abundant marsh frogs. Where there is mud and shallow water, you may have to puzzle out rare waders like broad-billed sandpipers among the more easily recognized stilts, avocets, green sandpipers, etc.. Among them run a bewildering variety of wagtails, for the many races of the yellow wagtail group, breeding in Asia and Russia, pass through Azraq. Water and red-throated pipits also like wet ground and will probably be there too. You will not fail to notice two or three marsh harriers quartering the reeds, and a smart gray male hen harrier or a pallid harrier may delight you.

Out on the Qa' proper you have a strange sense of spaciousness from the far shimmer of the flat sand stretches around you. A flock of short-toed larks feed on apparently bare ground, and scores of Kentish plovers sprint around you at high speed. If you have two or three hours in hand you can skirt the marshes and re-enter the nearby Druze village. On the way you will pass dozens of miniature lakes, very shallow but full of life, and much loved by storks, herons and waders, not to mention rarer visitors such as flamingoes, pelicans, gulls, terns, and kingfishers.

A June expedition, to be enjoyed, should be early or late in the day when it is cooler. Most of the birds you will see now are breeding here in Azraq. Though most are difficult to find, there are about 60 different breeding species to look for. The marshes hold little bitterns, two or three kinds of rail or crake—small birds that run rapidly and secretively among the reeds—and marsh harriers. On the dry islands exotic blue-checked bee-eaters nest, gleaming bright green as they chase insects. In the summer heat, the Qa' is bone dry; even the lagoons where the duck shooters spread their decoys are shrinking or gone, and soon Bedouin tents will sit where the ducks and coot dabbled. Pratincoles and plovers are nesting on the dry edges, and there are crested larks everywhere. Depending on the year and the level of water, you may find avocets and stilts nesting. Bush chats and desert wheatears are conspicuous in the dry area, and in the hot desert beyond the oasis life is far from absent. An astonishing array of larks and wheatears manage to breed, sometimes even among the shiny black basalt boulders which stretch for miles and become blistering hot in summer. On sandier ground, coursers make their nesting scrapes, and in a very few favored areas houbara bustards still survive.

A winter visit to Azraq also has its rewards. In January the tamarisks glow orange and the reeds have turned brown. The water has risen again, and vast areas of wet mud and shallow lagoons shine on the Qa'. Hordes of duck have appeared, and it is the season for hunting. Teal, by the thousands or tens of thousands, feed in the rich ooze; solid masses of elegant pintails rest far out, or feed in the shallow water with wigeon, shoveler, mallard and others. Deeper water, in the heart of the swamp, may yield diving ducks—tufted, pochard, ferruginous. The hunters may bring home some rare items—perhaps a falcated teal, a red-crested pochard, or even a cormorant, which should never have been shot at all. The winter sunlight is incredibly pure and lovely.

* * *

People who make the desert castle tour often plan to stop at Azraq for a picnic lunch. A shaded area by the oasis spring on the far side of Azraq village is the best place to enjoy a picnic.

On the left of the road, about a mile before the fort of Azraq, a secondary road leads to the Government Rest House which has a swimming pool with cabana-type rooms around it, and a large dining room in a large separate building.

WEST OF AMMAN

The Jordan Valley

Two main roads lead from Amman to the Jordan Valley. Either is a delightful drive through the ancient hills of Biblical history. From these heights of 2,500 feet above sea level the road descends to the lowest spot on the surface of the earth. Watch for a sign by the side of the road that marks the sea level point. Don't be alarmed if you feel dizzy or if your ears crackle from the sudden pressure. A few minutes' exposure to fresh air is all you need to make the adjustment.

As the road winds out of the Biblical wilderness into the valley, you see the Jordan River and the green valley floor stretching to the north and the silvery waters of the Dead Sea sprawling to the south. Here, in an area of ten square miles, are concentrated some of the world's most important sites of antiquity and Biblical history.

The Jordan River is only 200 miles long and less than a mile wide. It has no large cities on its shores. Yet, as the place of Jesus' baptism, the river has an immeasurable significance to Christians throughout the world. Visitors are often disappointed by the size of the Jordan, having imagined it as wide and majestic. Undoubtedly in Joshua's day the river was wider. Today, it would be easy to ford the stream in many places. But in Biblical times a miracle was required to roll back the waters so the people could cross by the Prophet's command.

Although there are no cities on the river now, archaeologists believe its banks were the site of the earliest communal life of man. The Cities of the Plain were in the Jordan Valley, possibly at the mouth of the river. Authorities say that volcanic activity around 2000 B.C. completely changed the landscape of the valley.

The main source of the river springs from a grove on Mount Hermon, long considered sacred by the ancients. After leaving the little grove the stream drops through a basalt gorge for six miles until the waters enter Lake Tiberias, or the Sea of Galilee (600 feet below sea level). From Galilee the waters flow south through the Ghor region and finally empty into the Dead Sea. Several tributaries enter the mainstream as it winds slowly through the Jordan Valley. A narrow floor of rich earth borders the river from Lake Tiberias to the Dead Sea, and is known in Arabic as al-Ghor.

The Jordan Valley is the northern strip of the Great Rift, a deep and massive depression in the earth's surface that extends as far south as Mozambique in Africa.

Although the east valley narrows to a width of 2.5 miles in some places, it stretches to a flatland almost 10 miles wide as it approaches the Dead Sea. Here, the perennial dream of making the desert bloom has become a reality. Al-Ghor is Jordan's natural greenhouse. The climate is almost tropical with long, hot, dry summers and mild, briefly wet winters when rainfall averages between 3 and 16 inches. In this climate, crops ripen two months ahead of those in surrounding countries of the Middle East.

Annual production in the east valley has reached over 330 million pounds of tomatoes, 44 million pounds of cucumbers, 110 million pounds of melons, and 36 million pounds of citrus fruits. The area that generates most of this output is a modest 30,000 irrigated acres, a fraction of the 23,650,000 acres that Jordan encompasses. But that is only the beginning. Adjoining the land now being cultivated are an additional 62,500 arable acres waiting only for water. Here the government has set its highest priority, and has built dams, canals, and irrigation systems and upgraded farming techniques. Through these improvements Jordan hopes to be self-supporting in food by the end of the decade.

Already farmers are growing enough vegetables and fruits in the valley to send tons of it to countries throughout the area. To keep pace with demand, some farmers are growing many crops in mini-greenhouses of plastic that lie in long, low tent rows across the fields. The method has revolutionized output, and it increased production sevenfold the first year it was introduced.

In addition to the major crops of tomatoes and cucumbers, there are oranges, lemons, pomegranates, honeydews, cantaloupes, radishes, bananas, plums, cauliflower, green peppers, cabbages, olives, wheat, corn, lentils, and beans. At present there are two growing seasons for most crops, but al-Ghor has the potential for three crops a year with its hothouse climate and expanded irrigation.

Since ancient times the Ghor has been one of the richest areas of the Levant. According to the Bible, the vegetation was as dense and impenetrable as a jungle. Lion, wild boar, wolves, and leopards roamed the river's shores: "Behold, he shall come up like a lion from the swelling of Jordan against the habitation of the strong" (Jer. 49:19). But over the centuries the land was denuded and neglected, and ultimately nature made it a wasteland. Now, it needs help.

Jordan began its first major development project to bring the valley under cultivation three decades ago with the Yarmuk River Irrigation Scheme. Despite repeated setbacks, a great deal was accomplished.

The 66-mile-long East Ghor Canal is now the vital bypass artery of the river. Built in stages over the past 25 years, it begins at the Yarmuk River in the north and extends to the Dead Sea. During most of its course, the canal is only slightly to the east of and parallel to the Jordan River. Along the route of the canal there are dams and waterways to collect and divert into it the waters of the Jordan's tributaries. In turn, the East Ghor artery sends out smaller canals to reach farmlands along the way.

Four dams have been built and are in service; others are being constructed or planned. The $35-million King Talal Dam, the newest, was completed in 1977. It has brought the waters of the Zerqa River into the canal to begin irrigating an additional 15,000 acres of new prime land in the valley. The dam is also providing power to generate 5,000 kilowatts of electricity for valley residents, and eventually will supply fresh water to the Amman region.

The government's grand plan for the valley gives equal priority to human needs. Before the 1967 war, there were 100,000 people living in the valley. By 1970 that number had diminished to 3,000, who lived in the constant insecurity of a military zone. In recent years, encouraged by growing stability and the accelerated efforts of the government, thousands have returned.

As irrigated areas are expanded and more people are needed to farm them, the government hopes to entice them to the valley by good incomes, new housing, and full community facilities. Schools, health centers, a social community center, and housing complexes have been designed specifically to attract the teachers, doctors, nurses, and other professionals required to run these facilities.

The government agency in charge is the Jordan Valley Development Authority (JVDA). Now, it has turned its attention to a massive rural development program to provide farmers with the amenities of a good life. The program includes:

—Thirty-six communities to range in size and services from four primary to eight secondary to 24 tertiary settlements throughout the valley, all with an equitable distribution of drinking water, electricity, and telecommunications.

—Nine educational zones, structured to provide all children with easy access to free schooling from primary through high school. JVDA is designing, building, and equipping the schools, then turning them over to the Ministry of Education to staff and operate.

—Health services that include emergency health posts in small settlements, resident doctors and maternity and child care in secondary communities, and hospital facilities in the four major towns.

—Long-term low-interest mortgages, available from public funds to low-income groups for housing. The estimate is that 24,000 new units will be required over the next several years, and the government wants to facilitate private home-building.

—A land-redistribution law under which the government is buying up large tracts of land that it has irrigated. It permits the owner to retain 20 percent, and resells the other 80 percent in small holdings with long-term payment facilities. It wants eventually to divide all land holdings in the valley so that no one farmer may own more than 50 acres of irrigated land.

JVDA is also helping farmers boost production and get higher income from their crops. It runs training programs in the valley to teach new irrigation and farming techniques. It has set up, as well, the Jordan Valley Farmers Association, whose membership includes all the farmers in the valley, with an executive committee of 15 members, ten elected by the farmers and five appointed by the government.

The Farmers Association imports and distributes to farmers the equipment they need—seeds, fertilizers, tools, and machinery. Another responsibility is grading and packing agricultural produce and then marketing it domestically and in foreign markets. To handle this operation JVDA has four centers in the central Ghor region.

Under this cooperative arrangement, all revenues return to the farmers. The Association also stands as a gilt-edged guarantor to any farmer seeking a loan; it can secure him quick credit with no other collateral than the potential produce of his land.

To accomplish all this, from dams to roads to housing, schools and public facilities, more than $250 million has been spent in the past several years. Most of the money has come from international funds and from Arab, American, and European aid.

It is an exciting development for Jordan and one that visitors can enjoy, too. The drive down to the heart of the valley can be combined with a picnic outing. It takes only an hour on the road northwest of Amman past Salt to the middle stretch of Highway 45 and Deir Alla, where every day (except Friday) is farmers' market day. Here you will find large quantities of freshly picked fruits and vegetables for a picnic or pictures.

Historic Sites

Deir Alla, which means House of God, is the site of an ancient sanctuary overlooking the green fields of the Jordan Valley. Scholars who have excavated the site have found evidence which they believe is potentially so important it could cause the rewriting of history—or at least provide an alternate interpretation from the one on which so much of our history is based.

The tell, which is a square approximately 600 feet on all sides, was first excavated by a Dutch expedition under Dr. H.J. Franken, Director of the Department of Palestinian Archeology at the University of Leiden. It was found to be from the late Bronze Age, c. 1500 to 1200 B.C., and the Iron Age, c. 1200 to 500 B.C., and much later a medieval Arab settlement.

On the northern slope of the tell the earliest settlers artificially heightened a temple mound on which to set their sanctuary—one that was so awesome, apparently, that it did not need protecting from the warring tribes of the valley, for there was no wall around it and no dwelling near it. The temple was active from the 16th to the 12th centuries B.C. In 1200 B.C., a date verified by an Egyptian faience vase bearing the cartouche of Queen Taouset found on the sanctuary floor, the temple was destroyed by an earthquake. It was abandoned and not rebuilt.

The site retained its character as a holy place, however, through the Iron Age, when remains of a large building with a different character appear. Here, many fragments of ritual vessels, particularly incense burners, were found. At the end of the second Iron Age the tell was abandoned for an unknown length of time. From artifacts discovered, it seems to have had a Persian settlement down to 330 B.C., and then was completely abandoned for centuries. During the medieval Arab era it was used as a cemetery by villagers who lived to the east of it.

In 1964 Dr. Franken came upon three clay tablets, inscribed in an unknown writing. The first tablet was in good condition. Its text was clearly incised in clay and divided into two registers, upper and lower, with dividing lines between the words. There are nine groups of letters. The second and third tablets are less well preserved. The third has lost its upper register, but the lower is complete and six words have been preserved.

Seven other tablets that bear mysterious dots in groups and series were also found. The writings are in an unknown type of alphabetic script, some letters having a likeness to the Phoenician Byblos script of Ahiram, others resembling a South Semitic writing.

An Aramaic text of the 7th century B.C. found written on a large fragment of plaster from a mud brick wall is very important. It speaks of a prophet named Bileam, son of Bear, as the head authority of the Deir Alla sanctuary. After studying the text, Dr. Franken declared that it conforms the archeological theory that Deir Alla was a sanctuary completely independent of the ancient Hebrew religion and of Hebrew cultural and political influence during the period of the Judean Kingdom.

In this region there seems to be an ancient site of historical or biblical significance at every turn in the road. **Tulul edh Dhahab,** the hills of gold, might be Phanuel, where Jacob struggled with the angel, according to the German Evangelic Institute, which has surveyed the site. **Tell Hajjaj** is thought to be Mahanaim, where David fled when his son Absalom revolted. **Tell Amta** is Amathus, one of the towns of Perea and apparently an important place in ancient times. **Tell es-Saidiyeh** is thought to be Zaretan or Zarethan, where the waters of the Jordan stood still while the Israelites crossed over (Jos. 3:16). The site was excavated in 1964 by James Pitchard of the University of Pennsylvania, and subsequent teams have worked here. It was occupied from the early Bronze Age through about 700 B.C.

At **Tell Mazar,** also from the Bronze Age, the University of Jordan and the Department of Antiquities has been excavating, trying to discover the relationship between the different ancient communities that were located in the area, and at the same time to give students at the university as well as foreign ones the experience of working on a dig. Upstream on the Wadi el Yabis, **Tell el Maqlub** has been identified as Abel-Meholah, the home of the prophet Elisha, where he was visited by Elijah.

Approximately 18 miles north of Deir Alla at Mashari a road on the right leads about two miles to the site of ancient **Pella,** one of the major cities of the Decapolis and the city to which early

Christians fled from persecution in Jerusalem in the 2nd century A.D.

In January 1979, Wooster College in Ohio and the University of Sydney in Australia together with the Jordan Department of Antiquities, began a 10-year project to excavate the site. When completed this year it is expected to be as extensive as Jerash.

Pella was named after the birthplace of Alexander the Great in Greece; locally it is known as Tabaqat Fahil. From excavations already completed at the site, archaeologists have established the fact that the area was inhabited as early as the Neolithic period around 5,000 B.C. and was continuously occupied in every major historical period down to the 14th century A.D. It was first mentioned in history in Egyptian texts of the 19th century B.C. by the name of Pihilum.

The ruins which have been uncovered and reconstructed to date are from the Greco-Roman period and include temples and a small theater of the 1st century A.D.

Pella reached its greatest size in the Byzantine period and had its own bishop as early as A.D. 451. The Bishop of Pella title remained in use in both the Roman and Eastern churches long after the site of Pella was lost to the Western World. The Byzantine period ended with the Arab conquest in 635, after which the city declined. Except for brief periods of occupation in the 12th and 13th centuries, the site was not occupied again until the last century.

Eventually researchers hope to reconstruct the history of Pella and understand its importance in the cultural, political and economic context of the region.

The valley road continues north to Adasiya on the Yarmuk or branches north east to Irbid. The valley road also continues south to meet a second road from Salt, which extends across a bridge to Jericho on the west bank of the river (it is not used by tourists).

Salt is the administrative center of the Balqa district, the second largest in the country, which extends from the Zerqa River to the Dead Sea. Salt has served as Jordan's capital several times in its history, and dates back to the Iron Age. A site nearby at **Tell Jadur** is said to be Gadara, capital of Perea at the time of Christ (but not the same as the Gadara of the Decapolis).

The road south of Salt leads to many sites that have been identified with the Old Testament—the Plains of Moab, Beth Nimrah near the village of Tell Nimrin, and Tell Bileibil. Tell ar-Rama, which is Liviasi, may have been Beth-Haram.

At **Tuleitat Ghusul** (Teleilat Ghassul), recent discoveries identify it as one of the oldest sites in the Jordan Valley. Wall frescos were found that have been carbon-tested to be 6,000 years old, and may be the second oldest in the world. An Australian archeological team headed by Professor Basil Hennessy, under the auspices of the Jordanian Department of Antiquities, completed its final season of excavations at the site in 1978.

The paintings, which decorate the walls of an early Chalcolithic building, are rendered in strong colors of red, white, yellow, and black. The frescos depict a group of figures standing before what is thought to be a religious shrine. The paintings are being restored by experts from UNESCO's School of Conservation in Rome.

South of the main road to Jerusalem is Suweimeh, located approximately a mile northeast of the Dead Sea. A road leads to the sea.

The Dead Sea

The Dead Sea, 1,306 feet below sea level, is the lowest spot on the earth's surface. In Arabic it is called Bahr Lut, the "Sea of Lot." The sea, 46 miles long and three to ten miles wide, has no outlet. By day it is silvery blue, and by night it glistens in the moonlight. The Dead Sea is a scenic oddity unique in the world. For miles around, arid hills eroded by wind form a silent moonscape that is at once eerie and beautiful.

The heavy salt content (33 percent) of the water makes animal life impossible, and makes swimming an unusual experience. It is almost impossible to sink. You can lie on your back in the water and read a magazine. When divers were searching for the sites of Sodom and Gomorrah, their suits had to have special weights to keep them from bobbing to the surface. You can be photographed having a cup of coffee or reading a newspaper as you float on top. You'll need a shower when it's over, because you will come out of the water with a nice, itchy coat of salt.

At Suweimeh there is a beach park with over a mile of seafront. Here there are facilities for a day's seaside outing—dressing rooms, indoor and outdoor showers, picnic area, and snack bar. The Dead Sea Beach Club has a restaurant. There are also cottages with kitchenettes, if you want to stay overnight. Sunset or moonlight on the Dead Sea is an extra bonus. If you want to avoid crowds, do not go on Fridays and Sundays.

In this region the effort to make the desert bloom is being followed by the even more colossal project of harnessing the power of the sun. A huge solar evaporation system is recovering 1.2 million metric tons of potash a year from the Dead Sea. Located at Safi at the southern end of the Sea, it is a joint effort of the Arab Potash Company and Jacobs Engineering Group of Pasadena, California. The $425 million project is the largest in the history of Jordan and one of the most complex and challenging of its kind undertaken anywhere. It makes Jordan one of the world's primary sources of potash, and at the same time potash is a major source of foreign exchange for Jordan. Potash is a key ingredient in the production of fertilizer, which in turn is vital to meet the growing food needs of the world. The mineral has been known since Biblical days when it was used as a fertilizer and in the making of soap.

The project was completed in three stages. The initial phase included field testing of the solar evaporation process, construction analysis of test dikes, and processing of test samples of potash in a pilot plant. The second phase included the construction of an elaborate network of evaporation ponds and dikes and related facilities. The third and final phase involved building the processing plant and the actual production and marketing of potash.

About 25,000 acres of dikes and manmade ponds covering 40 square miles were constructed at the southernmost end of the Dead Sea. The facility pumps 1.2 million tons of brine daily through a six-mile-long canal leading into a network of evaporation ponds. It has been estimated that 1.25 billion gallons of fuel oil a year would have to be burned to achieve the same results by conventional methods.

A refinery plant near Safi is fed with the coarse potash salts through a floating pipeline. After being purified and dried at the plant, the potash is hauled by truck along the newly constructed road from Safi to Aqaba, from where it is shipped to its world markets.

Safi is accessible from Kerak as well as by the new road, which runs through the Wadi Aqaba to Gharandal, Tel Khalifa, and thence to Aqaba. Another road from the north end of the Dead Sea connects with the new road at Safi. Completion of this project has given Jordan three parallel north-south highways: the Jordan Valley–Dead Sea–Wadi Araba; the Irbid–Jerash King's Highway; and the Mafraq/Azraq–Zerka Desert Highway.

THE WEST BANK

Jordan's Fertile Acres

The area west of the Jordan River, which became part of Jordan in 1950 and is known as the West Bank, has been under Israeli military occupation since the war of 1967. In order to cross the Jordan River to the West Bank visitors must follow the procedures detailed in Facts at Your Fingertips. *Over the past year Israeli military authorities have frequently banned travel in the West Bank. You must inquire locally. In any event, travel in a group organized by a U.S. or British tour operator or local travel agency is preferable to independent travel at this time.*

Jericho. Twenty-two miles east of Jerusalem, 853 feet below sea level

Jericho (*Ariha* in Arabic) and its surrounding area is one of the oldest continuously inhabited sites in the world. On a mount overlooking the Jericho oasis, excavations have uncovered settlements dating from 9000 B.C. and the oldest walled town (7000 B.C.) yet discovered.

Here, in the digs at **Tel-es-Sultan,** many layers of ancient civilizations are visible, all predating Joshua's attack, when he blew his horn and the "walls came tumbling down" (probably about 1250 B.C.). In the center of the site a massive, round, Neolithic defense tower dating from before 7000 B.C. has been cleared to bedrock. The original entrance to the oldest known stairs in the world is exposed. For details of the site, see K. Kenyon, *Digging Up Jericho.* (The late Miss Kenyon was the archeologist in charge of the excavations that uncovered the tower.) Tel-es-Sultan is open daily from 8 A.M. to 5 P.M.

In Roman times, Jericho was a garden of fruit and palm trees, from which considerable revenue was derived. Mark Antony presented it as a gift to Cleopatra—and what a magnificent gift!

Jericho reached its peak under Herod the Great. His winter palace and new town were located south of present-day Jericho along Wadi al-Qilt, the Valley of the Shadow of Death in the 23rd Psalm. From the old road from Jericho to Jerusalem a road on the north leads down the ancient Roman road into the Wadi. In Biblical times shepherds led their sheep down the Wadi in autumn and came back up in spring. The danger of flash-floods made the route treacherous.

It was on a street in Jericho that Jesus healed the blind beggar. Later he was entertained at the house of Zaccheus the publican. Byzantines, Arabs, and Crusaders also came to Jericho and left their mark.

Elisha's Fountain. The main water spring of the oasis is at the foot of Tel-es-Sultan. Tradition says it is the fountain that Prophet Elisha sweetened by casting a handful of salt into it (2 Kings 3:21).

Mount of Temptation. West of Jericho and overlooking the Jordan Valley is the wilderness where Jesus spent 40 days and nights fasting, and the mountain where Satan tempted him "and showeth him all the kingdoms of the world, and the glory of them; and saith unto him, all these things will I give thee, if thou wilt fall down and worship me" (Matt. 4:8-9).

The path to the top of the mountain is very steep, and passes by a Greek Orthodox monastery perched on one of the cliffs.

The road between Jericho and Jerusalem traverses the Wilderness of Judah, one of the most starkly beautiful landscapes that can be imagined. The muted pastels of the baked, barren hills rolling away as far as the eye can see are hauntingly lovely.

As you come from Jerusalem, elevation markers on the side of the road pace your descent. Even after you pass the one saying "Sea Level," you note that there's still a long way down . . . and the Dead Sea shimmers far below to your right.

The road forks, and Jericho is to the north; the other road continues to the Jordan River and the Dead Sea. A small road to the south leads to Nebi Musa (the Prophet Moses), which Moslems believed was the site of the prophet's tomb. The Bible, though, tells us that Moses' tomb is "unknown to this day" but lies somewhere in the Mountains of Moab. Tradition has placed it on Mt. Nebo, where it is marked by a chapel dating from the 5th century.

Hisham Palace. Three miles north of Jericho at Khirbet al-Mafjar, the palace was a country residence, probably built by the Umayyad Caliph Hisham Ibn Abdul Malik (A.D. 724–743). It is open daily from 8 A.M. to 5 P.M. Hisham, like most of the early Arab rulers, preferred the freedom of the desert to the city life of Damascus, their capital. The palace is a complex of buildings, baths, mosques, and colonnaded courts. Its mosaics and stucco ornaments are fine examples of Umayyad art and architecture.

Experts say an earthquake destroyed the buildings before they were completed. Thus the accumulated sand and debris helped to preserve the palace's lovely mosaics.

The mosaic floors of the baths are the major attraction for visitors. The Tree of Life (also called the Tree of Human Cruelty) is one of the most beautiful mosaics in the world. In the same room another mosaic pictures a Persian rug, complete with tassels.

Many of the carved stuccos from the palace are displayed at the Rockefeller Archeological Museum in Jerusalem.

In the Jordan valley east of Jericho is the farm of the Arab Development Society. It was the first of its kind, founded in the late 1940s by Oxford-educated Musa al-Alami. The Society has given life, hope, and education to hundreds of children orphaned by the Arab-Israeli wars. The farm is fed from underground wells, and its high-quality products are sold throughout the area.

For the Christian world the most important site on the Jordan is **Makhad al-Hajla** (the Ford of the Partridge), six miles from Jericho, where tradition says John baptized Jesus. For centuries pilgrims have come to this peaceful, shaded bend in the river, and many take home water from the sacred spot. Water from the Jordan is used for baptisms in churches around the world. There are several churches near the spot, the most distinctive being the Greek Monastery of St. John. A special service of blessing the water is held annually on Epiphany Sunday.

It should be noted that, although the tradition has placed the site of Jesus' baptism here, there is considerable question in the minds of biblical scholars as to its accuracy. Eugene Hoade's *Guide to Jordan* devotes considerable space to the site on the east bank that he believes to be the correct one, based on reports of early pilgrims and, of course, the text of the Bible. It is northeast of the Hussein Bridge in the Wadi Kharrar, which is the site of Bethania *(Bethany)* beyond the Jordan. Hoade writes: "These things were done in Betania beyond the Jordan, where John was baptising" (John 1.28). "The site of the crossing of the Israelites under Joshua is fixed at the same place as the Baptism of Jesus, and it is certainly the most probable of the fords suggested. The place is directly opposite Jericho and the land on both sides of the ford is more suitable than elsewhere for the crossing of a big number."

Khirbet Qumran and the Dead Sea Scrolls. Fourteen miles south of Jericho

The story of the Dead Sea Scrolls began in 1947, when, by accident, a Bedouin found several scrolls in clay jars hidden in a cave on a rocky cliff high above the Dead Sea. After the sensational discovery, Bedouin and archeologists, aided by the Jordan Department of Antiquities, searched every hole in these desolate hills and turned up one of the most exciting discoveries of modern times: Biblical manuscripts 2000 years old, predating by some 1000 years the earliest known Hebrew text of the Old Testament. Also among the finds were books of an unknown religious community, identified as the Essenes, a pre-Christian, mystical Jewish sect mentioned in ancient writings. The discoveries were important as verification of Biblical text and for the study of Biblical history. The writings in these scrolls covered a period of 300 years, including the birth of Christ. Thus they have unveiled part of the background on which the teachings of Christ and the early Christian church were based.

An Essene community lived in caves and dwellings at a site known as Khirbet Qumran (the ruins of Qumran), one of the world's most ancient "monasteries." Under strict rules of obedience and high ethical standards set down in their Manual of Disciplines, the "brothers" spent their lives studying the Holy Writ and praying for the coming of the Messiah.

At Khirbet Qumran the oldest ruins are a cistern and a square building that date from the 8th century B.C. At this time the site was probably a fortress. Apparently it was deserted for a long period until the Essenes came in the late 2nd century B.C.

The Essenes first erected small buildings around the earlier ruins. Later they expanded as the community grew. To cope with the problem of water on the waterless hilltop, an aqueduct was built to bring captured rainwater from nearby Wadi Qumran. Visitors will notice the large numbers of cisterns at the ancient site. Some were probably used for ritual ablution—a rule of the community.

In what was the upper story of a building, excavators found long, narrow tables and benches along the walls and two large inkwells. This, then, they concluded, was the very room in which the Essenes sat to write their now-famous scrolls. Excavations have also unearthed the ruins of a storehouse, a communal kitchen, workshops, the community bread oven, an assembly chamber, a pantry in which hundreds of bowls, dishes, plates, and jugs were found stacked in piles against the back wall, and a complete potter's workshop with a potter's wheel.

Experts believe the community fled the area during an earthquake in 31 B.C. After about 30 years they returned to repair their buildings and to settle again to a secluded life of prayer and study.

In A.D. 68 the settlement met an abrupt end. A Roman Legion en route to Jerusalem to put down the first Jewish Revolt destroyed it, and the members of the community fled after placing their precious manuscripts in the nearby caves for safekeeping. The site was not inhabited again except as a temporary hiding place during the second Jewish Revolt (A.D. 132). The settlement and its people were lost to history.

Among the thousands of scroll fragments that have already been identified, most of the books of the Old Testament are represented. The task of cataloguing and assembling the huge collection was entrusted to an international group of scholars. Other fragments have been found in caves at Wadi Murabbat about ten miles south of Qumran. These manuscripts include fragments from Genesis, Exodus, Deuteronomy, and Isaiah.

Displays of scroll fragments may be seen in the Archeological Museums in Amman and Jerusalem.

A road continues along the Dead Sea past 'Ayn Feshka to the southern end and to the Red Sea.

JERUSALEM

Shrine of Three Faiths

Few places in the world have commanded the devotion of so many people for so long a period as has Jerusalem. From your first day in the Holy City you will be awed by a sense of history and religious significance. Jerusalem is a city with a special destiny. Its effect on visitors is unique.

The origins of Jerusalem are lost in the remote past. Recent archeological excavations reveal that it is at least as old as the 15th century B.C. In Egyptian and Babylonian literature it is called Urusalimu. The first mention of it in the Bible is probably under the name of Salem, the city of Melchisedek, "Priest of the Most High God" (Gen. 15:18). It is afterwards referred to as Jebus. When David captured the Jebusite fortress of Zion, he made the city his capital and there placed the Ark.

Under Solomon the first great Temple was built upon Mount Moriah. After Nebuchadnezzar, King of Babylon, overran the city in 586 B.C., the Jews were taken into captivity. A half-century later Cyrus, King of Persia, allowed them to return and to rebuild the Temple and city on a modest scale. Among the city's subsequent conquerers were Alexander the Great in 332 B.C. and Antiochus Epiphanes in 168 B.C. Under the Maccabeans, and later the Herods,

173

Jerusalem was independent to a certain extent, although the Herodians were Roman vassals.

Under Herod the Great the Temple was rebuilt on a more grandiose scale and Jerusalem was enlarged and beautified. It was in the 36th year of his reign that Jesus Christ was born in Bethlehem.

Following a Jewish revolt in A.D. 70, the temple and city were destroyed by the Romans under Titus, son of the Emperor Vespasian. After a second revolt in A.D. 132, the Jews were expelled. On the ruins a pagan city was built by Emperor Hadrian and named Aeolia Capitolina.

In the 3rd century, under the reign of Constantine, Jerusalem became a Christian shrine. The Emperor's mother, Helena, ordered the construction of the Church of the Holy Sepulchre on the site she determined was the site of Christ's crucifixion. From established traditions, advice of the bishops and revelations in her dreams, Helena established a number of "official" sites connected with the life of Christ. These sites are still recognized today by most Christians. Some have been confirmed by archeological research; many have not, but all are hallowed by centuries of pilgrimage.

Early in the 7th century the city was sacked by the Persians, but by 637 the Arab armies had taken all the major towns from the Tigris to the Mediterranean, except Jerusalem, from the Byzantines. As they moved to take that city, the Greek Patriarch sent word that he would surrender Jerusalem without a struggle but only to the Caliph Umar in person.

As the story goes, Umar, who was in Damascus, hurried to the scene and entered Jerusalem alone, except for a servant. The priests mistook the servant for the caliph, much to Umar's amusement.

Once the confusion was cleared up, Umar asked the Patriarch to show him the city's holy places. He was led first to the Church of the Holy Sepulchre, where the Patriarch invited him to pray. Umar declined, saying that it might encourage his followers to convert the church into a mosque. Instead, he prayed outside. Today the spot is commemorated by a mosque in his name.

Umar offered the Byzantines the same treaty he had proferred to the Christians in Damascus. It stated that Umar "grants them security of their lives, their possessions, their churches, and crosses . . . they shall have freedom of religion and none shall be molested unless they rise up in a body . . . They shall pay a tax instead of military service . . . and those who leave the city shall be safeguarded until they reach their destination. . . ."

The religious tolerance established by Umar was continued by the Umayyads but deteriorated under later caliphs and disappeared under the Crusaders who captured Jerusalem in 1099. The European conquerors massacred most of the city's Muslims, burnt the small Jewish community in its synagogue, and slaughtered large numbers of the local Christians. They converted Muslim shrines to churches, including the Dome of the Rock.

A century later the Crusaders were driven out by the Arabs under Saladin, who restored the covenant of Umar. Jerusalem remained Arab for the next 800 years.

In 1517 the Ottoman Turks occupied Jerusalem, and governed the city until World War I, when it surrendered to the Allied troops under Allenby, the British commander. During the rule of Turkish Sultan Sulayman the Magnificent the present walls of the Old City were constructed in 1542.

After World War I, Jerusalem and Palestine were placed under British Mandate. When the British withdrew in 1948, hostilities broke out between the Jews and the Arabs. The United Nations Armistice line, drawn in 1949 as a result of this conflict, divided Jerusalem.

Following the war in 1967, Israel occupied all of Jerusalem and the West Bank of the Jordan. The area that had divided it from Israel, known as No Man's Land, has since been intensively built up with modern high-rise apartment buildings, greatly changing the timeless character of the area surrounding the ancient walled city. The area east of the old armistice line is known locally as East Jerusalem or Arab Jerusalem.

In this section of the book we will concentrate on East Jerusalem and the West Bank, where the majority of holy places are located, plus other sites and cities of particular religious significance. Travelers who are planning an extended visit can refer to *Fodor's Israel.*

THE OLD CITY OF JERUSALEM

Within an area of about one square mile of Old Jerusalem are concentrated some of the most important historical and religious shrines of the world's three great monotheistic religions, Judaism, Christianity, and Islam.

The Ancient Walls and Gates

The 16th-century walls that enclose the Old City contain eight gates: Jaffa (west), New (north), Damascus (north), Herod's (north), Lion's or St. Mary's or St. Stephen's (east), Golden (east), Dung (south), and Zion (south). The Golden Gate was closed by a Turkish governor in 1530. Legends say that the governor hoped to postpone the final judgment and the end of the world by closing the gate, which according to tradition would be the place of the last trumpet call and the resurrection of the dead.

Within the walls on the east and north are the Moslem quarters, containing the Haram esh-Sharif, or Dome of the Rock, the Aqsa Mosque, the Islamic Museum and the Wailing Wall. On the north and west are the Christian quarters, where the Church of the Holy

Sepulchre and the Via Dolorosa are located. The southwest contains the Armenian Quarter and the Jewish Quarter with the Wailing Wall.

Outside the present walls of the Old City on the south is the city of David, ancient Ophel. It is bounded on the east by the Valley of Kidron and on the south and west by the Valley of Hinnom, which meet at the Pool of Siloam. Opposite the east wall of the Old City is the Garden of Gethsemane on the slope of the Mount of Olives. Entering the Old City through the stately Lion's Gate will orient you best; the road leads directly into the Via Dolorosa and passes the main shrines.

Lion's, or St. Stephen's, Gate is the legendary site of the stoning of the martyr Stephen. It is also called Bab Sitti Miryam, or St. Mary's Gate, since several sites nearby are connected with the Virgin. The Crusaders named it the Gate of Jehoshaphat because it overlooked the valley of the same name. Many claim the present gate was built by the Crusaders because of its architecture. Others say the gate dates from the 16th century, citing as proof a tale about the Turkish Sultan Sulayman the Magnificent.

The Sultan dreamt he was being torn apart by four lions. When he asked for an explanation of the dream, a sheikh replied that the Sultan proposed to punish the inhabitants of Jerusalem for refusing to pay their taxes. The Sultan, intrigued by the dream and its explanation, made a pilgrimage to Jerusalem. There he was seized with an urge to do something for the city. As a result he had the walls rebuilt—and, as a reminder of the dream, he had the lions carved over the portals of the gate. One may walk along the top of the walls from Jaffa Gate to the New and Damascus gates from 9 A.M. to 4 P.M. There is an admission fee.

Al-Haram esh-Sharif, the Noble Sanctuary

On the left after entering St. Stephen's Gate is the sacred enclosure holding the Dome of the Rock and the Aqsa Mosque on the summit of Mount Moriah. It forms the southeast corner of the Old Walled City and was the site of the first and second Temples. The area with its colonnades and surrounding walls and gardens covers 30 acres. The site is associated with the Prophet Muhammed's nocturnal journey to Jerusalem on his visit to heaven. During his lifetime Muhammed faced Jerusalem while he prayed. Hence, the city was the first *qiblah* (the direction toward which Moslems face to pray) in Islam. The Rock acquired early sanctity in Moslem eyes and became second only to Mecca and Medina as a Moslem shrine.

Tradition holds that Mount Moriah is the site where Abraham prepared to sacrifice his son. Here at a later time Ornan (Araunah) the Jebusite had his threshing floor, which David bought and upon which he erected an altar. David's altar was superseded by Solomon's Temple, which was destroyed by Nebuchadnezzar in the 6th century B.C. A smaller temple was rebuilt by Zorobabel. On the same site Herod the Great built an enormous and splendid temple. Herod's temple was the one Jesus knew, and his prophecy of its destruction was fulfilled in A.D. 70 at the hands of the Romans. The lower course of the second temple on the southwest side came to be known as the Wailing or Western Wall after the temple's destruction by Titus in A.D. 70. After the second Jewish revolt Emperor Hadrian rebuilt Jerusalem and erected a temple dedicated to Jupiter on the site of the previous temples.

When Queen Helena, mother of Constantine, came to Jerusalem in the early 4th century she had all pagan shrines, including Hadrian's Temple on Mount Moriah, destroyed. The area was then abandoned because Christians believed it was cursed by God. Eventually it became the city's rubbish heap.

Early in the 7th century, when the Caliph Umar Ibn al-Khattab conquered Jerusalem, he helped clear with his own hands the accumulated refuse of centuries and had a simple mosque of wood built on the site. A half-century later the Umayyad Caliph Abdul Malik Ibn Marwan built the Dome of the Rock. It remains one of the most magnificent examples of Moslem architecture and one of the most beautiful monuments in the world.

The Dome has undergone reconstruction many times. The most extensive repairs were made in the early 1960s when King Hussein took a personal interest in its restoration. The gilded lead dome was removed altogether with its wooden supports and replaced by another made of gold-colored aluminum. The building's famous 16th-century tiles have been replaced with copies of the originals.

The focal point of the mosque is the Rock, from which Mohammed is said to have made his nocturnal visit to heaven. You can discern the spot from the railing around the Rock; there appears to be an imprint of a human foot. A small box near the footprint holds a few hairs of the Prophet. The cave dug into the Rock is called "The Well of Souls."

On the east side of the Dome of the Rock is the miniature Dome of the Chain, which is said to have been the model for the larger mosque.

South of the Dome, going through arched portals and past a large, ornamental fountain called El-Kas (The Cup), is the Mosque of al-Aqsa, built by Walid, son of Abdul Malik Ibn Marwan. Inside the mosque are some of the finest oriental rugs in the world. It was here that King Abdullah was assassinated in July 1951 as he was entering the mosque.

A curious legend attends two pillars standing cheek-by-jowl near the front of the mosque: those of the faithful who can squeeze through the space will also be able to pass through the gates of heaven. It's a pretty tight squeeze.

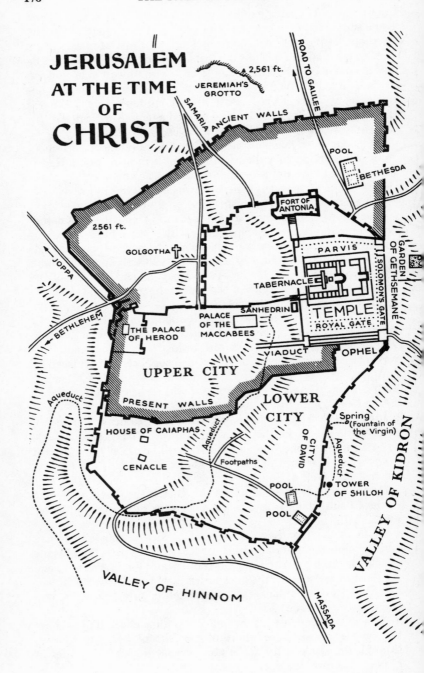

JERUSALEM
AT THE TIME
OF
CHRIST

2,561 ft.

JEREMIAH'S
GROTTO

SAMARIA   ANCIENT WALLS

ROAD TO GALILEE

POOL

BETH'ESDA

FORT OF
ANTONIA

2561 ft.

GOLGOTHA

PARVIS

JOPPA

TABERNACLE

SOLOMON'S GATE

GARDEN OF GETHSEMANE

SANHEDRIN

TEMPLE

BETHLEHEM

THE PALACE
OF HEROD

PALACE
OF THE
MACCABEES

ROYAL GATE

VIADUCT

OPHEL

UPPER CITY

LOWER
CITY

Spring
(Fountain of
the Virgin)

PRESENT WALLS

Aqueduct

HOUSE OF CAIAPHAS

Aqueduct

CITY
OF
DAVID

Aqueduct

VALLEY OF KIDRON

CENACLE

Footpaths

POOL

TOWER
OF SHILOH

POOL

VALLEY OF HINNOM

MASSADA

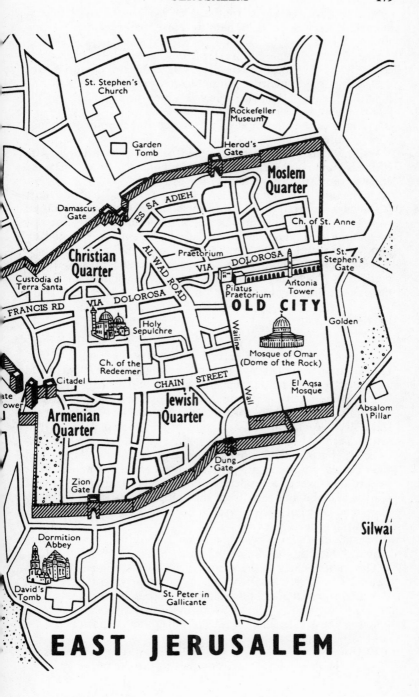

St. Stephen's Church

Rockefeller Museum

Garden Tomb

Herod's Gate

Moslem Quarter

ES SA ADIEH

Damascus Gate

Ch. of St. Anne

Christian Quarter

Praetorium

VIA DOLOROSA

St. Stephen's Gate

AL WAD ROAD

Custodia di Terra Santa

Pilatus Praetorium

Antonia Tower

FRANCIS RD

VIA DOLOROSA

OLD CITY

Holy Sepulchre

Golden

Wailing

Ch. of the Redeemer

Mosque of Omar (Dome of the Rock)

Citadel

CHAIN STREET

El Aqsa Mosque

ate ower

Jewish Quarter

Wall

Absalom Pillar

Armenian Quarter

Dung Gate

Zion Gate

Silwai

Dormition Abbey

David's Tomb

St. Peter in Gallicante

EAST JERUSALEM

Next to El-Aqsa on the southeast corner are the subterranean Stables of King Solomon. These were used later by the Romans and the Crusaders.

One of the eight gates of the Old City is within the Noble Enclosure. This is the Golden Gate, sealed up about five centuries ago.

On the northwest corner is a tall tower, the site of Herod's Antonia Fortress and the place where tradition says that Pontius Pilate condemned Jesus to death.

The area of the Haram also has smaller domes, minarets, fountains, shrines, a library, and the Islamic Museum.

Visiting hours for the Dome of the Rock are 8:30 to 11 A.M. The shrine is closed on Fridays and Moslem holidays. An entrance fee admits you to the Dome and to the Museum.

On the right after entering Lion's Gate is the Church of St. Anne. It stands on the traditional site of the house of Anne and Joachim, parents of Mary, at the time of her birth. Within the precincts of the church is the Pool of Bethesda, where Jesus healed the sick man who had waited faithfully for 38 years to be cured by its waters. St. Anne's Church was built during Crusader days on the remains of a 5th-century shrine. Northwest of the church are the remains of earlier Byzantine and Crusader churches.

The Via Dolorosa

The Via Dolorosa (Way of the Cross, or Way of Sorrows) is the road Jesus walked carrying his cross from the Praetorium to Calvary. The street winds through the narrow cobblestoned alleys of Old Jerusalem, past churches, chapels, bazaars, and ancient archways. The 14 Stations of the Cross are indicated by inscriptions in Roman numerals. Every Friday at 3 P.M. the Franciscan fathers retrace these steps accompanied by pilgrims of all denominations. A Pilgrim's Terminal opened recently at the beginning of the Via Dolorosa. Its purpose is to provide a gathering place for pilgrims and their guides, ministers, and priests before starting their walk. (The present-day level of Jerusalem is 20 feet higher that at the time of Christ, and the authenticity of the route is questioned by many Christian sects; but it has been accepted and made holy from centuries of pilgrims' devotion.)

First Station: Jesus was condemned to death, scourged and crowned with thorns (John 19:2-16).

The station starts at the site of Pilate's Praetorium (200 yards beyond the Church of St. Anne). In this courtyard Pilate placed the judgment seat and interrogated the populace. Christ was presented, scourged, to the public with the words "Ecce Homo" (Behold the Man). Pilate then washed his hands and condemned Jesus to death on the Cross.

El-Umariye School marks the first station and the Franciscan Convent of Flagellation stands on part of the site of the Praetorium. It has a rich museum and a special library for Biblical and archeological studies.

Second Station: Jesus received the Cross (John 19:17).

The station is fixed outside on the street, opposite the Chapel of Condemnation.

The Chapel stands on the Gabbatha or Lithostratas (the street by which Christ went out of the Praetorium to Calvary). A large part of the original pavement is visible in the Chapel of the Condemnation and in the Convent of the Sisters of Zion. The sisters will show you the flagstone street on which you can see traces of games played by the Roman soldiers. This is one of the few accessible places in Jerusalem that has been authenticated as the Jerusalem of Jesus' time. It is very likely that Christ actually passed along this pavement. The Chapel of the Flagellation, where Jesus was scourged, has a beautiful stained glass window behind the altar.

Third Station: Jesus fell the first time.

Marked by a small chapel that was once the main entrance to the baths. In back of the third station is a small museum.

(Here the Via Dolorosa turns sharp left onto al-Wad Road.)

Fourth Station: Jesus met his mother.

The station is marked by an altar outside the Armenian Catholic Church. On the altar rests a marble statue of Jesus meeting his mother.

(Twenty yards beyond the fourth station the Via Dolorosa turns sharp right on Tariq as-Serai.)

Fifth Station: Simon of Cyrene helped Jesus carry his Cross.

The station is marked outside on a building on Tariq es-Serai.

Sixth Station: Veronica wiped the face of Jesus.

The traditional site of the house of Veronica is marked by a fragment of column inserted in the wall. (The incline to Traditional Calvary begins here.)

Seventh Station: Jesus fell the second time.

The station is marked by a Franciscan chapel at the Souq Khan ez-Zeit. Apparently there was a city gate here where Jesus' death notice was posted.

Eighth Station: Jesus spoke to the daughters of Jerusalem.

At the Greek Orthodox Convent of St. Charalambos the station is marked by a stone with a Latin cross and the Greek word NIKA inserted in the wall. It is opposite the Station VIII Souvenir Bazaar.

Ninth Station: Jesus fell the third time.

At the Coptic Church the shaft of a column enclosed in a pillar of the door marks the station.

Stations 10 through 14 are located in the Church of the Holy Sepulchre. Just inside the church a red slab stone on the floor, the Stone of the Unction, covers the spot where the body of Jesus was anointed.

Tenth Station: Jesus was stripped of his garments (John 19:23).

Eleventh Station: Jesus was nailed to the Cross (Luke 23:33). The station is located in the Latin chapel.

Twelfth Station: Jesus died on the Cross (John 19:30). The station is located in the Greek chapel.

Thirteenth Station: The body of Jesus was taken down from the Cross (Luke 24:53).

The station is the Latin altar of the Stabat Mater Dolorosa between the eleventh and twelfth stations. The Chapel of the Discovery of the Cross is said to be the place where St. Helena discovered the original cross. The Chapel of the Division of the Raiment is supposed to mark the place where the Roman soldiers distributed the Savior's clothes.

Fourteenth Station: Jesus was laid in the sepulchre (John 19:40). This is the spot which marks the traditional burial place of Christ.

The Church of the Holy Sepulchre

The Church of the Holy Sepulchre is the holiest church in Christendom, erected upon the traditional site of the crucifixion, burial, and resurrection of Jesus Christ. The site on which the church stands was outside the city walls at the time and included Calvary and the tomb of Joseph of Arimathea where Jesus was buried.

The early Christians worshipped secretly at these places. When Titus attacked and destroyed the city in A.D. 70, Christians in Jerusalem fled across the Jordan. After the war they returned and continued to worship at Calvary and the Tomb.

In an attempt to wean Christians away from their faith and holy places, Hadrian built a temple dedicated to Venus on the site of Calvary. Ironically, his deed marked the spot forever. Upon Constantine's conversion to Christianity, his mother, Helena, ordered the erection of a magnificent basilica on the site. Over the centuries the church was destroyed and rebuilt several times. Today the building is approximately the same as the one restored by the Crusaders in the 12th century.

By a tradition established by Saladin to avoid misunderstandings among the different Christian sects, the keys of the Church were kept by the Moslem family of Joudeh, and the opener of the door was a member of the Moslem family of Nuseibah. At Easter, three sects are allowed to have the long, curiously-shaped key. On Holy Thursday it goes to the head of the Franciscan Monastery; on Good Friday, to the chief Dragoman of the Greek Orthodox Monastery, and on Holy Saturday to the head of the Armenian Orthodox Church.

An 18th-century decree gave six churches the right to share the sanctuary: Latin (Roman) Catholic, Greek Orthodox, Armenian Orthodox, Coptic, Syrian (Jacobite), and Abyssinian. The latter two are allowed the privilege only for special ceremonies during the year. No Protestant sect has the right to share the sanctuary.

The status quo and the designation of space within the sanctuary are jealousy guarded by each denomination, and regrettably have often been obstacles to restoration of the church.

The chapels in the church are elaborately decorated and the altars are cluttered with a bewildering array of statues, pictures, candelabra, and silver, gold, and bejewelled gifts.

Some people come to Jerusalem expecting to find the city as it was during Jesus' time. They imagine Calvary as a barren hilltop—even picturing it with the Cross of Jesus still standing. Upon entering the Church of the Holy Sepulchre, they are astonished and distracted by its glittering contents, the international parade of clergy, and the heavy air of burning incense. Their guides often rush them past crowded altars and through dimly lighted chambers so quickly there is little time for reflection or meditation. As a result, visitors are often critical and disappointed. If you find yourself in this situation, it will help to recall Mark Twain's visit to the Holy Sepulchre over a hundred years ago, which he described in *The Innocents Abroad* (Hartford, Conn., The American Publishing Co., 1869). Upon entering Jerusalem, Mark Twain wrote, "One naturally goes first to the Holy Sepulchre. It is right in the city, near the western gate; it and the place of the Crucifixion, and in fact, every other place intimately connected with the tremendous event, are ingeniously massed together and covered by one roof—the dome of the Church of the Holy Sepulchre . . ."

After describing the church and its history, he notes that "When one stands where the Saviour was crucified, he finds it all he can do to keep it strictly before his mind that Christ was not crucified in a Catholic Church."

Mark Twain ended his description with this paragraph:

And so I close my chapter on the Church of the Holy Sepulchre—the most sacred locality on earth to millions of men, and women, and children, the noble and the humble, bond and free. In its history from the first, and in its tremendous associations, it is the most illustrious edifice in Christendom. With all its clap-trap side-shows and unseemly impostures of every kind, it is still grand, reverend, venerable, for a god died there; for fifteen hundred years its shrines have been wet with the tears of pilgrims from the earth's remotest confines; for more than two hundred, the most gallant knights that ever wielded sword wasted their lives away in a struggle to seize it and hold it sacred from infidel pollution. Even in our own day a war, that cost millions of treasure and rivers of blood, was fought because two rival nations claimed the sole right to put a new dome upon it. History is full of this old Church of the Holy Sepulchre—full of blood that was shed because of the respect and the veneration in which men held the last restingplace of the meek and lowly, the mild and gentle, Prince of Peace!

Other Churches and Sites

The Church of Alexandros Nephki is near the Church of the Holy Sepulchre, to the southeast. This church, better known as the Russian Church or Excavations, will help you understand the orientation of the original Church of the Holy Sepulchre. Ruins dating from the time of Hadrian include the Triumphal Arch and part of the enclosure walls of the Temple. Open Monday to Thursday, 9 A.M. to 3 P.M. except holidays. Entrance fee. Tel. 283866.

On the west wall near Jaffe Gate stands the Citadel, known as David's Tower, open daily from 8:30 A.M. to 4 P.M. The fortification was built during the 14th century on the base of a 12th-century Crusader castle, which in turn had been built on an ancient foundation. The huge stones at the bottom of the big tower on the right of the entrance are the oldest part and are said to date back to the time of Herod the Great. It contains the Jerusalem City Museum on the history of Jerusalem. A spectacular multi-screen show can be seen daily. In English, Sunday to Thursday at 9 and 11 A.M.; 1 and 3 P.M., and nightly except Friday at 9 P.M.

South of the Citadel in the Armenian quarter is the Cathedral of St. James, an Armenian Orthodox Church, erected in the 12th century on the site where, tradition holds, St. James was beheaded by Herod Agrippa. Architecturally the church is very beautiful. One must be modestly dressed to enter; hours are from 8 to 12 A.M., and 2 to 5 P.M. daily except Sundays and holidays. Nearby the Church of St. Mark stands on the traditional site of the house of Mary, mother of John surnamed Mark. The Armenian Convent is believed to be the place of Caiaphas' Palace where Jesus was taken on the night of his arrest. Across from the Armenian compound is the Gulbenkian Library.

On the south side of the walls opposite Zion Gate is Mt. Zion, the hill that is crowned by the Church of the Dormition and its monastery, dedicated at the beginning of the 20th century. They stand on ground presented by the Turkish sultan to the German emperor. According to tradition, this was the spot where the Virgin Mary "fell into eternal sleep." The sanctuary is ringed by chapels, the walls are covered with medallions commemorating the kings of Judea, and the floor is adorned with symbols of the months, saints, and prophets. The crypt contains a stone sepulchre representing Mary in her last sleep. The inscription around the wall is from the Song of Solomon (II.13): "Arise, my love, my fair one, and come away." The chapels surrounding the crypt were donated by different countries.

The Cenacle, or Upper Chamber, is a Gothic room built on the site of the Last Supper. Seven weeks after the Passion the Holy Ghost appeared here to the assembled disciples. This was the origin of the Pentecost, as recorded in the Acts of the Apostles.

A medieval building leads to the Tomb of David. The cenotaph contains an impressive sarcophagus. Brocade hangings adorn the walls and the solid silver crowns of the Torah provide decoration. Although this site was not discovered until the 12th century, during the preceding 200 years people had been claiming that David's remains lay buried here.

The valley below once was forest land. On a certain day in that forest a tree was felled from which a heavy cross was fashioned. This event is commemorated by a medieval fortresslike structure called the Monastery and Church of the Holy Cross.

The road along the old walls from Zion Gate leads to Dung Gate, so called because the city's garbage was taken out through it in olden times, to be dumped down the slopes of the Valley of Kidron.

Dung Gate is also closest to the Wailing Wall, where Jews came to pray and bewail the destruction of the Temple.

The lower layers of the Wall are a section of the retaining and supporting wall of Herod's temple extension, while the upper layers were added by Sir Moses Montefiore in the middle of the 19th century. The claim that the huge lower blocks were from Solomon's temple has no foundation. Men and women pray at different sections of the Wall in accordance with Orthodox Jewish custom.

South of Dung Gate is the Church of St. Peter's in Gallicantu, built by the Assumptionist Fathers to commemorate St. Peter's denial of Jesus and the former's repentance.

From Dung Gate at the southeast corner of the city wall the road drops down and crosses the Valley of Kidron (Kedron), or Valley of Judgment. Below lie many tombs. Most prominent among them are Absalom's Pillar and the Tombs of St. James, Zachariah, and Josephat. In the walls of the city overlooking the valley is the Golden Gate. According to tradition this is the gate through which Jesus rode into Jerusalem on Palm Sunday. The tradition is substantiated by underground chambers and stonework dating from Herodian times. It was the only gate of the outer city wall that would have led directly into the site of Herod's Temple.

Farther down the valley road, on the right, is the Virgin's Fountain. Here, it is said, the Virgin Mary took water to wash the clothes of Jesus. The fountain is fed by the Spring of Gihon.

Gethsemane and the Mount of Olives

Across the Valley of Kidron and facing the Golden Gate lie Gethsemane and the Mount of Olives. On the north of the road before climbing the hill stands the Tomb of the Virgin, or the Church of the Assumption. According to tradition, this is the site of the Virgin's resting place before her ascent into heaven. The church in its present form was built by the Crusaders in 1130 to replace an earlier fifth-century basilica.

Further up the hill on the right is the Garden of Gethsemane. Here, in this peaceful grove of ancient olive trees, Jesus spent the evening with his disciples when he visited Jerusalem. The Grotto of Gethsemane is traditionally believed to be the cave mentioned in the Bible where Jesus was betrayed by Judas and arrested by the soldiers. The Basilica of the Agony, or the Church of All Nations, is built over the Rock of Agony, where Christ is believed to have prayed and wept before his arrest. It is one of the loveliest churches in the Holy Land. Many nations contributed funds to build it, and their coats of arms are displayed in the cupolas.

The Church of St. Maria Magdalena with its onion-shaped domes was built by Tsar Alexander III in 1888. It is open Monday and Thursday from 9 A.M. to 3 P.M. There is an entrance fee.

On the road to the summit of the Mount of Olives you come to the Church of the Ascension, said to mark the spot from which Jesus ascended into heaven. The chapel dates back to Crusader times and stands on the site of an earlier 4th-century church. After Saladin's recapture of Jerusalem in 1187 the church was made into a mosque. Inside there is a rock bearing what tradition holds is the footprint of Christ. Nearby, the Church of the Pater Noster marks the traditional site where Christ taught his disciples the Lord's Prayer. It was built for the Carmelite Nuns in 1875 by Princess de la Tour d'Auvergne on the ruins of a Crusader church. In the church are tablets of glazed tiles on which the Lord's Prayer is written in 44 different languages; these tiles were donated by Christians around the world.

At the summit of the Mount of Olives the Church of the Dominus Flevit rests on the traditional site where Jesus wept over Jerusalem before his entry into the city on Palm Sunday. The road rises to a crest here and stops in front of the Jerusalem Inter-Continental Hotel. From there is a view of the walled city of Jerusalem, the Judean Hills to the west, and the Judean wilderness.

Damascus Gate

On the north side of the city walls is Damascus Gate, the largest and most impressive of the entrances to the Old City. From ancient times it led to the road to the Syrian capital. The road leading into it today is called Nablus Road.

The Damascus Gate is a beehive of activity inside and out. In front of it is the bus terminus of East Jerusalem. From here buses leave for all parts of the West Bank. Most of the buslines going between East and West Jerusalem stop here, too. Nearby, "service" taxis sell seats in Mercedes limos to the main towns in the West Bank.

Within the great gate itself there are stalls and shops and the fantastic souks of the Old City. On the way to the Street of Spices there are moneychangers, souvenir shops, and coffee houses where men in partly Western, partly Oriental attire spend their social hours sipping Turkish coffee, smoking their narghilis and noisily playing backgammon, as their fathers and grandfathers have done for centuries before them.

The Garden Tomb: A short walk up Nablus Road from Damascus Gate outside the old walls there is a small path on the east side leading to an ancient tomb in a garden. Some Protestant groups believe this to be the place of Jesus' crucifixion and burial because it more accurately fits the description in the Bible. The site was located and excavated by General Gordon (of Sudan fame) in 1883. Nearby, a hill still used as a graveyard is believed to be the site of Calvary. (It is best seen from the garden.) It is known that Christ was crucified at "the place of a skull." Immediately in front of the Garden Tomb is a rock formation resembling a skull, which Gordon believed to be an obvious identification of the original site. The Garden is a lovely and quiet place for meditation.

Farther along, where Nablus Road intersects with Saladin Street, is the Tomb of Kings. This is a misnomer; it is actually the tomb of a queen and her family who came to Jerusalem in the first century A.D.

Back toward the walls on the corner of Nablus and Saladin is St. George's Cathedral, the largest Anglican edifice in the country and the Anglican Commission's center for the Holy Land.

Between Damascus Gate and Herod's Gate (also called the Flower Gate) there is a small iron grill door leading down to King Solomon's Quarries (closed to visitors). From these labyrinthine caves the stones for Solomon's Temple are believed to have been cut. The Masons consider it the birthplace of their order. The quarries have numerous galleries covering thousands of feet and, in a direct line, the quarry penetrates more than 700 feet into the Old City. Some people are convinced it stretches even farther. An alternate name for the quarries is Zedekiah's Cave. Legend has it that the last king of Judah fled into the cave to escape his Babylonian enemies. He emerged miles from Jerusalem, in the Plain of Jericho, only to be caught anyway.

Opposite King Solomon's Quarries, down a narrow street, is Jeremiah's Grotto. It is supposedly the dungeon into which the prophet was cast and whence he was rescued by Ebed Melech the Ethiopian.

Rockefeller Archeological Museum. Hours: 10 A.M. to 5 P.M. daily; Friday and Saturday, 10 A.M. to 2 P.M. Entrance fee. Northeast of the city walls near Herod's Gate is one of the finest museums in the Middle East. Built in the 1930s and maintained by a gift of John D. Rockefeller, Jr., it houses many treasures from years of excavation in the Holy Land. Only the best samples of each item are on display. The exhibits are arranged chronologically.

Among the most interesting is a collection of jewelry dating from 1700 B.C. to A.D. 700, a coin collection dating from 500 B.C. to A.D.

1600, and a group of oil lamps from the early Bronze Age to the Islamic period. Exhibits of the Stone Age include objects 200,000 years old. Wooden panels of the 7th and 8th centuries from the Aqsa Mosque in Jerusalem and carved stuccos and frescos of the same period from the Hisham Palace in Jericho are also on display. In a corner of one exhibit room you will see a copy of a tomb with skeletons and artifacts exactly as they were found in Jericho. Samples of the Dead Sea Scrolls are displayed in a separate room. You need at least two hours at the museum for even a brief look at all the exhibits.

North of the Archeological Museum is the area known as the American Colony, so named because of the American eschatologists who settled here in the late 19th century. Located in the vicinity are the U.S. Consulate, East Y.M.C.A., St. George's Cathedral, and the American Colony Hotel, one of the oldest, best, and most attractive in the Middle East. The original building dates from about 1850 and was the palace of a pasha. It is built around a beautiful old courtyard where, weather permitting, guests can dine or enjoy a drink and coffee. Upstairs, the Pasha's Room, where folklore evenings are held, has a lovely, elaborately painted ceiling. Saturday brunch is an all-you-can-eat meal. There is a swimming pool. Tel. 282421.

The West Y.M.C.A., built in 1933, is probably the most beautiful Y in the world. Tel. 282375. It has a restaurant and sports facilities. There is an excellent view of the Old City from its tower. It houses the Herbert Clark Collection of Middle East Antiquities. Open daily except Wednesday and Sunday, 10 A.M. to 1 P.M. Entrance fee.

The *Shrine of the Book* is open daily from 10 A.M. to 5 P.M., Tuesday to 10 P.M., Friday and Saturday to 2 P.M.

The *Islamic Art Museum* is open daily except Friday from 10 to 12:30 A.M. and 3:30 to 6 P.M. Wednesday until 9 P.M. Saturday to 1 P.M.

Model of Ancient Jerusalem, within the grounds of the Holy Land Hotel. The model shows Jerusalem in the first century A.D. with its monuments, splendid public buildings, palaces, fortifications, and temple.

Other Sites

In addition to the Dome of the Rock and al-Aqsa Mosque, there are 29 mosques and dozens of churches within the Old City of Jerusalem.

From the roof of Notre Dame de Sion or the Tower of the Lutheran Church near the Church of the Holy Sepulchre you can get the best view of the Old City of Jerusalem.

The French School of Biblical and Archeological Studies in Jerusalem conducts specialized tours of the Old City. A different place is selected each week as the focal point. The school also sponsors trips outside Jerusalem. The tours are led by professors from the school, and lectures are in French.

At the Pilgrim Office of the Franciscans on St. Francis Street in the Old City you may obtain a "Pilgrim Certificate" as a memento of your visit to Jerusalem. The tradition was established during the Crusades, and the certificate is given to pilgrims of all denominations.

Holy Days

The traditional holy days of Christianity are observed throughout the year by both Eastern and Western churches in Jerusalem.

The Eastern Church follows the old Julian calendar, which is 13 days behind the Gregorian. Consequently Eastern and Western religious feasts seldom coincide. Christmas and Easter are the major celebrations in which thousands of pilgrims and tourists from all over the world participate. Programs listing the major celebrations and services are available from churches, the Tourism office, leading hotels, and travel agencies.

Christmas in Bethlehem

Christmas has three dates in the Holy Land: Western Christmas is celebrated on December 25, the Orthodox one on January 6, and the Armenian Christmas on January 19.

Christmas Eve, December 24, in the little town of Bethlehem is a memorable experience. About 1 P.M. the Latin Patriarch makes his ceremonial entrance into Bethlehem. He is followed by a colorful procession of churchmen and choirboys, and is met upon arrival by church organizations in Bethlehem of all denominations, by groups of school children, and by a large crowd of townspeople and visitors.

At dusk the YMCA holds a service in English and other languages at Shepherd's Field, where the angels appeared to the shepherds "as they sat watching their flocks by night." The congregation joins the choir in singing well-known Christmas carols. It is a beautiful moment to hear the familiar words of "Silent Night" as the first stars of evening appear overhead. At the end of the service, a traditional supper of bread and meat is served to the congregation. For the service at Shepherd's Field buses leave from the YMCA in Jerusalem at 3 P.M and return about 7 P.M. Sometimes the weather is cold and windy. Wear warm clothing and comfortable shoes.

At nine o'clock in the evening, you may join the community carol singing in the Church of the Nativity courtyard. Bethlehem is gaily lighted and a festive spirit is in the air.

At midnight, a Pontifical High Mass is celebrated in the Franciscan Church of St. Catherine, adjacent to the Church of the Nativity. At the moment the choir sings the Gloria, a huge star over the altar is set aglow and the bells of Bethlehem are rung. The little town's special message of "Glory to God in the highest, and on earth, peace and good will toward men" is carried throughout the world.

Tickets for the service are limited; be sure to request yours far in advance. They may be obtained through travel agents and the Pilgrim Office. The church always overflows its capacity, so plan to arrive early. The Mass is long and most of the congregation stand throughout the service. Wear warm clothing and comfortable shoes.

On Christmas morning, services are held in almost every church in Jerusalem. A pamphlet lising the hours of services at the major churches is available from the Tourist Office.

Christmas cards mailed from Bethlehem on Christmas Day bear a special postmark. You may also arrange in advance at the post office in a basement on Manger Square opposite the Church of the Nativity to have cards mailed from Bethlehem.

In recent years, the Bethlehem area has been closed 48 hours over Christmas for all except those with special permits.

Easter in Jerusalem

Few ceremonies rival in pomp, pageantry, and piety the Easter services in Jerusalem. The very names associated with the celebration—the Washing of the Feet, the Exposition of the Column of the Flagellation, the Service of the Imperial Hours, the Ceremony of the Holy Fire, the Bridegroom's Arrival, the Abyssinian Search—intensify the devotion of pilgrims.

During Holy Week many processions are held. On Palm Sunday the Anglican procession begins at the ruins of the Crusader Castle in Bethany and proceeds along the ancient footpath over the Mount of Olives to Gethsemane, and then to the Anglican Cathedral of St. George in Jerusalem.

Among the most splendid rituals of Holy Week are those of the Roman Catholic Church. They begin at 6:30 A.M. on Palm Sunday with the ceremonial entry of the Latin Patriarch into the Church of the Holy Sepulchre, followed by his Blessing of the Palms. Each member of the congregation carries an olive or palm branch to symbolize the reception of Christ entering Jerusalem. After blessing the Palms, the patriarch leads a procession three times around the Rotunda of the Holy Sepulchre, once around the Stone of Unction, and concludes with the Pontifical Mass before the Holy Tomb.

The Exposition of the Column of the Flagellation (a three-foot cylindrical column to which Christ was bound when He was scourged) takes place on Holy Wednesday in the Chapel of the Flagellation.

At 9 A.M. on Maundy Thursday in front of the Holy Tomb in the Church of the Holy Sepulchre, the patriarch, divested of his miter and cope, performs the Washing of the Feet, as did Jesus before his last Passover (John 12:5). (The ceremony is colorful and crowded; be sure to arrive early. Weather permitting, the ceremony is now performed in the courtyard in front of the Church of the Holy Sepulchre.) In the evening at eight, Mass is said at the Garden of Gethsemane. The Lutherans walk from their Church of the Redeemer near the Holy Sepulchre along the Via Dolorosa to the Garden of Gethsemane.

The next day, Good Friday, at 11 A.M. the Franciscan Fathers lead a procession from the site of Pontius Pilate's court along the Via Dolorosa, pausing for brief service at each of the 14 Stations of the Cross. Many orders of priests and nuns carry heavy crosses.

This service is widely attended and is very crowded. The pilgrimage is divided into sections according to language. You should join the section you wish to attend at the first station. The procession inches along at a snail's pace. Persons in weak health should stay near the back.

In the Burial Service later in the day at 7 P.M., a procession visits the Stations of the Cross within the Church of the Holy Sepulchre. When the procession reaches the Cross, an effigy of Christ is taken down and wrapped in a winding sheet. It is then carried to the Stone of Unction where it is anointed, spiced and scented with incense. The effigy is laid to rest in the Holy Tomb, and the Good Friday services are concluded with a memorial sermon.

The Russian Orthodox Good Friday begins with the Service of the Imperial Hours ("Imperial" refers to the universal empire of the Lord) at the Church of Alexandros Nephki, and ends in the evening with the Burial Service in St. James Cathedral. Between these two services a solemn procession begins at the Greek Orthodox Convent of the Prison of Christ and traces Christ's steps along the Via Dolorosa to Calvary.

The Armenian Church has special ceremonies for the Holy Week. They are held in the Armenian Chapel of St. John and the Chapel of the Second Calvary.

The Coptic Ceremony of the Washing of the Feet is held in the Coptic Church of St. Anthony. The feet of the "disciples" are not actually washed. Instead, the Coptic Patriarch marks with olive oil a cross on one knee of each of the 12, and afterwards on the knee of any member of the congregation requesting anointment.

The Syrian Orthodox Church is entitled by custom to hold its Burial Service in the Church of the Holy Sepulchre. Other services of the Church are performed in the Chapel of St. Nicodemus and the Church of St. Mark in the Syrian Orthodox Convent. In the latter the Ceremony of the Bridegroom's Arrival is celebrated on Palm Sunday.

The Abyssinian Orthodox Church, established in Ethiopia 16 centuries ago and having rights to the sanctuary of the Holy Sepulchre, does not have an altar inside the Church. Its tiny altar is located on the roof of St. Helena's Chapel near the entrance to the Church of the Holy Sepulchre. There, in the Chapel of the Saviour, the Abyssinian Orthodox Church celebrates the services of Holy Week. The most colorful is a small procession known as the Abyssinian Search. The group moves about in a symbolic search for the risen body of Christ. The service is held on the night before Easter Sunday; the ceremony is unique—and very crowded.

The Roman Catholics celebrate another Pontifical High Mass on Holy Saturday before the tomb and hold the Blessing of the Fire.

At the same time, in the Greek Orthodox Church the congregation moves in procession to the tomb of Lazarus (Lazarus Saturday) in the town of Bethany on the road to Jericho. There Lazarus lay for four days in his tomb until Christ raised him from the dead (John 12:1).

The Ceremony of the Holy Fire is the major service of the Eastern Churches and one of the most ancient. It symbolizes the Resurrection, when Christ, the Light of the World, rose from the tomb. The ceremony is at least a thousand years old, for it was mentioned by Bernard the Wise in the ninth century. Although the Syrian, Armenian Orthodox, and Coptic Churches participate, the ceremony is mainly Greek Orthodox and is conducted by the Greek Orthodox Patriarch.

At 11 o'clock on Holy Saturday the door to the empty Tomb of Christ in the Rotunda of the Church of the Holy Sepulchre is closed. A white ribbon passed through the door handles is sealed with a large piece of hot wax.

Exactly at noon the Greek Orthodox Patriarch enters the crowded Rotunda. The ribbon and seal are removed, and the unlit silver Holy Lamp is placed in the Tomb. At 12:30 the service begins. The Patriarch, preceded by members of leading Greek Orthodox families of Jerusalem carrying 13 banners, leads a solemn procession three times around the Rotunda. The Patriarch removes his cope and miter and enters the Holy Sepulchre, accompanied by the Bishop of the Armenian Church. At this moment the crowd in the tiny Chapel of the Angel is silent.

The Patriarch prays before the Holy Tomb of Christ. The Holy Lamp is lighted, and from it torches are ignited by the Patriarch and the Bishop. Their flaming torches are raised to small openings above the Holy Sepulchre, where the fire is received on one side by the Greek Orthodox congregation, on the other by the Armenians. The instant the fire is seen the crowd rushes frantically forward with candles and torches to receive it. Lasting honor is bestowed on the one whose candle is lit first. As the light of the Holy Fire appears, the massive bells of the church are rung, and the fire passes rapidly from candle to candle until the entire church is aglow.

The candles of churches in the Jerusalem area, which are extinguished on Good Friday, are lighted on Easter from this fire. All year one candle in each church is kept lit from the holy flame.

On Easter Sunday, Roman Catholics hold mass in the Holy Sepulchre without pause throughout the day.

Hotels: Hotels in East Jerusalem range from luxurious (such as the Jerusalem Inter-Continental) to simple, and are rated from five stars to one.

A complete list of hotels is available from the Tourist Office in Jerusalem. Generally hotels in East Jerusalem are lower in price than those in West Jerusalem and range from $60 for a double in a five-star hotel to $35 double in a three-star one.

Post Office: Main post office remains open from 8 A.M. to 6 P.M.; branches from 8 to 12:30 A.M.; 3:30 to 6 P.M. Wednesday to 2 P.M. Telegrams can be sent from all post offices and hotels.

Tourist Information Offices: 24 King George St., tel. (02) 241281; Jaffe Gate, tel. (02) 282295; 24 Jaffe St., tel. (02) 228844.

SOUTH OF JERUSALEM

The sites described in the following section can be covered in a half-day; however, those who want to spend time in Bethlehem should allow a full day.

Bethany: 1¼ miles

Bethany was the home of Lazarus and his sisters, Mary and Martha, and Simon the Leper. On the site where Jesus called forth Lazarus from the tomb (John 11:43) stands a Franciscan church built on the foundations of earlier Byzantine and Crusader churches.

Jesus sent two disciples from Bethany to Bethpage on the Mount of Olives to fetch a donkey, which he rode into Jerusalem on Palm Sunday (Matt. 21:1). Today the exact site of Bethpage is no longer known, but the name is given to the enclosure of the Franciscans. Its chapel contains a cubical stone with paintings and Latin inscriptions discovered in 1876. Past the church, going up a hill, is the entrance to the Tomb of Lazarus. The key is with the people who run the souvenir stand opposite. For a small fee you are taken down 24 slippery steps into a dark cave which is always cool no matter how warm it may be outside. There you may view the tomb, which rests in a lower vaulted room. Above is the Greek Orthodox Church of Lazarus.

On Palm Sunday, following a tradition set in the 4th century, Bethpage is the starting point for the procession that ends at the Church of St. Anne in the Old City.

Rachel's Tomb: 6 miles

On the right of the road before Bethlehem a small 19th-century domed building marks the traditional site of the tomb of Rachel, wife of Jacob. The structure was originally built by the Crusaders, but in subsequent years was altered many times. The tomb is open daily from 8 A.M. to 5 P.M.

Bethlehem: 7 miles

As the birthplace of Christ, the charming town of Bethlehem has a sweeter meaning to Christians than any place on earth. Its origins are lost in history. The first mention of it in the Bible is in connection with the death of Rachel. Bethlehem was the scene of the idyll of Ruth the Moabite and Boaz. In Bethlehem Samuel anointed David King of Israel.

The Church of the Nativity, facing Manger Square in the center of Bethlehem, stands above a cave, the traditional site of Jesus' birth. The first Church of the Nativity was built at the time of Constantine about A.D. 326. It was destroyed two centuries later, but rebuilt in the 6th century by Justinian. The present-day structure is basically the same as the 6th-century one.

All the outside entrances to the Basilica are closed except one, which is entered from the courtyard. According to tradition, the passages were blocked to prevent Turkish soldiers in bygone days from entering the church on horseback. The one door remaining open, called the Door of Humility, was made smaller so that visitors must bow upon entering the small passageway.

The length of the church is divided by four rows of columns in reddish limestone. The wooden ceiling is made of stout English oak, a gift of King Edward IV. The vast amount of lead the monarch donated to cover the roof is said to have been melted down by the Turks to use as ammunition.

Three Christian denominations share rights in the church—Roman Catholic (Franciscan), Greek Orthodox, and Armenian. Each has its own chapels and altars. Rivalries in the past have been so intense that fighting has broken out among the religious orders. The status quo that is now adhered to was the result of compromises worked out by the British High Commissioner during the Mandate. Peace is maintained by the three communities' strictly observing their schedules. For example, the Greek Orthodox must have finished censing the Altar of the Nativity by 4:30 A.M., when the Catholics hold their first mass. The Armenian mass begins at 8 A.M., after which the Grotto is open to the public.

Beneath the protective floor boards of the church are fragments of the beautiful mosaics of the church built by Justinian. During the Persian conquest of Palestine in A.D. 614, most Christian places were devastated. According to legend, the Persians spared the Church of the Nativity because its mosaics pictured the Magi dressed as Persians. (These mosaics were only uncovered in 1933.) Fragments of other mosaics dating from the 12th century and uncovered in the 1950s decorate the inside walls of the church.

On each side of the altar steps descend to the Grotto of the Nativity, wherein lies the manger (Luke 2:7). A silver star marks the birthplace. Seventeen lamps burn day and night above the altar. The original star was placed here by the Roman Catholic Church in 1717 but was removed by the Greeks in 1847. The Turks replaced it, but the incident was said to be a contributing factor to the outbreak of the Crimean War.

Next to the grotto is the Chapel of the Manger. Catholics are forbidden to use the Altar of the Nativity, but they may burn incense over the star. They use the Altar of the Manger, which is marked by a Latin inscription saying that the newborn Jesus was placed here by His mother.

North of the Basilica is the Church of St. Catherine. On Christmas Eve, the Latin Patriarch takes a wooden image of the infant Jesus from the Franciscan Church of St. Catherine and solemnly places it on the Altar of the Manger, where it remains until Epiphany. Here on Christmas Eve the church bells are rung during the midnight mass, announcing the dawn of Christmas around the world.

The Milk Grotto (entered from stairs beneath the Church of St. Catherine) is near the Church of the Nativity. Tradition holds that while Mary was nursing Jesus, drops of her milk fell on the rock and turned it white. The original church is said to have been built in the fourth century.

A description of Bethlehem's history with Biblical references and details on the Church of the Nativity are available in Eugene Hoade's *Guide to the Holy Land.*

A road to the east just before Manger Square in Bethlehem leads down to Beit Sahour and Shepherd's Field (Luke 2:8-10). On Christmas Eve before sunset services are held in the field next to the YMCA Hostel. Services of the Catholic and Orthodox Churches at the nearby Shepherd's Field are held earlier in the day.

On the Jerusalem–Bethlehem road immediately after Rachel's Tomb the road forking right leads south to Hebron.

Tourist Information Office: Manger Square, tel. (02) 742-591.

Qala'at el Burak (Castle of the Pools): 13 miles

Two miles beyond Bethlehem on the Hebron road on the east is a fortress built by the Turks in the 17th century for the protection of Solomon's Pools. These three ancient reservoirs are set in a beautiful grove of pine and cypress trees. Upon seeing the enormous reservoirs empty, you may wonder if enough water could ever flow from the surrounding area to fill them.

According to scholars, the pools are misnamed. Solomon probably came to the spot to enjoy the gardens and springs, but history records that Pilate, not Solomon, built the great aqueduct which supplies water to Jerusalem. It is possible, of course, that an earlier water supply system existed. The reservoirs still provide Jerusalem with part of its water.

Herodion and Mar Saba

Five miles southeast of Bethlehem lie two interesting and historic sites: the fortress and burial place of Herod and the Monastery of Mar Saba.

Herodion, a huge circular bastion, was one of a string of fortresses built during Herod's reign and was apparently one of his proudest, for he was buried here. Built on a height of 2,500 feet above sea level, it commands a view of the Judean Wilderness and the Dead Sea. The defensive walls were built over 70 feet high and the great towers over 100 feet from the floor of the fortress.

Closer to the Dead Sea, clinging to the very wall of a high canyon, is Mar Saba, a monastery founded by St. Saba of Cappadocia in the 5th century. Long a center of theological literature and poetry, the monastery has had as many as 5,000 monks in residence at one time. Today it is tended by only a few.

Isolated as it is, the monastery was destroyed many times through the centuries by invading armies and bandits. It was sacked for the last time in 1835 and was rebuilt by the Imperial Russian Government in 1840. The fantastic, fortresslike complex has 110 rooms with living quarters on five stories.

Only men are permitted to visit the monastery. Women—and even female animals, it is said—are forbidden to enter. Women may, however, look out on the monastery from a special tower to the south of the building.

West of Bethlehem is the village of Beit Jalla, set among olive groves and vineyards, where the Cremisan Monastery is located. The friars make a popular wine, bottled under their name, which can be sampled and bought here.

Continuing toward Hebron, the road passes through some of the highest parts of the Judean hills. At the village of Halhul on the east there is a tall tower, which local tradition claims is the tomb of the prophet Jonah, Nebi Yunes, who is revered by Moslems as well as Christians.

At Mambre, the Mamre of the Bible, on the east one mile before Hebron, stand the ruins of Haram Ramet el-Khalil (Enclosure of the High Place of the Friend). It is the traditional site of the Oak of Mamre, where Abraham received the three angels of God (Gen: 18). Ruins from the Abrahamic period have been excavated, although only those from the times of Herod, Hadrian, and Constantine are visible.

Hebron: 28 miles

Al-Khalil, as Hebron is called in Arabic, means "the Friend [of God], *i.e.,* Abraham. In ancient times it was known as Kirjah Arba, "the town of four," because of its position on four hills. Situated at an altitude of 3,000 feet, Hebron has been continuously settled for 5,000 years. It lies in a valley identified with the Biblical Valley of Ephron (Gen.24:17) as well as the Valley of Eshkol, where Moses sent his scouts to spy out the fields near Hebron. They returned with pomegranates, figs, and grapes in clusters so large that it took two men to carry them (Num. 13:21–24).

The Bible relates that Abraham "moved his tent and came and dwelt in the plain of Mamre, which is in Hebron, and built there an altar unto the Lord." After the death of his wife Sarah, Abraham bought the Cave of Machphelah from a Hittite and buried her there (Gen. 24:17). Later, Abraham was buried beside her. In the years that followed, Isaac and Rebecca, Jacob and Leah were also buried there.

Hebron was captured by Joshua, and later, for a brief period, was David's capital. The story of the cave disappeared from history until the time of Herod, when a temple was built on the site.

After the Moslem conquest of Palestine in the 7th century, Hebron, because of its association with Abraham, became one of the four sacred cities of Islam. To the Moslems, Abraham was the first Moslem.

In 1100 the Crusaders took Hebron, but later it was recaptured by Saladin. It has remained predominantly Moslem since that time. Today it is the seat of government for the southern district of the West Bank.

Al-Haram al Ibrahimi al Khalil (The Sanctuary of Abraham, the Friend) is a mosque built on the traditional site of the Caves of Machphelah. The building is massive; the wall is about 50 feet high and almost ten feet thick. The lower part dates from the time of Herod. The main part of the building was formerly a Crusader Church which was an enlargement of the original Byzantine basilica used by Christian pilgrims en route to Abraham's Oak at Mamre. The upper part and four minarets (of which only two remain) were added by the Mameluks.

The mosque is divided by four pillars into a nave and two aisles. The cenotaph on the right as one enters the mosque is that of Abraham; the one on the left, that of Sarah. The cenotaphs are enclosed in chapels above the tombs, which lie in the cave below. The cenotaphs are covered with green velvet tapestries embroidered with golden threads, presented by a Turkish sultan over a century ago. The stained-glass window over the main entrance dates from the 12th century.

The *mihrab,* or prayer niche facing Mecca, is made of multicolored marble and fine mosaics. Next to it the carved walnut *minbar,* or pulpit, is a masterpiece of intricate workmanship. It was constructed without a single nail. An inscription on it explains that it was made in the 11th century by order of the minister of the Fatimite Caliph of Egypt.

In front of the *mihrab* stand the two black-and-white marble cenotaphs of Isaac and Rebecca, and to the north are the two similar tombs of Jacob and Leah. The bodies of the patriarchs and their wives lie in the cave below. The cave itself may not be visited, but you may look through an opening in the floor by the dim light of a suspended oil lamp into the eerie subterranean chambers below. Visiting hours: Sunday to Thursday, 7:30 to 11:30 A.M.; 1:30 to 4 P.M. Closed on Fridays, Saturdays, holidays, and during Moslem prayers.

The mosque is approached on foot. You leave your car or bus in a parking lot and climb up a road that is lined with shops, all eager to sell to tourists. Along the way you will have a view of the wares of the town—Hebron glass, pottery, sheep, goat skins, and woodcarvings.

As the place of David's anointment and the burial of the patriarchs, Hebron is holy to Jews as well as to Moslems. Because of the religious fervor that this town inspires, it has frequently been the scene of conflict between Arabs and Israelis and tight security limits its access to tourists.

Hebron is a conservative town. Some of the Moslem women wear veils of flowered material, which, when viewed from afar, are weird and startling. You should be very cautious about photographing in Hebron. Ask your guide about taking pictures, especially in the area of the mosque.

In the bazaar near the mosque as well as on the road into Hebron there are small glass factories where hand-blown glass is made. It has been a trade of Hebron since the Middle Ages. You may watch the men at work around their ancient furnaces, turning and blowing the green, blue, or amethyst glass into vases, pitchers, candlesticks, and beads. The glass items can be bought here as well as in Jerusalem.

NORTH OF JERUSALEM

The trip from Jerusalem to Sabastiya (Sebaste), with stops at major Biblical and archeological sites along the way, can be made in a hurried half-day. For the trip as far north as Jenin one should allow a full day. The trip to Nazareth and the Sea of Galilee is an overnight excursion.

Going north toward Ramallah on the Nablus Road, a you can see tall minaret on a high rise on the left. This is Nebi Samwil, one of the sites where the prophet Samuel is said to be buried. From the top of this mosque one can see the entire breadth of the Holy Land, from the Mediterranean to the Mountains of Moab. From this vantage point, over 3,000 feet above sea level, pilgrims in medieval times often caught their first glimpse of their goal—Jerusalem. The height was thus dubbed Mount of Joy.

East of the road from Jerusalem to Ramallah, Tel el-Ful is the site of Bigeah or Gabaath, the birthplace and residence of Saul. At Er-Ram, ancient Ramah, the prophet Jeremiah was freed from the convoy of captives on its way to Babylon. At Tel en-Nasbeth, the site of Mizpah, Saul was elected the first king of Israel.

About ten miles from Jerusalem on the Ramallah highway a road leads west to the village of El-Jib, identified as Gibeon, "where the sun stood still" (Josh 10:12–13). Excavations are located south of the village. In his book *Gibeon Where the Sun Stood Still* James Pritchard provides valuable diagrams and descriptions which aid in viewing the site, especially the cistern and stairs cut in solid rock, giving access to springs which surface outside the walls.

About three miles further along this road is Qubeibeh, traditionally believed to be the place on the road to Emmaus, where Jesus appeared to the disciples Cleophas and Simon on the third day after his burial. Later Jesus broke bread with them in the house of Cleophas. A Franciscan church, reconstructed on the foundation of an earlier Crusader church, stands on the traditional site of Cleophas' house.

One mile before Latroun was the small village of Amwas (Imwas), believed by many Biblical scholars to be the correct site of Emmaus; it and two other tiny villages were leveled after the 1967 war and are now Canada Park. Further on at Latroun the *Abbey of the Trappist Monks,* built about 50 years ago, stands on the ruins of a 12th-century Crusader castle. The abbey is known for its good wines bottled under the name of Latroun.

Ramallah: 15 miles

In the year Columbus discovered America a small Christian community in Shobak in southern Jordan fled north to avoid the marriage of one of their daughters to the son of the chief of the Moslem tribe. As a child, the daughter had been promised by her father to the chief's son. The little community settled by a well, one day's journey north of Jerusalem, near Bireh, a Moslem village that was named for the well. In the centuries that followed, the two settlements grew and today, the Christian town of Ramallah and the Moslem town of Bireh form a single adjacent community.

Situated at 2,900 feet above sea level with a view of Jerusalem and the Mediterranean in the distance, Ramallah means "Height of God" in Arabic. Traditionally it has been a popular summer resort. It is connected with Jerusalem by a four-lane highway and is a 30-minute drive through the suburbs of Jerusalem that have sprung up under Israeli occupation.

Ramallah has several good restaurants. The town is known for the chocolates and ice cream made there. The American Friends (Quakers) opened their first school in Ramallah in 1866.

While Ramallah itself does not have known sites of antiquity, the town is surrounded by places familiar to us from the Bible.

Bireh (Bira), mentioned above, was the first stopping place for caravans from Jerusalem to Galilee, and is therefore believed to be the place where Mary and Joseph missed the 12-year-old Jesus. Afterwards they returned to Jerusalem to find him in the Temple. Rentis, a village near Bir Zeit northeast of Ramallah, was said to be the home and burial place of Samuel.

A mile or so north of Ramallah a small road to the right leads to Beit-el, thought perhaps to be biblical Beth-El (House of God). It is repeatedly mentioned in the Book of Genesis, first as the place by which Abraham pitched his tents and built an altar to the Lord in the land of Canaan, later when Abraham returned here from Egypt with his nephew, Lot. Beit-El is most closely associated, however, with the story of Jacob and his dream of a ladder reaching to heaven. Jacob took the pillow of stone he had rested his head on when he slept and set it up as a pillar (Gen. 28:18–19). Today, it is the Israeli military occupation administrative center for the West Bank.

North of Ramallah and Bireh en route to Nablus the road passes through the olive groves of Wadi el-Haramiyah (Valley of the Robbers). The area is dotted with Biblical sites, and the ruins of a khan at Ain al-Haramiyah (the Robbers' Spring) mark the major pass on the route from Jerusalem to Nablus. From earliest times small forts were used to defend the pass against robbers; hence the name.

About half way to Nablus a road on the right leads to Kirbet Seilun, the site of ancient Shiloh (Silo). After the conquest of Palestine, the tabernacle and the Ark of the Covenant were placed in Shiloh, where they remained for two centuries until the Ark was captured by the Philistines. From excavations at the site authorities believe that Shiloh was destroyed by the Philistines about 1050 B.C.

Farther along the Nablus road Ain Berkit, near Khan al-Lubban, marks the traditional frontier between the northern kingdom of Israel and the southern one of Judea.

Jacob's Well: 34 miles

The famous well believed to have been dug by Jacob near his camp outside Shechem is located less than one mile east of Nablus. Here Jesus met the Samaritan woman and asked her for a drink of water. He revealed himself to her as the Messiah and she believed (John 4:5–25).

In the early 4th century, a church was built over the well. Apparently destroyed during the Samaritan revolts of the 5th century, it was later restored under Justinian. In Crusader days a new church was built over the old one.

The area containing the Crusader church ruins was acquired by the Greek Orthodox Church in 1860. Reconstruction was begun in the 19th century but had to be stopped after World War I, when funds from the Church of Russia were discontinued.

The Greek Orthodox monk in attendance will lower a bucket into the well and bring up clear, fresh water for you to drink.

Joseph's Tomb

Joseph had requested that upon his death his body be buried in the Land of Canaan. Four centuries later Moses brought Joseph's mummy on the Exodus and buried him near the site of Jacob's well. The tomb is marked by a white dome. Northeast of the tomb is Askar (Sichar), the village home of the Samaritan woman.

On the northeast of the road immediately before reaching Nablus, the suburb of Balata is the site of ancient Shechem (Sichem), the first capital of ancient Samaria. Behind the village at Tel Balata excavations reveal the ruins of two city gates and a large temple built about 1600 B.C. Apparently the temple was used for four succeeding centuries. About 800 B.C. a granary was built over the temple site. Shechem was probably first settled by the Canaanites in the fourth millennium B.C. It is mentioned in the Bible in connection with Abraham and Jacob.

Nablus: 35 miles

Between Mount Garizim and Mount Ebal lies Nablus. The town is located in an area that has an abundant water supply. Its gardens and fields are irrigated from 16 springs. The Nablus area is known for its olive crop and the production of oil and soap. Kanafa, one of the best oriental sweetmeats, is also a specialty of Nablus. If you have time, stop in one of the town's pastry shops to enjoy the delicious dessert.

Nablus, the largest town of the West Bank, was founded in A.D. 72 by Roman legionaries under Titus. In 636 the town was taken by the Arabs and, except for a brief period during the Crusades, has remained predominantly Moslem to the present day. The town's main ancient building is the Great Mosque. It was originally a Byzantine basilica, rebuilt as a church by the Crusaders.

In addition to its small Christian minority, about 300 Samaritans live in Nablus. Their high priests (Cohanim) are the direct descendents of Levi, the descendant of Aaron, the son of Jacob. A modern synagogue has replaced the ancient one, which was destroyed by an earthquake in 1927. Here you can see an ancient Pentateuch Scroll or Torah written in Samaritan script, akin to Hebrew. (These are the five books of Moses and the only part of the Scriptures accepted by the Samaritans.) The Samaritans claim that the document is the original copy of the words of Moses—hence the oldest one in existence. In fact, however, scholars say the oldest part of it goes no farther back than the 10th or 11th century A.D..

Mount Garizim, the holy mountain of the Samaritans, is located south of Nablus. The Jews, after their return from captivity (538 B.C.), refused to consider the inhabitants of Samaria as Jews because they had intermarried with Gentiles. The Samaritans, on the other hand, had retained the old Judaic teachings and rejected the new ideas acquired by the Jews during their 49 years in Babylon. The Samaritans, believing that Mount Garizim fitted Abraham's description better than Mount Moriah, built a rival temple to the one in Jerusalem. Although the temple has long since been destroyed, the Samaritans celebrate the feasts of the Passover, Pentecost, and Tabernacle near the site. Also on the summit are the ruins of a mosque and an octagonal church, the earliest known one dedicated to Mary. The panoramic view of the Holy Land from the summit of Mount Garizim is magnificent.

In the valley between Mt. Garizim and Mt. Ebal the 12 tribes of Israel assembled. By Joshua's orders the six nobler tribes stood for blessings on the side of Mt. Garizim, while the lesser tribe stood on Mt. Ebal. The priests, judges and elders gathered around the Ark of the Covenant placed in the valley between the two.

The Samaritans point out a rock on Mt. Garizim that, they say, was the place where Abraham prepared to sacrifice Isaac. They also show the 12 rocks Joshua was supposed to have set up for the tribes of Israel, although the Bible puts this on Mount Ebal.

To the Samaritans Moses is the only prophet and God is one and incorporeal. Annually on Mount Garizim, the Samaritans hold their unique Passover feast on the evening before the full moon of Nisan (April), following every word of the Mosaic Law literally, up to and including the slaughter, roasting, and eating of the Paschal lamb. A year-old lamb is struck with a knife. If it is not killed on the first blow, another one is presented. Only a Samaritan is allowed to touch the sacrifice. The blood of the lamb is poured into bowls and used to mark the first-born son of each family. The carcasses of the lambs are boiled after the entrails have been removed and burnt. After defleecing, the lambs are roasted in rock-hewn ovens and the meat is distributed to Samaritans to eat.

Sabastiya (Sebaste): 48 miles

At a fork in the road northwest of Nablus the route west leads to Tulkarm; the one to the north proceeds to Sabastiya, the capital of ancient Samaria. On a hill above the new town lie the ruins of many ancient civilizations.

History tells us that Omri, the sixth king of Israel, bought an isolated and defensible hill for two talents of silver from Shemer. There he built a city called Samaria and made it his capital. The city was embellished by his successors, one of whom was Ahab. Under the influence of his Phoenician wife, Jezebel, Ahab built a temple in honor of Baal. For Ahab's blasphemy the prophets foretold that Samaria would be "a heap of stones in the field." After Israel's defeat by the Assyrians and later Babylonian captivity, the prophecy came to pass. The area was subsequently settled by the Chaldeans, but destroyed again by Alexander the Great in 331 B.C. and later by John Hyrcanus in 108 B.C.

After the Roman conquest the town was rebuilt by Pompey. Later Augustus bestowed it on Herod the Great, who called it Sebaste and embellished it to its former opulence. According to one legend, here Salome danced for the head of John the Baptist. Other legends, however, say it was at Jericho, and still others claim it was at Machaerus, south of Madaba. Ruins of a 5th-century church built on the traditional site contain frescos representing a beheading.

In Sabastiya are the ruins of the Crusader Church of St. John the Baptist built on the remains of a Byzantine basilica. On the hill above the village the site of ancient Sebaste includes the ruins of a Roman forum, colonnaded street, theater, temple to Augustus, and palace of Omri.

About 14 miles north of Sabastiya is the site of ancient Dothan, where Joseph was sold by his brothers and taken to Egypt (Gen. 37:17–28).

About 27 miles north of Nablus is the town of Jenin, ancient Engannin. There, according to tradition, Christ cured the ten lepers. At Jenin there is an excellent view of the Plain of Esdraelon and a glimpse of Nazareth.

The road leads through cultivated fields into the Esdraelon (Jezreel) Valley to Afula, ten miles away, believed to be the site of ancient Ophir.

Galilee

The border of the West Bank ends above Jenin. The editors have included Galilee, however, because of its important Christian sites.

Galilee, the country of Jesus, is one of the most fertile and highly cultivated areas of the region. But for all its lushness and religious significance, it was also one of history's bloodiest battlefields. A natural trade and migration route between Europe, Africa, and Asia, it was fought over for thousands of years by the Egyptians, Canaanites, Philistines, Israelites, Romans, and Crusaders, to name a few.

All roads in this region of craggy hills and cultivated valleys lead to an inland freshwater lake known as the Sea of Galilee, whose waters spring from Mt. Hermon and cascade in a torrent or trickle in a stream into the basin 684 feet below sea level. At the southern end of the Sea of Galilee (or Lake Tiberias) the waters flow southward through the Jordan Valley.

Galilee is a region of extremes, from green farmland to parched hillsides strewn with basalt boulders to grand mountain peaks such as Mount Meron (3,964 feet), Mount Canaan (3,150 feet), and Mount Tabor (1,929 feet).

On the east is Mount Gilboa where Saul and his three sons died in battle with the Philistines (1 Sam. 31). Nine miles southwest of Afula is Megiddo, a stronghold on the Via Maris, the ancient caravan route between Egypt and Mesopotamia and the key to controlling the valley and the trade and supply route to and from the sea and the hinterland. In the Bible the very sound of its name was a trumpet call to war. Armageddon is where St. John predicted the last great battle between good and evil will be fought (Rev. 16:16).

The great Egyptian pharaoh Thutmose III ordered his victories over Megiddo in 1478 B.C. to be carved in detail upon stone. Solomon considered it necessary to maintain a garrison there, and the tax he levied for the walls of Jerusalem also had to finance the fortification of Megiddo. As a shrewd soldier he was aware that the outcome of battle on a plain depended on the cavalry, and he kept the garrison well stocked with horses and chariots. Josiah was killed here in 610 B.C. trying to stop the advance of Nechao, king of Egypt, who had nevertheless told him, "My quarrel is not with thee."

Twenty levels of settlement have been brought to light by scholars at Megiddo since 1925, covering the period from 4,000 to 400 B.C. The oldest remains uncovered so far are those of the Canaanite temples, built to face the rising sun. A museum at the foot of the mound houses some of the finds, together with models to help visitors understand the site. The museum is open from 8 A.M. to 5 P.M. The archeological site is open from April to September, 8 A.M. to 5 P.M.; October to March, 8 A.M. to 4 P.M.

From the top of the hill there is a magnificent view of the entire valley.

A road from Afula continues north to Nazareth and the Biblical sites of Kafr Kana (Cana) or eastward to Mount Tabor.

Nazareth

Nazareth is a Christian and Moslem Arab town. Its greatest site is the Basilica of the Annunciation, the biggest and richest in the Middle East, and the Mosque of Peace. Both were completed in 1965. The Basilica stands over the grotto where the Archangel Gabriel appeared to Mary to announce the coming birth of Christ (Luke 1:26–35). A Greek chapel now stands on the site of the temple where Jesus preached.

In this cradle of Christianity all sects are represented, and their members here, as elsewhere, wage a cold war. Outside of the Basilica there is the Roman Catholic Church of St. Joseph, built on the traditional site of his carpenter's shop. The oldest Church of the Annunciation (300 years), dedicated to St. Gabriel, is Greek Orthodox and built over the well where Mary is said to have drawn water. The Greek Orthodox also believe it is the site where Gabriel appeared to Mary. It is open daily 8 A.M. to 12 P.M. and 2 to 5 P.M.

The Melchite community has a Greek Catholic church near the marketplace. The Maronites, originally from Lebanon, have in the Latin quarter of Nabaa a Maronite church where Mass is said in Arabic and Aramaic. The Anglican Church is located near Casanova Street. The Southern Baptist Convention built their temple next to the Greek Orthodox church about 45 years ago, and a small Coptic church was added in the eastern part of the town in 1952.

The Salesian Order of St. John Bosco has a beautiful church, also known as the Church of the Boy Jesus, on a hill above the town. It can be seen from afar. Lastly, west of Nazareth on another summit stands the Greek Church of St. Joseph.

Nearly all the streets of Nazareth slope uphill. Casanova Street in the center of town gets its name from the Latin words *casa* and *nova* and has nothing to do with the amorist. In olden days the Franciscans had a hospice in Nazareth to house pilgrims. When it began to deteriorate they built another and called it the new house, *casa nova,* to distinguish it from the old one. The town has a dozen hospices, convents, monasteries, and hostels of denominations which lodge pilgrims and travelers.

In the time of Jesus the town had a somewhat bad reputation. The people of Galilee looked down on it: "Can any good thing come out of Nazareth?"

Today the site of the temple where Jesus spoke is a Greek Catholic church. A chapel, Our Lady of Fright, belonging to the Franciscan Order of Nuns, the Holy Clairs, was built on a hill south of town at the place where Mary was supposed to have been seized with fear for her son's life. A mile or so from Nazareth at Jebel-el-Qafse you will be shown the hill from which angry townsmen wanted to push Jesus.

The cave where the annunciation was said to have taken place, a site hallowed by tradition, is under the present Basilica. For 1,600 years chapels, churches, and basilicas have been built and rebuilt here. The site was confirmed only a few years ago by an archeological discovery: an inscription reading "Hail Mary" in the ruins. The old Greek Orthodox Church of the Annunciation had laid claim for 300 years to the glory of standing on the site of the miracle.

The present Basilica was built over a very old altar bearing the words "And the Word was made flesh" (John 1, 14). That alone matters. The early Christians, the Crusaders, and generations of pilgrims for the past 2,000 years have knelt here in awe. Four times in the course of centuries the Byzantines, the Crusaders, and twice the Franciscans have borne witness to their faith and that of millions by building a church here.

One should allow a minimum of an hour to tour the Basilica of the Annunciation. It contains many works of art. Masses are said at 7, 8, 9, and 10:30 A.M. and at 6 P.M. Entry is forbidden to persons dressed in shorts or with bare shoulders. Photographs cannot be made of the interior. The Tourist Information Office is located on Casanova Street, tel. (065) 70555.

Seven miles to the northeast of Nazareth on the main road is Kfar Kana, old Cana, where Jesus attended a wedding feast with his mother and turned the water into wine (John 2: 1–11). As in Nazareth, two churches lay claim to the spot. A first chapel was built in the fourth century by St. Helena. Later, the Crusaders built a church on the ruins, and even later the Franciscans added the church that now stands on the site. There is a water jar on display that they claim is one of the originals. On the other hand, the Greek church also claims to stand on the ruins of the old house where the water was changed to wine. And still another tradition places Cana eight miles north of Nazareth!

A few miles to the west on a hilltop lies Zippori, which means "bird." A simple village now, it is said to have been the most important town in Galilee in Jesus' time. A church, built on the ruins of a Crusaders' church, marks the birthplace of Mary in the house of her mother, Anne, and her father, Joachim.

Tiberias, 18 miles northeast of Nazareth, was built by Herod Antipas in honor of his emperor. One can take a boat to the northern shores of the lake where Christ preached and where so many of the miracles took place. A boat crosses the sea, from east to west, departing Tiberias at 10:30 and 12 A.M. and 1:30 P.M.

The *Tourist Information Office* is located at 8 Alhadef St., tel. (067) 20992.

Sea of Galilee

The Sea of Galilee, 13 miles long and seven miles wide, lies 686 feet below sea level. Its waters appear calm, but they are deceiving. Unexpected violent storms can whip up from nowhere.

Like Jerusalem and Nazareth, the sea is linked with the name of Jesus. He walked on its waters (Mark 4: 45–56); He becalmed the storm (Mark 4:35–41); He filled the empty fishing-net (Luke 5:4–7); He gathered together His followers Simon, Andrew, James, and John (Matt. 4:18–22). We meet Him almost everywhere—in Tabgha, in Migdal, in Capernaum; however, He avoided the town of Tiberias.

In the 4th century, beginning with Constantine, the first emperor to be converted to Christianity, churches went up among the temples of Tiberias; afterwards the Arabs built their mosques. The earthquakes of 749 and 1033 destroyed the town. The survivors moved nearby to settle in what is now the old town. After defeating the Crusaders, Saladin captured Tiberias in 1187. It was again leveled by earthquake in 1837.

The landscape around Tiberias is still beautiful but it had more trees and supported a larger population in Biblical days.

The main road along the lake, heading north, leads to famous New Testament locations. Each year thousands of pilgrims visit these shrines. Three are at lakeside—Migdal, Tabgha, and Capernaum—and another, the Mount of Beatitudes, is on a beautiful hilltop. Mount Tabor is a half-hour's drive to the southwest, near Nazareth.

Following the shore of the lake northward, one should see the Monastery of St. Peter, kept by the Franciscans. The apse of the old Church of the Crusaders is still shaped like a ship's prow, a reminder of Peter the Fisherman. Further on there is an Antiquities Museum.

Migdal, the old Magdala, four miles from Tiberias, gave its name to the renowned sinner Mary Magdalen, who was born here. Having fled from Nazareth, Jesus stopped near a tower, *migdal,* and met the woman who, through Him, was to see the light. The meeting place is marked by a small whitewashed dome.

Formerly the people of Migdal salted fish from the Sea of Galilee. Now the village is simply a suburb.

There is a camping ground and, on the shore of the lake, a youth hostel.

Tabgha, four miles north, is the site of the multiplication of the loaves and fishes. Here the Benedictine Order has a monastery built in the gray volcanic stone of Galilee. The monks make a very good dry wine, and show the traveler the magnificent mosaics in the old Byzantine basilica. It pictures the miracle in a wonderful setting of plant and animal life.

When Jesus heard of the death of John the Baptist, "He departed thence by ship into a desert place apart." This place seems to be Tabgha, or Tabigha, from the Greek word *heptapegon*, "seven springs." "When the people had heard thereof, they followed Him on foot." Evening came, and the crowd had no food. The disciples had "but five loaves and two fishes." Jesus handed them out, "and they did all eat, and were filled: and they took up of the fragments that remained twelve baskets full. And they that had eaten were about five thousand men, beside women and children" (Matt. 14:13–21).

It would also be in Tabgha that the Lord appeared, and "this is now the third time that Jesus shewed Himself to his disciples, after that He was risen from the dead" (John 21: 14). And "when they had dined"—following a second catch of fish—"Jesus saith to Simon Peter . . . Feed my lambs . . . Feed my sheep." A Franciscan church in honor of St. Peter was built there during World War II.

Mount of Beatitudes

The Mount of Beatitudes is two and a half miles from Tabgha. On the hill top, at about 330 feet, there is a hospice kept by an Italian Order of Franciscan nuns, and a chapel. The shrine was built in 1937. Within, the eight sides of the dome list the beatitudes uttered by Jesus in the opening to His Sermon on the Mount (Matt. 5). The signs of the seven virtues are inlaid in the floor. The view from here is lovely, with the Sea of Galilee spread out below, a fitting end to the rolling landscape. To the north, Mount Hermon lifts its snowy peak.

According to tradition, it was on the Mount of Beatitudes that Jesus chose His 12 apostles from among His followers: "And He goeth up into a mountain, and calleth unto Him whom He would . . . and He ordained twelve, that they should be with Him" (Mark 3:13–14). On going down, Jesus went into Capernaum.

Capernaum is today a graveyard of old stones worked by the hand of man. There are traces of a 2nd- or 3rd-century temple, probably built over the one where Jesus preached. For, on coming from Nazareth (Matt. 4:13), He made of Capernaum the "center of His teaching." The "village of Nahoum," on the road from Syria to Egypt, must have been of some importance, since it called for a Roman garrison and a customs house. In spite of His prodigies of healing there—Simon's mother, the man possessed of an unclean spirit, the centurion's servant—the people of Capernaum mocked Jesus, who proceeded to denounce them: "And thou, Capernaum which are exalted unto Heaven, shalt be brought down to hell."

There is a Franciscan monastery, open daily from 8:30 A.M. to 4:30 P.M. Entrance fee.

Mount Tabor

The best road to Mount Tabor is from the southern tip of the lake. The climb up the mount is steep, with many hairpin bends, and so narrow that if two cars meet, one has to back off to a widening in the road to allow the other to pass.

As you drive up the sun beats fiercely down onto the treeless, stony path. But, having ascended 1,900 feet, the traveler is rewarded at the top by a panorama of tranquility. Mount Tabor is topped by a tableland, on which stand the Basilica of the Transfiguration and the Hospice Casa Nova, both kept by the Franciscan Order. There is also a Greek church named for St. Elias. The Mount is the site where Christ was transfigured before Peter, James, and John (Matt. 17). The Basilica is open daily from 8 A.M. to 12 noon and from 3 P.M. to sunset.

The hill has a historic past, but it owes its renown to St. Cyril of Jerusalem, who in the 4th century named it the scene of the Transfiguration. The evangelists had merely spoken of a high mountain, which many had thought was Mount Hermon (Luke 9:28).

Two passages in Luke have served as the starting point for the architects who over the centuries have been called upon to rebuild the Church of the Transfiguration. The latest one has three triangles on the front, recalling the three tabernacles (Matt. 17:1–8). The effect of the Transfiguration can be seen at sundown when the rays of the setting sun, falling slantwise through an opening, shine on the golden mosaics of the rounded vault.

The first Church of the Transfiguration was built in the 4th century in the form of three chapels. The present altar is said to be on the former site of the biggest chapel, that of Jesus. The two others are today marked by chapels daubed with frescos; one recalls the meeting of Elias with the priests of Baal.

From the terrace of the Hospice Casa Nova there is a breathtaking view stretching from Upper Galilee to Mount Gilboa. One can make out the town of Na'ine (Nain), where Jesus raised a widow's dead son (Luke 7:11–16).

At the foot of Gilboa lies Ein Dor, famous in the story of Saul, who came there to speak with the witch on the eve of the battle that was to cost him his life (1 Sam. 28:7–25).

Dabburiya is the town where 2,000 years ago nine followers waited with Peter, James, and John for Jesus to come down from the "high mountain."

A road west leads to the Arbel Valley, wedged between the Horn of Hittin on the left and Mt. Arbel on the right. Here is the place where Saladin defeated the Crusaders in a decisive battle. One may continue from here to Tiberias.

The Pilgrim's Map of the Holy Land (see Reading List) lists the Biblical references to the sites and is particularly helpful in touring Galilee.

INFORMATION FOR CHRISTIAN VISITORS

CHRISTIAN HOSPICES. For Christian visitors making a pilgrimage to the Holy Land, hospices of all denominations are available. They offer board and accommodation at more reasonable prices. Facilities vary greatly from hospice to hospice. In addition, each hospice has its own rules regarding length of stay, who may be admitted, etc. You should write to them directly or inquire from the Christian Information Office, Jaffa Gate, open from 8:30 A.M. to 12:30 P.M., and from 3 to 5:30 P.M. in winter; 3 to 6 P.M. in summer.

Jerusalem

Casa Nova PP. Franciscans (Roman Catholic)
Near Jaffa Gate (Buses 1, 19, 20)
P.O.Box 1321
Tel. (02) 282791

Christ Church Hostel (Anglican—British)
  Jaffa Gate (Buses 1, 19, 20)
P.O.Box 14037
Tel. (02) 282082

"Ecce Homo" Convent; Notre Dame-de-Sion (Roman Catholic)
Via Dolorosa (Buses 3, 12, 27)
P.O.Box 19056
Tel. (02) 282445

Evang. Lutheran Hostel (Lutheran—German)
St. Mark's Street
Old City (Buses 1, 5, 20)
P.O.Box 14051
Tel. (02) 282120

Filles de la Charite (Roman Catholic—French)
Bethany Shiya (Buses 36, 43, 63)
P.O.Box 19080
Tel. (02) 284726

Sisters of Nigrizia (Roman Catholic—Italian sisters)

Bethany Shiya (Buses 36, 42)
P.O.Box 19054
Tel. (02) 284724

Sisters of Notre Dame-de-Sion (Roman Catholic—French)
En Karem (Bus 27)
P.O.Box 17015
Tel. (02) 419609; 415738.

Sisters of the Rosary (Roman Catholic—Arab)
14 Agron Street (Buses 22, 30)
P.O.Box 54
Tel. (02) 228529; meals only during the summer.

St. Andrew's Hospice (Church of Scotland),
near railway station
(Buses 4, 6, 7)
P.O.Box 14216
Tel. (02) 717701

St. Charles Hospice; Order of St. Karl Borromaeus (Roman Catholic—German)
German Colony (Buses 4, 6)
P.O.Box 8020
Tel. (02) 637737

St. George's Hostel (Anglican/Episcopal)
Nablus and Saladin Streets (Buses 3, 12, 27)
P.O.Box 19018
Tel. (02) 283302
Notre Dame of Jerusalem Center
P.O.Box 20531
Tel.289723

Mount Tabor

Franciscan Convent of the Transfiguration; Roman Catholic (Italian)
P.O.Box 16
Tel. (067) 67489; (067) 67497

Nazareth

Casa Nova Hospice; Franciscan (Roman Catholic)
P.O.Box 198
Tel. (065) 71367

Greek Catholic St. Joseph Seminary (Greek Catholic)
P.O.Box 1548
Tel. (065) 70540

Religieuses de Nazareth; Roman Catholic (French)
306 Casa Nova Street

P.O.Box 274
Tel. (065) 54304

St. Charles Borromaeus (German Sisters; Roman Catholic)
House 12, 316 Street
Tel. (065) 54435

Tiberias

Church of Scotland Centre; Church of Scotland (British-Scottish Hospice)
Old Town
P.O.Box 104
Tel. (067) 90144

Terra Sancta; Franciscan (Roman Catholic)
Old Town, on shore of the Sea of Galilee
P.O.Box 179
Tel. (067) 205160; 205160

Y.M.C.A.—on western shore of Sea of Galilee advance reservations
through Jerusalem Y.M.C.A., P.O.Box 192;—tel. (067) 20685 or phone
directly to Tiberias.

CHURCHES IN JERUSALEM. Christian churches of just about every
denomination abound in Jerusalem. Be sure to call for the schedule of services.

Name/address	Phone	Denomination
Armenian Patriarchate III Station Chapel Via Dolorosa	(02) 284262	Catholic
Basilica of the Holy Sepulchre	(02) 284213	Franciscan
Basilica of all Nations Gethsemane	(02) 283264	Franciscan
Church of the Dormition P.O.Box 22	(02) 719927	Benedictine
Church of St. Anne St. Stephen's Gate	(02) 283285	Catholic
Church of St. Stephen Nablus Road	(02) 282213	Catholic
Church of the Agony Gethsemane	(02) 283964	Catholic
Church of the German Hospice St. Charles Hospice	(02) 637737	Catholic

Name/address	Phone	Denomination
German Colony P.O.Box 8020		
Dominus Flevit Mt. of Olives	(02) 285837	Franciscan
Flagellation Convent (Via Dolorosa)	(02) 282936	Franciscan
Franciscan Convent Close to the Cenacle (Mount Zion)	(02) 33597	Franciscan
Greek Patriarchate Jaffa Gate	(02) 282023	Catholic
Grotto of Gethsemane		Catholic
Latin Patriarchate of Jerusalem Jaffa Gate	(02) 282323	Catholic
Maronite Vicariate Maronite Convent Rd.	(02) 282158	Catholic
Pontifical Biblical Institute 3 Emil Botta Street P.O.Box 497	(02) 222843	Jesuit
Saint Saviour's Church Saint Francis St.	(02) 282354	Franciscan
Seventh (VII) Station of the Way of Cross		Franciscan
St. James Beit Hanina	(02) 854694	Catholic
American Gospel Church 55 Habevi'im Street	(02) 234804	Protestant
Anglican Services St. Abraham Chapel Holy Sepulchre		Anglican
Association for Unification of World Christianity P.O.Box 14015		Protestant
Baptist House 4 Narkis Street	(02) 225942	Baptist

Name/address	Phone	Denomination
P.O.Box 154		
Baptist Southern Worship Rashid St.	(02) 284165/ 284415	Baptist
Christ Church Anglican Jaffa Gate P.O.Box 4037	224584(202) 282082	Anglican
Christian Assembly	(02) 723968	Protestant
Church of Christ Al-Zahra St. near New Victoria Hotel P.O.Box 19529	(02) 282205	Protestant
Church of God Mt. of Olives near Palace Hotel P.O.Box 19287	(02) 284436	Pentecostal
Church of the Nazarene Centre 33 Nablus Road P.O.Box 19426	(02) 283828	International
Church of the Redeemer P.O.Box 14076	(02) 282543	Lutheran

Collegiate Church of St. George
   the Martyr, commonly called
    St. George's Cathedral
Nablus Road and Saladin St.
P.O.Box 190018
	(02) 282253/
	287708
		Anglican/
		Episcopal

First Baptist Bible Church Salah-el-Din St.	(02) 282118	Independent
Garden Tomb near Damascus Gate P.O.Box 19462	(02) 283402	Interdenomina- tional
Pentecostal Church 33 Hanevi'im Street Zion House		Protestant (American)
Seventh Day Adventist Advent House, near Y.M.C.A. P.O.B.10184	(02) 221547	Protestant
The Scottish Church of St. Andrew Harakevet Street	(02) 37701	Protestant
Armenian Orthodox Patriarchate	(02) 282331	Armenian

Name/address	Phone	Denomination
St. James Cathedral near Jaffa Gate		
Church of Jesus Christ of Latter Day Saints Nablus Rd., Sheikh Jarrah		Mormon
Gethsemane (Tomb of the Virgin)		Armenian
Holy Sepulchre	(02) 284347	Armenian
St. James Tomb	(02) 282331	Armenian
Blessed Virgin Mary Chapel (room on façade)		Coptic
Coptic Orthodox Patriarchate Old City	(02) 282343	
Holy Sepulchre	(02) 284213	Coptic
St. Anthony (Main Church Patriarchate)	(02) 282343	Coptic
St. George (St. Mitri)		Coptic
St. Helene (before Patriarchate on right before the one leading to 9th station)		Coptic
Der es-Sultan (Holy Sepulchre)	(02) 282848	Ethiopian
Ethiopian Orthodox Church Ethiopia Street	(02) 286871	Ethiopian
Paradise Ethiopia St.		Ethiopian
Patriarchate Church (Harat el Nasara)		Ethiopian
Church of the Holy Sepulchre	(02) 282025	Greek
Parish Church of St. James (beside Holy Sepulchre)		Greek
Orthodox Patriarchate of Jerusalem Convent of Patriarchate	(02) 284917	Greek
St. Michel of Arch (St. John Chrysostom)		Greek

Name/address	Phone	Denomination
St. Nicolas Church		Greek Orthodox
St. Simeon Church Katamon		Greek
Russian Orthodox Church (outside of Russia) St. Mary Magdalen (Mt. of Olives)	(02) 282897	Russian
Russian Orthodox Church (outside of Russia) St. Alexander 25 Dabbagha Street	(02) 284580	Russian
Gethsemane Tomb of the Virgin		Syrian
Holy Sepulchre	(02) 284347 (02) 284213	Syrian
St. Marks Church St. Marks St.	(02) 283304	Syrian

SUGGESTED READING

AIDS TO SIGHTSEEING

Browning, Iain. *Petra.* London: Chatto & Windus, 1973; Noyes, 1974. The most extensive book in print on Jordan's major tourist attraction, this is a wonderfully detailed volume that can be used as a guide as well as for pleasurable background reading. It is available in Amman bookstores.

Fistere, John and Isobel. *Jordan, The Holy Land.* Beirut: Middle East Export Press, 1965. An inexpensive travel and picture book to take home as a souvenir of your visit to Jordan. The authors are American writers who have lived in the Middle East for the past 25 years and have been closely associated with Jordan tourism.

Harding, G. Lankester. *The Antiquities of Jordan.* London: Praeger, 1967; paperback, 1974. An absolute must for anyone going to Jordan and a guide to be used while there. The book is well written and easy to read. It will generate an interest in Jordanian antiquities, even though you may have had no previous attraction to the subject. Mr. Harding was the Director of Antiquities in Jordan for 20 years, and his enthusiasm for his subject is contagious.

Hoade, Fr. Eugene, O.F.M. *Guide to the Holy Land.* Jerusalem: Franciscan Press, 1962. Although written as a guide for Catholics, this is the standard and most thorough guidebook available. It is indispensable for its detailed information on Biblical sites. The book includes maps, diagrams, mileages, and itineraries.

Father Hoade's later book, *East of the Jordan* (1966), was revised and released in 1977 under the name *Guide to Jordan* by the Franciscan Fathers. It is available in Amman bookstores, and is particularly valuable for those who are exploring Jordan on their own.

Huxley, Julian. *From an Antique Land.* New York: Crown Publishers, 1954. As an introduction to the Middle East this is one of the best books available. The writer was a scholar, an enthusiastic traveler, and a keen observer. The photographs are excellent.

Morton, H.V.C. *Through Lands of the Bible.* London: Methuen, 1959. *In the Steps of the Master.* London: Methuen, 1962. *In the Steps of St. Paul.* London: Methuen, 1959. *The Women of the Bible.* New York: Dodd, 1941. The first-named book has the widest general interest, but a Morton fan will want to read them all. It is a entertaining way to absorb vast amounts of information on the Holy Land. Some of the books are out of print and are now collector's items.

Nelson, Bryan. *Azraq: A Desert Oasis.* London: Allen House, 1973; Ohio University Press, 1975. A specialized book on one of Jordan's important historic and naturalist sites.

Osborne, Christine. *Insights and Guide to Jordan.* Longmann, 1981. A new book that will fill in some of the details about modern Jordanian life that this book did not cover.

BIBLICAL/ARCHEOLOGICAL/HISTORICAL

Albright, William. *The Archaeology of Palestine.* New York: Penguin Books, 1960. A basic treatment of the subject by one of the world's leading scholars.

The Archeological Heritage of Jordan, Part 1: The Archeological Periods and Sites (East Bank). Amman: Department of Antiquities, 1973. Published to mark the 50th anniversary of the Department of Antiquities, this volume reviews the archaeological work done during this period. The Department also publishes annual reports which include summaries of all activity by foreign expeditions excavating in Jordan.

Avi-Yonah. *The Holy Land.* New York: Holt, Rinehart & Winston, 1972. An architectural survey from an historic point of view of the major buildings and sites in the Holy Land.

Baly, Denis. *The Geography of the Bible,* rev. ed. New York: Harper and Row, 1974. Indispensable as a reference book; one of the most authoritative available.

Cross, Frank Moore, Jr. *The Ancient Library of Qumran,* The Haskell Lectures, 1956–1957. New York, 1976; *Qumran and the History of the Biblical Text.* Cambridge: Harvard University Press, 1975. The first is readable and authentic, although it is now a bit out of date, since subsequent research has augmented the early work on the scrolls.

Fosdick, Harry Emerson. *A Pilgrimage to Palestine* (1926) 1977 reprint. A readable account of a trip through the Holy Land.

Glueck, Nelson. *The River Jordan.* New York: Philadelphia Publication Society of America, 1945 (out of print). For those seriously interested in the archaeology of the Holy Land, Glueck's books are standard reading. The author is recognized as one of the leading scholars of this century. His survey of the Holy Land was the first scientific one undertaken. Subsequent works by the author are *Dieties and Dolphins: The Story of the Nabataeans,* Farrar, Strauss & Giroux, 1965, and *The Other Side of the Jordan,* American School of Oriental Research, Cambridge, Mass., 1970.

Grollenberg, L.H. *Shorter Atlas of the Bible.* Penguin, 1977. Valuable for reference and background reading.

Guillaume, Alfred. *Islam.* Penguin Books, 1956 (paperback). A standard introduction to Islam.

Hitti, Phillip. *History of the Arabs.* London: Macmillan, 1970 (paperback). The classic work, indispensable for serious students of the area. A shortened version by the author, *The Arabs: A Short History* (Chicago: Henry Regnery, 1956), is also available in paperback and is recommended as a primer.

Keller, Werner. *The Bible as History.* New York: Morrow, 1956. Also available in paperback: Bantam, 1974. The standard work on the subject, and the one to read for a Holy Land visit.

Kenyon, Kathleen. *Digging up Jericho.* New York: Praeger, 1957. *Archaeology in the Holy Land.* New York: Praeger, 1960; London: Ernest Benn, 1970, paperback. *Digging Up Jerusalem.* New York: Praeger, 1974. *Royal Cities of the Old Testament.* New York: Schocken, 1973. Miss Kenyon was one of the leading archaeologists to work in Jordan. To her goes the credit for uncovering the oldest walled city in the world. The story of that dig is described in the first book; the second is a good one for beginners.

Lambert, Michel John. *Jerusalem.* New York: Putnam, 1958. (Out of print.) The leading book on the history of Jerusalem. It contains photographs, maps, and charts; and it will provide pleasurable reading after you get home.

Moore, Elinor. *The Ancient Churches of Old Jerusalem.* Beirut: Khayat, 1961. *Early Church in the Middle East.* Humanities Press, 1968. The author traces the origins and history of some 50 churches in Jerusalem, based on accounts written by pilgrims from the years A.D. to 1750. The first title is out of print and difficult to find in the U.S.

Pritchard, James. *Gibeon: Where the Sun Stood Still.* Princeton: Princeton University Press, 1962. *Archaeology and the Old Testament.* Princeton, 1958. The author was head of the excavations at Gibeon during the 1950s. He has authored many books on archaeology in the Middle East.

Runciman, Steven. *History of the Crusaders.* 3 vols. Cambridge University Press, 1954. The standard treatment of the subject.

Sanger, Richard. *Where the Jordan Flows.* Washington, D.C.: Middle East Institute, 1963. Provides extensive Biblical and historic chronological data, and is a valuable guide for visitors with academic interests.

Sheen, The Most Rev. Fulton. *This Is the Holy Land.* Conducted by Rev. Sheen, photographed by Yusuf Karsh and described by H.V. Morton. New York: Hawthorn Books, 1961. (Out of print.) Three famous men combine their knowledge and abilities to take the reader on a pilgrimage through the Holy Land.

Thubron, Colin. *Jerusalem.* Boston: Little, Brown, 1969. With 64 pages of color photographs by Alistair Duncan. *Jerusalem* Great Cities Series. New York: Time-Life, 1976. An esthetic description of Jerusalem and nearby holy places.

Wilson, Edmond, *The Dead Sea Scrolls.* Oxford University Press, 1969.

National Geographic Society, *Biblical Times.* In the high-caliber tradition of the National Geographic Society, this large picture book will introduce you to the Holy Land before your trip, and be a pleasant reminder of it upon your return. The Society has also published many maps and articles on Jordan and the Holy Land over the years, which are useful to read as you prepare for your visit.

MODERN HISTORY

Antonius, George. *The Arab Awakening*. New York: Putnam, 1965. A necessity for anyone who plans to stay in Jordan for an extended period and wants to understand the background of the modern Middle East.

Glubb, John B. *A Soldier With the Arabs*. New York: Harper and Bros., 1959. *The Story of the Arab Legion*. Da Capo, 1976. *Peace in the Holy Land*. London: Hodder & Stoughton, 1971; Verry, 1971. Few foreigners have known Jordan and the Jordanians better than Glubb, who for many years was head of the Arab Legion and Chief of Staff of the Jordan Army. And fewer persons were as close to events in the Middle East during the 1940s and 1950s.

Harris, George. *Jordan: Its People, Its Society, Its Culture*. New Haven: Human Relations Area Files, 1958. A thorough treatment. Especially good background reading for anyone planning to live in Jordan.

Hussein, Ibn Talal, King. *My War With Israel*. New York: William Morrow, 1969. *Uneasy Lies the Head*. Toronto: Heinemann, 1962. Jordan's tumultuous history as seen by the man at center stage is indispensable reading for all who are genuinely interested in the country and the Middle East.

Johnston, Charles. *The Brink of Jordan*. London: Hamish Hamilton, 1972.

Knowles, John. *Double Vision*. New York: MacMillan, 1964. (Out of print.) A journalistic account with many human interest stories, for background reading.

Lawrence, T. E. *Seven Pillars of Wisdom*. New York: Penguin, 1976. (Paperback.) If seeing the film *Lawrence of Arabia* didn't lead you to read this book, a trip to the Middle East should. Read it before you go.

Memoirs of King Abdallah. Gives a picture of the country from 1920 to 1945.

Peake, F.G. *A History of Jordan and Its Tribes*. Coral Gables: University of Miami Press, 1958. (Out of print.)

Snow, Peter. *Hussein: A Biography*. London: Barrie & Jenkins, 1972.

Sparrow, Gerald. *Hussein of Jordan*. Toronto: George Harrop, 1960.

P.J. Vatikiotis. *Conflict in the Middle East.* London: Allen & Unwin, 1971. The author is one of the leading scholars of modern Middle Eastern history today.

MISCELLANEOUS

Foley, Rolla. *Song of the Arab: The Religious Ceremonies, Shrines and Folk Music of the Holy Land Christian Arabs.* New York: Macmillan, 1953. The major religious folk rites of the Christian Arabs are described. The book provides background information on the pageantry, traditions, and folklore of the Holy Land.

Gubser, Peter. *Politics and Change in Al-Karak, Jordan.* London: Oxford University Press, 1973.

Montfort, Guy. *Portrait of a Desert: The Story of an Expedition to Jordan.* London: Collins, 1965.

Mufti, Shawkat. *Heroes and Emperors in Circassian History.* Beirut: Librarie du Liban, 1972.

Nevins, Ed, and Theon Wright. *World Without Time—The Bedouins.* New York: John Day, 1969. (Out of print.)

Pilgrims' Map of the Holy Land for Biblical Research; The Journeys and Deeds of Jesus Christ. Details the Holy Land at the time of Jesus and locates the sites mentioned in the Old and New Testaments, together with an index of the Bible references. The map is on sale at bookshops in Amman and other major towns and antiquities sites.

GLOSSARY

There are many systems for the transliteration of Arabic words into their English equivalents. In the following glossary, the system has been made as simple as possible.

—All long vowels appear as double vowels except "a," which is written with a circumflex: â.

—The letter *ain* in Arabic has no English equivalent. Its presence (when necessary to avoid confusion with other words) has been indicated by: '.

—The *hamza*, a glottal stop, is indicated by: '.

—H, h: the first is hard, the second is like the English "h" in *hat*.

—T, t: the first is hard, the second is like the English "t" in *tip*.

—D or th (like the "th" in *this*) are almost the same sound in Jordanian speech: hatha, ooDa.

—The sound indicated by "kh," pronounced gutturally, as the German "ch" in *Bach*.

Greetings

Good morning	*SabaH el khair*
(reply)	*Sabah el noor*
Good evening	*masa-l khair*
Good night	*laileh sa'eedi; tisbaH 'ala khair*
Good day	*nahârak sa'eed*
(reply)	*nahârak wa'eed sa-mbârak*
Hello	*marHaba*
(reply)	*marhabtain*
Greetings (Peace be with you)	*as-salâm 'alaikoom*
(reply)	*'alaikoom salâm*
Goodbye (the one departing)	*b-khatirkum*
(the one remaining)	*ma'-salâmi; fi amân illah*
How are you?	*keef Hâlak*
Well, thank God	*mabsut (a) elHamdu lillâh*
Welcome (host says)	*ahlan wa-sahlan*
(reply)	*ahlan bekum*

Useful Phrases

Yes	*na'am*
No	*lâ*

Please	*min fadlak, min fadlik (f.)*
If you please	*a'mel ma'roof*
After you, I beg you to (enter, eat, take)	*tfaDDal, tfaDDali (f.)*
If God is willing	*inshallah*
Thank you	*shukran; mamnoonak, mamnoonik (f.)*
What is your name?	*shu ismak? Shu ismik? (f.)*
My name is	*ismi . . . .*
Do you speak English?	*btiHki ingleezi*
I do not speak Arabic	*ana ma baHki 'arabi*
How? (In what way)	*keef?*
How much? (cost)	*adaysh?*
How many?	*kam?*
What?	*shu?*
What is that?	*shu hatha?*
What is it? What's the matter?	*shu fee?*
What do you want?	*shu biddak?*
Who?	*meen?*
Why?	*laish?*
For what purpose?	*min shân aish?*
I do not want	*ma biddi*
I do not have	*ma fee, ma 'indi*
I am hungry	*ana ju'an, ana ju'ana (f.)*
I want to eat	*ana bidee akul*
Give me	*'ateeni*
Bring me	*jibli*
Excuse me	*mut'asif, ma ta'aKhizni*
Take care, watch out	*ou'a*
Go away!	*imshi, rooh*
Hurry up	*Yallah*
Get up	*qoom*
Stop	*waqqif, uqaf*
Stop, enough	*bass*
Slower please	*'ala mahlak minfadlak*
Slowly	*shway, shway*
Take me to the hotel	*khudni 'al otel*
Wait here!	*istenna hoon*
Open the door!	*iftaH el bâb*
Shut the door!	*sakkir el bâb*
Let me see!	*farjeeni, warreeni*
Come here!	*ta'a la hoon*
I do not know	*ma ba'raf*
See!	*shoof!* I saw *shuft*
Never mind	*ma'laish*
Again, also	*kaman*
Another time	*marra tâni, kaman marra*
Once	*marra*
Twice	*marratain*
Everything	*kull*
All of us	*kulna*
Together	*sawa*
Here	*hawn*

There	*hoonak*
Yet	*lissa*
Not yet	*ma lissa*
When	*emta*
After	*ba'd*
Later	*ba'dain*
Never	*abadan*
Always	*daiman*
Perhaps	*yimkin*
It is possible	*mumkin?*
Please wash these	*minfadlik, ighsil hatha (f.)*
Please press these	minfadlik, ikwi hatha (f.)

At the Airport

Airport	*MaTâr*	Porter	*hammal, attâ*
Car, taxi	*arabiyeh; taxi;*	Office	*maktab*
	sayyara	Suitcase	*shanta*
Customs	*gumruk*	Ticket	*tezkara*
Handbag	*juzdan*	Trunk	*sanduq*
Money	*fuloos*		

In Town

Bridge	*jisr, qantara*	Place	*maHal*
Church	*kaneesah*	Hospital	*mustashfa*
District	*Hye, Hara*	House	*bait*
Harbour	*mena*	Shop	*dukkân, makhzen*
Market	*souq*	Square	*midân*
Mosque	*jami*	Street	*shâri'*
Museum	*matHaf*	Town	*medineh; balad*

At the Hotel

Ashtray	*manfatha, mtakkeh*
Bed, mattress	*farsheh*
Bath	*hammam*
Blanket	*hrâm*
Door	*bâb*
Doorman	*bawwâb, concierge*
Floor (storey)	*tâbiq*
Hotel	*otel, lukanda*
Hot water	*mye sukhni*
Lamp	*Daw*
Light	*noor*
Lightbulb	*lamba*
Pillow	*makhadda*
Room	*ooDa*
Sheet	*sharshaf*
Soap	*saboon*

Towel	manshafa, bashkir
Window	shubbâk
Is there air-conditioning?	fee tabreed?
Is there heat?	fee tadfi'a
Show me a room	farjeeni ooDa
Where is the toilet?	wain bait-el-mye?

On the road

Above, up	fooq
Behind	wara
Under	taHt
East	sharq
Far	ba'eed
Gasoline	benzeen
Go down	inzal
Go up	iTla'
In front	'uddam
Inside	juwwa
Left	shemal
Near	'areeb
North	shamâl
Over	'ala
Outside	barra
Right	yameen
Road, highway	tareeq
South	jannub
Straight ahead	dughri
Village	day'a, qarya
Where	wain
Where is the road to . . . . ?	wain et-tareeq 'al . . . . ?
Is the road far from here?	et-tareeq ba'eed min hoon?
How many kilometers?	kam kilometer?

In the Restaurant

Bill	fatoora, hisab	Matches	kibreet
Breakfast	ftoor	Plate	saHn
Cigarette	sigara, sagayer (pl.)	Restaurant	mat'am
Dinner	'asha	Spoon	mal'aqa
Fork	shokeh	Table	tawla
Glass	kubbayeh	Table napkins	foota
Knife	sikkin	Waiter	walad; garçon
Lunch	ghada		

Food

Apricot	mishmish	Grapes	'enab
Banana	mooz	Green beans	loobiyeh, fasulia
Beef	laHm baqar	Honey	'asal
Beer	bira	Ice	talj

Bread	*khubz*	Milk	*Haleeb*
Butter	*zebda*	Olive	*zaitoon*
Cabbage	*malfoof*	Olive oil	*zait*
Cheese	*jibneh*	Onions	*basal*
Chicken	*djâj*	Oranges	*bortuqâl, bort'ân*
Chick peas	*Hummos*	Peaches	*durrâq*
Coffee	*'ahwi*	Pepper, black	*filfil aswad*
Cracked wheat	*burghul*	Preserves	*murabba, tatli*
Cucumber	*khiyar*	sweet	*bhâr hellu*
Cutlet	*castaletta*	Pistachio	*fustuq halebi*
Eggs	*baid*	Pine nuts	*snobar*
hard boiled	*baid maslooq*	Plums	*khûkh*
soft boiled	*baid brisht*	Rice	*ruzz*
omelette	*'ijje*	Salt	*milH*
Eggplant	*batinjan*	Salad	*salata*
Figs	*teen*	Soup	*showraba*
Fish	*samak*	Squash	*koosa*
Fruit	*fawakeh*	Sugar	*sukkar*
Garlic	*toom*	Tea	*sky*
Lamb	*kharoof*	Tomatoes	*banadura*
Lemon	*limoon*	Veal	*laHm 'ijl*
Lentils	*'adas*	Vegetables	*khudra*
Lettuce	*khass*	Vinegar	*khall*
Meat	*laHm*	Water	*mye*
Roast	*rosto*	Watermelon	*baTTeekh*
Skewer	*meshwi*	Wine	*nbeed*
Melon (yellow)	*shammâm*	Yogurt	*leban*

Useful Words

Antiquities	*athar*	Donkey	*Hmâr*
Baker	*khabbâz, farrân*	Dress	*fustân*
Barber	*Hallâk*	Elder man	*sheikh*
Bedroom	*ooda-t noom*	Eyeglasses	*naDDarat*
Book	*kitâb*	Fever	*harâra; Humma*
Bookseller	*maktabji*	Fire	*nâr*
Bookshop	*maktabeh*	Girl	*bint, benât (pl.)*
Camel	*jamel*	Headache	*waja' râs*
Candle	*sham'a*	Heaven, sky	*sema*
Caravanserai	*khân*	Holiday	*'eed*
Carpet	*sijjâda*	Horse	*Hosân*
Castle	*qasr, qal'a*	Iron (metal)	*Hadid*
Chair	*kursi*	(instrument)	*makwa*
Coat	*kaboot*	Jar	*jarra*
Column	*'âmood,*	Judge	*qâDi*
	'awamid (pl.)	King	*malak*
Consul	*'unsul*	Kitchen	*matbakh*
Diarrhea	*is-hâl*	Letter	*maktub*
Dining room	*ooda-t sufra*	Living room	*sâlon*
Doctor	*Hakeem, doctoor*	Monastery	*deir*
Dog	*kalb*	Money-changer	*sarrâf*
Dome, cupola	*qoobah*	Moon	*qamar*

New moon	*hilâl*	Seamstress	*khayyâta*
Pain	*waja'*	Servant (maid)	*khadmi (f.)*
Pilgrim	*Hâjji*		*khaddam*
Pilgrimage	*Hâjj*	Shirt	*qamees*
Policeman	*bolees*	Shoes	*kundara*
Police station	*markaz bolees*	Shrine	*mezâr*
Prophet	*nebi*	Stone	*Hajar*
Prayer-niche	*miHrâb*	Sun	*shams*
Pulpit	*minbar*	Tomb	*qabr*
Reception room	*diwan, dar*	Toothpick	*miswâk*
Religion	*deen*	Trousers	*bantalon*

Numbers

zero	*sifr*	six	*sitte*
one	*wahad*	seven	*sab'a*
two	*etnain*	eight	*tamanya*
three	*talata*	nine	*tis'a*
four	*'arba'*	ten	*'ashra*
five	*khamseh*	eleven	*hedasher*

INDEX

The letter H indicates hotels. The letter R indicates restaurants.

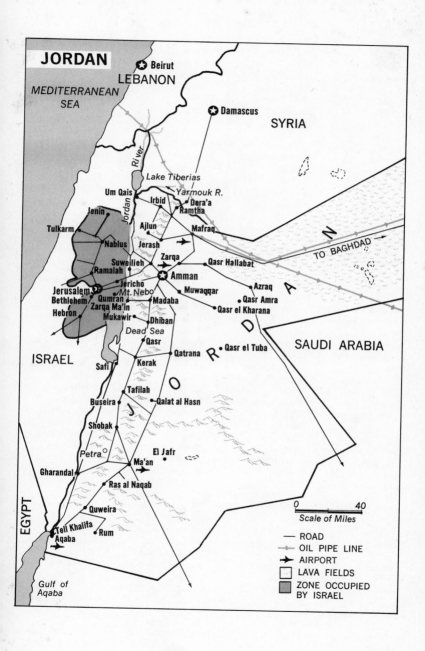

JORDAN

MEDITERRANEAN
SEA

LEBANON

Beirut

Damascus

SYRIA

Lake Tiberias

Yarmouk R.

Um Qais

Irbid

Dera'a

Ramtha

Jenin

Ajlun

Mafraq

Tulkarm

Nablus

Jerash

TO BAGHDAD

Suweilieh

Zarqa

Ramalah

Qasr Hallabat

Jericho

Amman

Jerusalem

Mt. Nebo

Muwaqqar

Azraq

Bethlehem

Qumran

Madaba

Qasr Amra

Hebron

Zarqa Ma'in

Qasr el Kharana

Mukawir

Dhiban

Dead Sea

Qasr

ISRAEL

Qatrana

Qasr el Tuba

SAUDI ARABIA

Safi

Kerak

Tafilah

Buseira

Qalat al Hasn

Shobak

Petra

El Jafr

Gharandal

Ma'an

Ras al Naqab

EGYPT

Quweira

Tell Khalifa

Rum

Aqaba

Gulf of
Aqaba

0   40
Scale of Miles

—— ROAD
OIL PIPE LINE
AIRPORT
LAVA FIELDS
ZONE OCCUPIED
BY ISRAEL

Fodor's Travel Guides

U.S. Guides

Alaska
American Cities
The American South
Arizona
Atlantic City & the
  New Jersey Shore
Boston
California
Cape Cod
Carolinas & the
  Georgia Coast
Chesapeake
Chicago
Colorado
Dallas & Fort Worth
Disney World & the
  Orlando Area

The Far West
Florida
Greater Miami,
  Fort Lauderdale,
  Palm Beach
Hawaii
Hawaii (Great Travel
  Values)
Houston & Galveston
I-10: California to
  Florida
I-55: Chicago to New
  Orleans
I-75: Michigan to
  Florida
I-80: San Francisco to
  New York

I-95: Maine to Miami
Las Vegas
Los Angeles, Orange
  County, Palm Springs
Maui
New England
New Mexico
New Orleans
New Orleans (Pocket
  Guide)
New York City
New York City (Pocket
  Guide)
New York State
Pacific North Coast
Philadelphia
Puerto Rico (Fun in)

Rockies
San Diego
San Francisco
San Francisco (Pocket
  Guide)
Texas
United States of
  America
Virgin Islands
  (U.S. & British)
Virginia
Waikiki
Washington, DC
Williamsburg,
  Jamestown &
  Yorktown

Foreign Guides

Acapulco
Amsterdam
Australia, New Zealand
  & the South Pacific
Austria
The Bahamas
The Bahamas (Pocket
  Guide)
Barbados (Fun in)
Beijing, Guangzhou &
  Shanghai
Belgium & Luxembourg
Bermuda
Brazil
Britain (Great Travel
  Values)
Canada
Canada (Great Travel
  Values)
Canada's Maritime
  Provinces
Cancún, Cozumel,
  Mérida, The
  Yucatán
Caribbean
Caribbean (Great
  Travel Values)

Central America
Copenhagen,
  Stockholm, Oslo,
  Helsinki, Reykjavik
Eastern Europe
Egypt
Europe
Europe (Budget)
Florence & Venice
France
France (Great Travel
  Values)
Germany
Germany (Great Travel
  Values)
Great Britain
Greece
Holland
Hong Kong & Macau
Hungary
India
Ireland
Israel
Italy
Italy (Great Travel
  Values)
Jamaica (Fun in)

Japan
Japan (Great Travel
  Values)
Jordan & the Holy Land
Kenya
Korea
Lisbon
Loire Valley
London
London (Pocket Guide)
London (Great Travel
  Values)
Madrid
Mexico
Mexico (Great Travel
  Values)
Mexico City & Acapulco
Mexico's Baja & Puerto
  Vallarta, Mazatlán,
  Manzanillo, Copper
  Canyon
Montreal
Munich
New Zealand
North Africa
Paris
Paris (Pocket Guide)

People's Republic of
  China
Portugal
Province of Quebec
Rio de Janeiro
The Riviera (Fun on)
Rome
St. Martin/St. Maarten
Scandinavia
Scotland
Singapore
South America
South Pacific
Southeast Asia
Soviet Union
Spain
Spain (Great Travel
  Values)
Sweden
Switzerland
Sydney
Tokyo
Toronto
Turkey
Vienna
Yugoslavia

Special-Interest Guides

Bed & Breakfast
  Guide: North America
1936...On the
  Continent

Royalty Watching
Selected Hotels of
  Europe

Selected Resorts
  and Hotels of the U.S.
Ski Resorts of North
  America

Views to Dine by
  around the World